Business and the Culture of the Enterprise Society

Business and the Culture of the Enterprise Society

JOHN DEEKS

Q

QUORUM BOOKS

Westport, Connecticut • London

Library of Congress Cataloging-in-Publication Data

Deeks, John.
   Business and the culture of the enterprise society / John Deeks.
      p.   cm.
   Includes bibliographical references and index.
   ISBN 0–89930–791–4 (alk. paper)
   1. Corporate culture.   2. Industry—Social aspects.   I. Title.
   HD58.7.D427   1993
   302.3′5—dc20   92–34951

British Library Cataloguing in Publication Data is available.

Library of Congress Catalog Card Number: 92–34951
ISBN: 0–89930–791–4

First published in 1993

Quroum Books, 88 Post Road West, Westport, CT 06881
An imprint of Greenwood Publishing Group, Inc.

Printed in the United States of America

(∞)™

The paper used in this book complies with the
Permanent Paper Standard issued by the National
Information Standards Organization (Z39.48–1984).

10 9 8 7 6 5 4 3 2 1

Copyright Acknowledgements

Acknowledgement is gratefully extended to the following for permission to use copyright material:

Excerpts from *Pravda: a Fleet Street Comedy* by Howard Brenton and David Hare, published by Methuen, London, 1986. Used by permission of Octopus Publishing Group Library.

Excerpts from *The History of Haute Couture, 1850–1950* by Diana de Marly, London, Batsford, 1980, used by permission of the publisher.

Excerpts from *Channels of Desire* ((c) McGraw-Hill, 1982; Revised edition, (c) University of Minnesota Press, 1992) by Stuart Ewen and Elizabeth Ewen. Used by permission of Stuart Ewen and Elizabeth Ewen.

From Kernan, Alvin; *The Imaginary Library*. Copyright (c) 1982 by Princeton University Press, Reprinted by permission of Princeton University Press.

From Pacey, Arnold; *The Culture of Technology*, (c) Arnold Pacey 1983, published by The MIT Press. Reprinted by permission of the publisher.

Excerpts from *An Occupation for Gentlemen* by Fredric Warburg, London, Hutchinson, 1959. Used by permission of Graham C. Greene, Literary Executor.

Excerpt from THE GREAT AMERICAN NOVEL by Philip Roth. Copyright (c) 1973 by Philip Roth. Reprinted by permission of Farrar, Straus & Giroux, Inc.

For Linda Marie

Contents

FIGURES AND TABLES   xi

ACKNOWLEDGEMENTS   xiii

Chapter 1. INTRODUCTION: BUSINESS, THE THIRD
            CULTURE   1

Chapter 2. BUSINESS, SOCIETY AND CULTURE   9

            Business, Society and Social Change   9
            Business, Culture and Cultural Change   12
            "What Do They Know of Cricket, Who Only
            Cricket Know?"   15
            Toward Defining the Conditions of a Business
            Culture   19

Chapter 3. THE MARKET: FROM MORAL PARIAH TO
            MORAL PRINCIPLE   23

            The Gift-Exchange Economy   23
            Development of the Market Economy   29
            The Culture and Morality of the Market   34
            "Market Relationships May Seriously Damage
            Your Health"   40

Chapter 4.   TECHNOLOGY: FROM TOOL TO TALISMAN   45

"If You Can't Win a Nobel Prize, the Next Best
Thing Is to Start Your Own Company."   45

Technology and Culture   46

Technology and Technology Practice   51

Space Technology: Reclaiming the Human
Territory   52

Computer Fetishism   58

Technology and Consciousness   60

Chapter 5.   THE LANGUAGES, SIGNS AND SYMBOLS
OF THE BUSINESS WORLD   67

The Bizarre Bazaar: Semiology and the Language
of Advertising   67

"Last Year's Words Are as Dated as Last Year's
Hats."   71

"Fictitious Values as Evanescent as Rainbow
Gold."   74

"Pecuniary Truth" and the "Permissible Lie"   77

Jesus as Ad-Man   80

Language and Consciousness   84

Chapter 6.   IMAGE AND REALITY IN THE CARTOON
WORLD OF THE BUSINESS EXECUTIVE   87

The Cartoon World   87

Business Relationships, Sexual Stereotypes and
Other Themes in the Cartoon World of Business   90

The Medium and the Messenger   99

The Cartoonist as Fool, Sage and Psychoanalyst   102

The Cartoonist as Business Critic   105

Chapter 7.   THE BUSINESS OF LITERATURE AND THE
LITERATURE OF BUSINESS   111

The Consciousness Industries: Culture and the
Medium of Communication   111

Publishing: From "Gentlemanly Profession" to
"Real Business"   119

The Literary Reaction to Fiction as Commerce   124

The Businessman as Anti-Hero   126

Electronic Culture: Television As Socio-Cultural
Agency   130

Chapter 8.   FASHION AND SOCIETY   137

The Language and Images of Fashion   137
Fashion and Social Control   140
Dress Codes   143
Sex Roles and Erotism   146
Fashion and the Zeitgeist   149

Chapter 9.   "THERE'S NO FASHION IF NOBODY
              BUYS IT"   153

Haute Couture and the Aristocracy of Fashion   153
The Denim Democracy   156
Fashion and Consumer Sovereignty   159
The Commercialization of the Self   162
Fashion and the Business Mode   166

Chapter 10.   PACKAGED AUTHENTICITY: TOURISM
              AND CULTURE   173

From Grand Tour to Cook's Tour   173
The Cultures of Travel and Tourism   179
"Wherever You Go, There You Are": The
Sociology and Psychology of Tourism   183

Chapter 11.   SPORT: "IT IS NOT LIKE AMERICAN
              BUSINESS, IT IS AMERICAN BUSINESS"   191

Sport as Culture   191
The Ideologies of Sport   195
Sport and the Market   200
Sport as Entertainment   203
Sports Sponsorship   207

Chapter 12.   SCHEMES FOR DREAMS: COMMERCE
              AND CULTURE   213

Culture and Counterculture   213
Technocratic and Craft Utopias and the
Engineered Society   216

x   Contents

Business and Postmodernism   223
Business Culture: Reprise   228

BIBLIOGRAPHY   233

INDEX   245

Figures and Tables

Figure 1. Diagrammatic Definitions of "Technology" and "Technology Practice"   53

Figure 2. Business Modes in the World of Fashion   171

Table 1. Relationships Portrayed in 361 *New Yorker* Cartoons, 1985–1989   91

Table 2. Themes of 361 *New Yorker* Cartoons, 1985–1989   93

Table 3. Business Practices and Values   99

Acknowledgements

A number of people, knowingly and unknowingly, contributed ideas to and inspiration for this work, made encouraging noises at appropriate times, directed me into further research or reading on a specific topic, or goaded me to completion of the book. My thanks to them all. I am especially indebted to the following colleagues and friends who offered detailed critiques of individual chapters: Jo Atkinson, Nigel Haworth, Steve Jones, Nick Perry, Michael Powell, Don Smith and Linda Robinson. I hope they will not be disappointed in the results. Thanks also to Lorri O'Brien for wordprocessing advice and to Kate and Harriet Russell for help with the preparation of the index. The staff of the Greenwood Publishing Group who have turned my manuscript into printed form have done a fine job. My special thanks to Eric Valentine, Publisher, Quorum Books; Margaret Maybury, Manager, Editorial Administration; William Neenan, Production Editor; and Krystyna Budd, Copy Editor.

The completion of this work was greatly facilitated by the University of Auckland's provisions for research and study leave.

CHAPTER 1

Introduction: Business, the Third Culture

This book is about "seeing" aspects of our everyday world that are frequently taken for granted yet have a major impact on our lives. It is about books, newspapers, advertisements, television, computers, clothes, travel, and sport. Such things reflect and shape the values of our societies and are intrinsic elements of our culture. In Western societies they are largely the products of business activity. What we read, wear, view on film and television, how we travel from place to place, the nature of the games we play and watch, are the consequences of a myriad of business decisions. Indeed, so integral is business activity to our way of life that we can play with, and explore, the idea that our culture is a "business culture." In such a culture business practices and values dominate the material, intellectual and spiritual life of the whole community.

The role of business practices and business institutions in mediating our encounters with the everyday world may seem self-evident. Yet the idea of a business culture remains relatively unexplored. When, for example, the English scientist-novelist C. P. Snow delivered his 1959 lecture "The Two Cultures and the Scientific Revolution," he raised a storm of controversy in the bitchy world of British academic politics. Snow described a deep divide between the world of science and technology and the world of literature. At one pole were the scientists and technologists; at the other, the writers and literary intellectuals. The divide between them stemmed from the lack of a shared language of communication, a shared education and a shared set of values. Notwithstanding the virulent and, in some cases, very personal criticism of Snow and his thesis, the idea of two cultures—a culture of science and technology on the one hand and a literary culture on the other—became entrenched in the English-speaking world. It still provides a productive paradigm for the analysis of contemporary society.

Criticized for restricting his discussion to merely two cultures, Snow later mooted the idea of a third, a culture based in the social sciences and in social history and "concerned with how human beings are living or have lived" (Snow 1964: 70). The idea that this third culture might appropriately be labelled a business culture was not considered by Snow or his contemporaries. Yet the world of business has progressively expropriated the worlds of science and technology, art and literature, dispossessing them of their claims for pre-eminence in shaping our social and cultural experience. A key theme of this book is the centrality of business activity to all aspects of life in Western society—economic, social, psychological, cultural. However, business both shapes and is shaped by society. It is not a one-way street. Contemporary business practices and values are themselves the product of particular social, cultural and economic histories. They are embedded in culture and not readily separated from it, even for analytical purposes. The intent here is to tease out this ebb and flow of shaping and being shaped, to explore the tensions that arise in the development of a business culture, and to examine the mechanisms through which business values become the dominant values in society.

The range of material available in such an ambitious enterprise is vast. To make the task more manageable, a simple structure is used, one that evolved from the development of the idea of an extended business culture. Chapter 2 defines the concepts of business, society and culture, identifies the role of business in social and cultural change, and outlines the distinctive characteristics of this extended business culture. It suggests that a number of core building blocks are needed to understand the dynamics of cultural developments related to the activities and values of the business world, namely markets, technology, language and symbols, consciousness, and ideology. It is these core blocks that underpin both the idea of an extended business culture and the structure of the book.

Chapter 3 discusses markets. It traces the history of exchange systems, from gift-exchange to the modern market economy. It highlights the social and political impacts of the market. It illustrates how attempts have been made to make the operations of the market compatible with social and cultural values, and how market values have progressively displaced other values as guides to social behavior and moral conduct.

Chapter 4 analyzes the role of technology in cultural change, utilizing a distinction between technology and technology practice. The institutionalized technology of the space program, and the portrayal of that program by Tom Wolfe and Norman Mailer, provide a basis for exploring the tension between Snow's two cultures, the world of science and technology and the world of literature. The chapter goes on to discuss computer language and computer fetishism and to examine the impact of technology on consciousness—of transport technology on concepts of time and space, and of computer technology on the way in which we apprehend the world around us and our place within it.

Chapters 5 and 6 focus upon business language and symbols. Chapter 5 takes a critical look at the signs, symbols and language of advertising—the semiology of advertising. Drawing upon advertising history and literature, it explores the critiques of advertising and some of the constraints that have been imposed upon advertising practice. It highlights the contest in the public domain for control of the language in which the values and ethics of the broader society are expressed.

Chapter 6 analyzes the world of business as seen in the simplest of symbolic representations, the drawings of a number of America's leading cartoonists. It discusses some explanations for the image that cartoons foster of the characteristics of U.S. business practice and the concerns of American executives.

Chapter 7, on "the consciousness industries," expands the discussion about the role of business in the industrialization of the mind. The chapter traces the history of street literature and early journalism. It outlines the development of the publishing business from a gentlemanly profession to a conglomerate investment, and it explores the literary reaction to this process of commercialism.

Chapters 8 and 9 explore the intermeshing of social values and business values in the world of fashion. Ways in which business reflects, creates, exploits and responds to social and cultural values are described and analyzed. Because clothing has so many richly symbolic aspects, the world of fashion provides an excellent medium in which to examine the interplay between business values and other social and cultural values.

Chapter 8 concentrates primarily on the social aspects of fashion. It highlights ways in which the symbolism of the fashion world is carried through tension between recurring images of change, novelty and freedom on the one hand and conformity, stability and conservatism on the other. Attention is given to the role of fashion in status placement and enhancement and in the maintenance of hierarchical social structures. In particular, dress codes, especially occupational costumes and business dress codes, together with stereotypical attitudes toward male and female attire, allow social controls to be enforced through the control of fashion behavior.

Chapter 9 gives a more explicit focus to the business aspects of fashion. Haute couture and ready-to-wear fashion are described, with particular attention to the origins of fashion changes and the respective roles of designers, manufacturers, retailers and consumers in influencing clothing styles. Links between fashion merchandising practices and concepts of personality expressed through dress are examined. Finally two predominant modes of fashion business operation are discussed, a managerial mode and an entrepreneurial mode.

Chapter 10 looks at the tourist industry as a locale in which the cultural values of business inevitably collide with traditional non-business cultural values. It traces the history of tourism and explores the psychology of travel with particular reference to the development of tourist attractions and "authentic" tourist experiences.

Chapter 11 uses the medium of sport to bring together a number of the themes of the book. It looks at the impact of industrialization on sport and at the ideologies linking sport to education and to achievement. It traces the development of professionalism and commercialism in sport and the decline of the ethos and values associated with the amateur. Attention is also directed to the role of the media, particularly television, in the development of sport, both in the changing structures of games themselves and in their cultural contexts. The link between sport and business through sponsorship is discussed, as is the common ground between the languages of sport and the languages of business.

Chapter 12 utilizes utopian writing to explore different conceptions of the structure and role of business in an idealized society. Finally it draws together the key themes of the book in a general discussion about commerce and culture.

As can be seen from this brief synopsis, throughout the book material from a number of industries is used to illustrate different facets of the interface between business and culture. A variety of "texts" have been drawn upon, both within particular industries and across the broader spectrum of business. These include the texts provided by the lives of particular entrepreneurs and business men and women and by the business and management practices of their organizations. They include reference to some visual texts, particularly the images of business projected through advertising and through cartoons. In addition, literary and dramatic texts—novels, plays, television dramas, and films—are used where appropriate to allow for a broader social commentary on the business world and to place that world within its rich cultural context.

Such texts are used as a means to discuss general issues without losing touch with the particularity of specific events. In an issue as broad as that of business culture, such a particularity helps to avoid the danger of writing at too abstract a level. It also gives author and reader a basis for testing out agreement and disagreement. It provides the opportunity and the confidence to work from within the limitations of our own special knowledge and expertise out into areas that are more speculative and uncharted, to mix what we know with what we think it means, to add interpretation to description. The intention is to facilitate general observations about the world of business in its cultural context but to ground these observations in concrete events and in the symbols and artifacts of business activity. The texts, then, are entry points designed to provide a fruitful basis for a broader analysis of business and cultural issues.

In the choice of texts and illustrative materials I have been anxious to avoid being influenced by preconceived notions and theories. I have tried to draw theory and general observation from the textual material rather than seeking out examples to illustrate pet theories. However, the choice of texts is inevitably idiosyncratic, and I make no claim that they are representative. The bias in their selection arises both from the availability of published work (although there is a certain randomness in which published works come to one's attention) and from a preference for the colorful, telling and amusing anecdote. The best to be hoped for is that the chosen texts are exemplary, that the selection of alternative texts would not have led to markedly different interpretations.

The approach adopted is more akin to that of the literary critic, the historian, or the anthropologist than to the mainstream of business books. Although this work is grounded in specific texts, events, and artifacts, it is important to understand something of the social and economic contexts of these texts, events and artifacts, to understand their broader impact and relevance, their place in the culture of the period from which they are drawn as well as their place in our culture now. Like Jeremy Hawthorn (1983: x), I do not share the position of those "who argue the pointlessness of trying to establish any links between social life, history and literature." Connections are precisely what I am seeking to make, connections across an eclectic range of material drawn from economics, sociology, anthropology, history, art, literature, and computer science, integrated by the common thread of business. By using a collage of literary, dramatic and visual texts alongside material on entrepreneurship and business management, I hope to enter the world of business imaginatively. Such an approach is the corollary to the idea of business culture, and it is integral to discussion and analysis of the impact of business on the ways in which we interpret and understand the modern world.

Two examples will illustrate the influences behind the approach adopted. Jeremy Hawthorn, in his book *Multiple Personality and the Disintegration of Literary Character*, sets literary portrayals of personality disintegration alongside clinical accounts. He illustrates the common themes shared by literary and clinical perceptions and descriptions of personality and personality disorders. These themes change over time in response to changes in social life. Similarly one can anticipate some interplay between the behavior and characteristics of entrepreneurs and business managers in particular historical periods and the portrayal of entrepreneurs and business managers in the literary and dramatic works of those periods. The present work, however, while attuned to business history, is not a business history. It is beyond this work's scope to adequately root the texts it uses in their particular cultural contexts. I am sensitive of the need to look to the changing *context* of business—to changes in the social, cultural and economic environment—for explanation of changes in the *content* of particular texts, whether entrepreneurial, literary, dramatic or visual. I am aware of the danger of interpreting the past through the perceptions and prejudices of the present but am unable here to reconstruct the kind of cultural milieu in which the texts used were created and might, therefore, come to be regarded as exemplary. Nevertheless, in so far as historical texts can provide useful commentaries on contemporary realities, they reinforce a sense of continuity rather than discontinuity in business culture.

The second example is that of Robert Darnton's *The Great Cat Massacre*, an investigation of ways of thinking in eighteenth-century France in which Darnton set out "to show not merely what people thought but how they thought—how they construed the world, invested it with meaning, and infused it with emotion." Darnton's approach is to follow up "the surprises provided by an unlikely assortment of texts: a primitive version of "Little Red Riding Hood," an account of a massacre of cats, a bizarre description of a city, a curious file kept by a police inspector—*documents that cannot be taken to typify eighteenth-century thought but that provide ways of entering into it*" (my emphasis). He did not look for representativeness or typicality in his texts but

pursued what seemed to be the richest run of documents, following leads wherever they went and quickening my pace as soon as I stumbled on a surprise. Straying from the beaten path may not be much of a methodology, but it creates the possibility of enjoying some unusual views, and they can be the most revealing. I do not see why cultural history should avoid the eccentric or embrace the average, for one cannot calculate the mean of meanings or reduce symbols to their lowest common denominator. This confession of nonsystematism does not imply that anything goes in cultural history because anything can pass as anthropology. The anthropological mode of history has a rigor of its own, even if it may look suspiciously like literature to a hard-boiled social scientist. It begins from the premise that individual expression takes place within a general idiom, that we learn to classify sensations and make sense of things by thinking within a framework provided by our culture. It therefore should be possible for the historian to discover the social dimension of thought and to tease meaning from documents by relating them to the surrounding world of significance, passing from text to context and back again until he has cleared a way through a foreign mental world. (Darnton 1985: 14)

Business history has its own rich supply of documents, its own curiosities, legends and mythologies. The cultural frameworks and mind sets that made the Paris sewers a major tourist attraction in the late nineteenth century, that produced Kink no More, a preparation to straighten "the most stubborn Negro hair" manufactured and advertised in the early years of this century (Schuyler [1931] 1969), or that made Bruce Barton's business-Jesus books bestsellers in the 1920s have both differences from and similarities with the cultural frameworks and mind sets that in our own time produce teenage mutant Ninja turtles, the Simpsons, psychohistory, televangelism and cryofreeze funeral rites. In rummaging through the business trashcan and in contemplating the monuments of the business world, I have selected what strikes my fancy and accumulated an unusual anecdotal hoard. Such magpie methods, however, are not designed to ransack the past or plunder the present for the sake of a good storyline. Rather I have sought to use the eccentric, the bizarre, the unexpected, to alert ourselves to the strangeness of the things around us, to "see" the everyday with new eyes and fresh insights.

CHAPTER 2

Business, Society and Culture

BUSINESS, SOCIETY AND SOCIAL CHANGE

Definitions of "business," "society" and "culture" are a necessary preliminary to examination of the interrelationships between them. Business is the least difficult term to define precisely. It can be tied down to a precise set of institutions and organizations that together make up the business community. A definition of business provides for inclusion in, or exclusion from, that community. For our purposes here business is "those profit-seeking organizations that are set up to provide a product or a service, together with those institutions funded by such profit-seeking organizations to represent their interests." Business includes, therefore, a first line of commercial enterprises, whether privately, publicly or state owned, that operate with the principal objective of making a profit; and a second line of organizations, such as trade associations and employers' federations, established to represent and advance the interests of the owners of those first-line enterprises. Banks, supermarkets, multinational pharmaceutical companies, profit-seeking state trading corporations, monopoly suppliers of a particular product, a manufacturers' association or business roundtable, are all part of business no matter what the structure of their ownership or the nature of the markets within which they operate. In contrast, voluntary, community and other organizations not primarily established to make a profit or to represent the interests of profit-seeking organizations are not part of business as defined, even though they may be providing products and services in the marketplace. Consequently whether or not a school, university, hospital, library, sports team, or government department is a business depends upon whether or not the organization concerned is primarily there to make a profit for its owners.

The first key element in the idea of society or a social system is the existence of groups. Without group activity—some basis on which individuals associate with each other—there can be no society. In most societies the primary group is the family. Whether single-parent, nuclear or extended, the family provides our first experience of association with others, our initial awareness that we are not isolates abandoned at birth to survive as best we can in an atomistic and hostile world. Other important forms of group activity may be political, social, religious or economic. In all cases of group activity it is possible, though not necessary, that groups will set up formal organizations or institutions to give concrete identity to their common interests. Such institutions and organizations, the second key element in the idea of society, evolve naturally from group activities. They will be set up to promote particular group interests or to protect group interests in an environment that is perceived to be hostile. Giving a group an institutional or organizational form is a way of consolidating its membership and increasing its influence and power.

Out of the existence of groups and their representative institutions and organizations emerges social structure, the third key element of a social system. Sociologists describe the components of social structure in terms of hierarchies of prestige and status and a corresponding specification of roles for members of a particular group or community. Prestige and status, for example, may be ascribed to individuals on the basis of race, ethnicity, caste, gender or family membership. In such a society hereditary factors will largely dictate who can fill leadership roles within the community and what occupational and social roles are available to different individuals. Alternatively, where prestige and status can be achieved through mastery of a particular skill, such as oratory, combat or business, then leadership and other roles will be attainable on the basis of expertise and ability rather than accidents of birth. Variations in the structures of societies will also reflect the group affiliations of members of the community and the relative power and influence of the institutions and organizations those groups have established to look after their interests.

The fourth key element of society is social control. The behavior of members is controlled through a mix of customary practices, or "norms" of behavior; legal codes of conduct; shared religious or other beliefs; and the power, influence and prestige of particular individuals and groups within the community. Social controls are made effective by providing rewards for those who observe them and sanctions against those who ignore them. Individuals' respect or disrespect for these controls will stem from their socialization, education and experience.

Society, then, contains a variety of institutions and organizations including, in most modern societies, the institutions and organizations that we have defined as business. Business is an integral part of society and not something that should be thought of as separate from it. Unfortunately the tendency in many books and educational programs is to think in terms of business *and* society, to focus on the relationship *between* business and society as though they were two discrete entities. In practice it is more fruitful and realistic to think of business *in* society. If we look at the key elements of society, we find business institutions and organizations integrally involved in aspects of social structure and social control. As market economies have developed, business has played an increasingly important part in shaping the structures of societies and in challenging traditional values regarding leadership and the transmission of leadership roles. The increasing power and influence of business has also been reflected in the changing precedence given to different systems of social control. In particular the market itself and the ethics of the market have, in most modern societies, become important means through which social as well as economic behaviors are encouraged, modified or constrained. This is a matter looked at in more detail in the next chapter.

Change in a society can come about in a number of ways. It can be imposed by ecological and environmental changes, either natural or man-made. Thus desertification may force formerly nomadic tribes to become urban dwellers, in the process destroying their traditional social structures. Population growth may also impose unwelcome changes. If the resources of the land cannot sustain the growing number of people in the community, various displacements and adjustments will occur. In Tonga, Western Samoa, and other South Pacific island nations, for example, emigration to New Zealand, Australia and Hawaii has been common in the years since World War II, partly in response to population pressures at home, partly in response to the perception of better economic opportunities abroad. The regular repatriation of money from overseas families to their communities in the islands is now an important component of the national economies of these South Pacific countries. It also has a major impact on the status and role of family members in these societies and hence on the indigenous social structures.

Social change may also result from revolution. New political or religious groups acquire power, overturning the former social structures and social controls. Thus the Bolsheviks and their successors in the Soviet Union transformed Russia and the societies of Eastern Europe, and the Islamic revolution in Iran replaced a monarchy with a theocracy. Less cataclysmic but equally significant and revolutionary change may flow from technological developments. Indeed, whole eras and societies may be defined in relation to technology—the Industrial Revolution, the machine age, the nuclear age, the Global Village, the post-industrial society, the computer age, the information society, the space age. As Chapter 4 indicates, many of these developments in technology are inextricably bound up with business activity.

Ebbs and flows in the relative power and influence of groups and their institutions and organizations may also precipitate social change. The development of entrepreneurial activity, trade and business has been a major source of social change, bringing pressure to bear on political and social systems in which business owners were excluded from positions of power and prestige. During the Industrial Revolution in England, for example, the growing class of manufacturers sought to break the stranglehold that the landed aristocracy maintained over positions of privilege in the English social structure. The development of the professions and of a professional managerial class, and the development of trade unions, create similar tensions within the prevailing social order and generate pressures for change.

Finally, change in a society may arise from that society's exposure to other social and economic systems. In traditional societies change often stemmed from the development of trading relationships with other communities. During the period of colonial expansion of the European powers, many societies were exposed to ethnocentric, self-confident and aggressive Europeans. The cultures of the European colonists, backed by their economic and military strength, overwhelmed a number of indigenous societies and created crises of identity for those that survived. More recently exposure to other societies and their values through modern communications media, particularly through television, has been viewed as a new form of imperialism, a colonization of consciousness that surreptitiously changes the socialization and social controls in the recipient societies. This is an issue explored further in Chapter 7.

BUSINESS, CULTURE AND CULTURAL CHANGE

The feature that distinguishes human societies from the societies of other species is the existence of culture. The nature of a society of monkeys or bees can be examined and discussed, identifying the formation of groups in those societies, their social structures, their hierarchies of status and prestige, their designation of roles, and the predominantly biological or physiological social controls that establish or sustain appropriate behaviors by their members. And the ways in which those societies adapt to changing environmental conditions or to the existence of predators can be observed. But we do not ascribe culture to them.

The term "culture" is particularly difficult to define adequately. In the early 1950s two United States anthropologists identified 164 definitions of culture and then added their own (Kroeber and Kluckhohn 1952). The intricate historical development of the word has been traced by Raymond Williams. In its early uses culture described the tending of crops or animals and later the nurturing of human development. In England it gradually acquired broader connotations of a more general civilizing process in society and took on class overtones, the cultured class being those members of society who, through breeding or education, had developed the sensibility and taste to appreciate the finer things in life. In this latter sense it still lives on in the notion of high or minority culture and its antithesis of pop or mass culture. But it is also used more generally to describe "the works and practices of intellectual and especially artistic activity. This seems often now the most widespread use: culture is music, literature, painting and sculpture, theater and film. A Ministry of Culture refers to these specific activities, sometimes with the addition of philosophy, scholarship, history" (Williams 1983: 90).

Another strand in the development of the word arose toward the end of the eighteenth century with the introduction of the idea of cultural variations between historical periods, between nations, and indeed between different economic and social groups within the same nation. This concept of culture had entered into the mainstream of European thought by the early twentieth century and is now common usage in sociology and anthropology. It allows for discussion and writing about national culture, folk culture, traditional culture, working-class culture, the culture of the organization, twentieth-century culture, even the culture of specific machines and their acolytes and accessories (the computer culture, the car culture), the culture of artifacts in general (material culture), and the culture of market commodities in particular (consumer culture). It is this meaning of the word culture that is central to the concerns of this book. Culture, for our purposes here, is defined as "a whole way of life, material, intellectual and spiritual" (Williams 1961: 16), "whether of a people, a period, a group or humanity in general" (Williams 1983: 90).

There are a number of key elements in this idea of culture or a cultural system. The first is symbolling. Cultures attach meanings to behaviors and objects that to outsiders are not readily apparent from the behaviors or the objects themselves; behaviors or objects may be symbolic, that is, representative of something else. The wearing of a diamond engagement ring becomes a symbol of eternal love. The eating of fish on Fridays, or of food that is kosher, or of animals slaughtered by halal methods, becomes a symbol of religious belief. Over a period of time quite simple objects can acquire encrustations of symbolic meaning that are largely impenetrable to non-members of the culture. Lowell Edmunds, for example, took a simple object like the martini glass and wrote a whole book about the symbolism of the martini and its cultural significance in the United States. The martini, he wrote is "as American as apple pie," a "totem-drink that binds together the members of the tribe." The mixing of the martini "is a rite, whether performed by the host or by the bartender, either of whom may assume the role of priest" (Edmunds 1981: 8). In American culture, Edmunds argued, the martini was male, upper class, metropolitan, optimistic and conservative, civilized yet idiosyncratic, and its consumption provided, for some, a ritual communion with their ancestors.

Language is the second key element of culture. Language allows objects and behaviors to be invested with symbolic meaning, for it is through the medium of language that the extrinsic associations and connotations attached to objects and behaviors are communicated. Cultures develop around the core of a shared language and the preservation of that language becomes integral to the preservation of the culture. This key role for language applies as much to the development of a group culture and identity among computer hackers or rap music fans as it does to national languages. Languages are themselves elaborate structures of symbolling and take a variety of forms—spoken, written, visual, mathematical, musical. In the context of business a number of special languages develop. Some, like the language of advertising, obtain a broad currency. Others, like programming languages or the shared insider languages of particular business specialists, remain largely sealed off from those without the requisite educational, organizational or professional initiation, the rites of passage into group membership.

The third key element of culture is an ideological component: some body of ideas that incorporates the beliefs shared by the members of the group or the society. Symbolling involves the attachment of meanings to objects and behaviors. It therefore needs to draw upon some system of beliefs within which those meanings make sense. Thus if the culture believes in the divine right of kings, then kingly symbols of divine authority will be found to reflect that belief and appropriate symbolic behaviors will be expected in those who approach the god-king. Orbs, scepters, crowns, maces, axes, wigs, chains, have all been used to symbolize authority. But without some underlying ideology to sustain that authority these elaborate symbols either disappear into museums or revert to their common uses.

Change in a culture implies, then, change in one or more of these key elements—in the symbols used to express meanings, in the ideologies that give rise to those symbols, or in the language. In practice, given the inter-dependence of these three elements, cultural change is likely to involve simultaneous change in all of them. Such change will be precipitated by much the same forces that create changes in societies. Social and cultural anthropologists suggest that there are three principal processes of cultural adaptation and change: evolution, acculturation and cultural diffusion. Evolutionary change involves new techniques and ways of doing things developing within a culture and being embedded in that culture in ways that are compatible with existing beliefs, traditions and practices. It is a process of change from within. Acculturation is the opposite process in which change is imposed from outside the culture. Through military or economic or ideological intrusion from outside, an indigenous culture is largely replaced by an alien culture with a totally incompatible ideological base. In this process of acculturation the members of the submerged culture adopt the alien culture as their own. Cultural diffusion implies a less closed process of change than evolutionary development and a less one-sided process of change than acculturation's cultural imperialism. It recognizes that as a consequence of the interactions between cultures, new words will be introduced into the indigenous languages, new symbols will become available for the expression of meanings, and traditional ideas and beliefs will be modified. Such changes are seen as potentially enriching the interacting cultures rather than destroying or impoverishing them.

"WHAT DO THEY KNOW OF CRICKET, WHO ONLY CRICKET KNOW?"[1]

Developments in the sport of cricket illustrate these alternative modes of cultural adaptation and change. The major countries playing international cricket are England, the home of the game, Australia, New Zealand, the West Indies, India, Pakistan, Sri Lanka and, after re-admittance to this international community in 1991, South Africa. Cricket in these countries had its origins in the activities of English colonists and administrators during the nineteenth-century expansion of the British Empire. Until the 1970s this most English of games remained largely unchanged in its basic format and rules. Although by then largely professionalized at the international level, the game was rooted in gentlemanly amateur codes of conduct developed in Victorian Britain. Its image was of a slow-paced, leisurely, genteel game accompanied, in England at least, by polite applause from the cognoscente of spectators who appreciated its subtleties; fans they were not. The phrase "it's not cricket" became synonymous with unsporting and ungentlemanly behavior in any walk of life.

In Australia and New Zealand, with their large numbers of English immigrants, cricket was readily established in its traditional guise. Unlike various forms of football, it never held much appeal for the indigenous peoples, the Aborigines and Maori respectively. In contrast, on the Indian continent and in the West Indies, the game was widely adopted by the local populations. Styles of play were often more expansive and flamboyant, and the behavior of spectators a far cry from the "breathless hush" around the hallowed turf of English arenas. Nevertheless, the format of the game, and the English values entrenched in the desirable mode of its playing, were adopted without revision. In these latter countries cricket was part of a process of acculturation.

However, the present international cricketing nations were not the only countries in which cricket developed during the expansion of the British Empire. Cricket was also introduced by English missionaries in a number of South Pacific countries. It was one of those British games established by the mission churches in an effort to provide entertaining substitutes for inter-tribal warfare and to encourage the spread of a new morality based upon Christian values. A 1975 film directed by anthropologist Jerry Leach describes how in 1903 the Rev. M. K. Gilmour, a Methodist missionary, introduced cricket, played according to the official English rules, to the Trobriand Islands southeast of Papua New Guinea. In the Trobriands, however, the English version of polite non-political competition was soon transformed into a form of cricket more in tune with the local culture. The first set of changes were changes to the traditional rules, structures and organization of the game. The restriction of 11 players to a team was lifted. If 40 or 50 players turned up to play for one village, then the opposing village would match that number. The overarm bowling of the ball was abandoned in favor of a spear-throwing delivery action. The capture of an opponent's wicket was accompanied by ritual "out-songs" and "out-dances," and the whole game played in an atmosphere of intense excitement created by the noise and shouts of spectators and players alike and by their comic, rude and erotic chants.

The second set of changes made by the Trobriand Islanders were changes to the technology of the game. The shape of the bats, the composition of the balls, the disposition and scale of the wickets, were all adjusted to take account of the new local rules and of local materials available for their manufacture. Finally, there were major changes to the symbolism surrounding the game. The approved white mission clothes were replaced by elaborate face painting and self-decoration, the dress of war. Long, curved cricket bats were developed locally, decorated in the war colors of black and white, and fortified by magic in a manner similar to that in which warriors had traditionally fortified their spears. Magic was also used by players, spectators and the umpire (a member of the batting side) to protect wickets or change the course of the ball. The social and political organization of matches placed the game of cricket in a context of ritualized political competition between villages. Matches were accompanied by ritual displays of prestige food and gifts, and they culminated in elaborate ceremonies accompanying the exchange of these items between rival villages. The result of the game itself was integrated into the broader framework of gift exchange between communities; the local or host side always won, but not by too much.

The cultural transformation of cricket in the Trobriand Islands has continued into modern times with a variety of creative and continuing adaptations. Jerry Leach shows how a number of the ritual dances of village cricket teams assimilated influences not only from the traditional dances of the village and from the natural environment of village life but also from the presence of World War II military bases in the islands. One cricket team called The Aeroplane, for example, was from a village where a wartime airstrip had been built. Their ritual entrance and exit dances for cricket matches mimed the takeoff and flight of aircraft in military formation. Another village team, at each successful capture of an opponent's wicket, performed an out-dance called PK. The chant for this out-dance, which included the refrain "PK are my hands," likened the surehandedness of the team's fielders to the stickiness of Wrigley's PK chewing gum.

Trobriand cricket provides an illustration of some of the processes of cultural diffusion. Potentially hostile alien cultural influences are adapted and accommodated in a manner that both brings them under the control of an indigenous culture and its traditions and, at the same time, establishes new practices and behaviors within those traditions. Rather than being swamped by features of a powerful external culture, the Trobriand Islanders, in their cricket at least, are able to reassert their own sense of cultural identity. Whatever the reasons for this cultural resilience—and they may lie in some mix of geographical isolation, a close-knit self-sufficient community life, inter-tribal political traditions, and an exchange-based economy—it is not exclusively a feature of the Melanesian Trobriand Islands. The Pacific island nations of Polynesia, including Hawaii and American Samoa, play a similar form of cricket known as Pacific cricket or Kilikiti. Competition between them culminates in a major tournament of Pacific cricket held in Auckland, New Zealand, each January.

Although initially triggered by Europeans, the development of Pacific cricket has been largely driven by cultural forces from within Melanesia and Polynesia. In contrast, the significant developments of the 1970s that transformed cricket among the major international playing countries were largely driven by business considerations. These were changes that led to increased marketing and promotion of test matches between these countries, to new structures of administration and management and to the establishment of one-day international cricket matches as popular entertainment. The one-day matches in particular, some of them played in the evenings under floodlights, draw large spectator audiences both to the venues and for television coverage. For these games a number of new rules governing field placements and bowling rates were introduced to make the game more entertaining, together with limitations on the number of balls that could be delivered by a single bowler. In addition, the traditional all-white dress codes for players were abandoned in favor of team colors for each competing nation.

Henry Blofeld (1978) identified three main ingredients in the initiation of changes that radically altered international cricket in the late 1970s: the professional players, Australian media mogul Kerry Packer, and the Australian government's quotas for locally produced television programs. The top professional cricketers desired to increase their incomes and rewards from the game. In comparison with other professional sports at that time, the salaries of top cricketers were low. In Australia some of the players' agents approached Kerry Packer, the owner of the Channel 9 television network, suggesting the development of a sponsored one-day cricket series to be broadcast live on the network. Kerry Packer's media organization had been taking a strategic look at future marketing opportunities and trends and concluded that the greatest potential for its television network lay in the development of sports programming. Sports programs could attract both sponsorship and the advertising revenue that would flow from delivering a mass viewing audience to the advertisers. They also overcame a contractual hurdle established by the Australian government in its granting of a television license to an independent network like Channel 9, namely that at least one-quarter of its transmitted programs should be produced in Australia. Locally produced sports programs not only fulfilled this condition of the government license but were, compared with other local "cultural" productions, relatively cheap to put on air.[2]

Packer, however, faced a problem. The television rights to international cricket matches played in Australia were under the control of the Australian Cricket Board. It had been the board's practice to sell the rights to the government-owned Australian Broadcasting Commission (ABC) for transmission on the ABC network. Packer needed exclusive rights to these matches for Channel 9 if he was to be able to deliver the size of audience necessary to attract advertisers. And he needed the potential of the advertising revenues to generate the income that would pay for the high cost of purchasing exclusive coverage rights in the first place. The hostility of the Cricket Board toward Packer and his ideas for greater commercialization of the sport were made clear when he failed to obtain from them exclusive rights to the coverage of, first, the 1975–76 test match series between Australia and the West Indies and, the following year, the series between Australia and Pakistan. In each case the board sold coverage rights to the ABC, in the latter case at a price lower than that offered by Channel 9. The upshot was that a frustrated Packer, when approached by the players' agents with the proposal for a one-day series, decided to try to break the Australian Cricket Board's monopoly of test matches by promoting his own series of five-day international games. The Packer organization signed up a large number of the world's top players at salaries up to ten times greater than they could obtain in the traditional structures of the sport and, in the Australian summer of 1977–78, World Series Cricket, or the Packer "Circus," was successfully launched with a series of matches between Australia and a Rest of the World XI. In contrast with the traditional organization of the game, almost half of World Series Cricket's revenues in its first year came from advertising and a large proportion of its expenditures went to the payment of the players.

World Series Cricket was part of a pattern of commercialization of sport set in train by the successful development of Jack Kramer's professional tennis circuit in the 1950s. This was a pattern in which, "in response to the apparent lack of marketing expertise displayed by the established authorities and the attraction of large potential profits, entrepreneurs [began] to challenge the sporting establishment by attracting away star players and mounting their own tournaments" (Sloane 1980: 70). In cricket as in other sports it eventually led to some accommodations between the new entrepreneurs and the traditional sporting administrations. In Australia, for example, the Australian Cricket Board and World Series Cricket came to an agreement in 1979 under which a Packer company, PBL Sports Pty.Ltd., was given exclusive rights to promote and market the board's cricket program, and the

Channel 9 network was given exclusive rights to televise Australian test and inter-state matches. Although the program of Packer's Circus was abandoned, many of its innovations remained a permanent feature of international cricket, particularly those associated with the one-day game; "we have come to terms," said the chairman of the Australian Cricket Board, "with the commercialism."

In the development of Trobriand cricket the game was changed to bring it into line with the rituals and symbolism of gift giving that were fundamental to Trobriand society's traditional exchange-based economy; cricket became culturally integrated. In the "Packer Revolution" the game was changed to make it compatible with the demands of the media, entertainment and advertising industries. If the cultures of the countries that play this form of international cricket could be described as "business cultures," then it would be arguable that the Packer-led changes were also in the direction of cultural integration. In both the Trobriand case and the Packer case cricket would have been subsumed in a larger cultural system: in the first, a system where the game was subordinated to ritual and, in the second, a system where the game was subordinated to business and commercial values. What does it mean, however, to describe a culture as a business culture?

TOWARD DEFINING THE CONDITIONS OF A BUSINESS CULTURE

Consideration of the role of business in society has focused primarily on the place of business in the social structure and the ways in which business activities impinge on social issues. Sociologies of business, for example, identify and describe the managerial and capitalist classes, their origins. characteristics and ideologies. They assess the status and prestige accorded to these classes and the roles they play in the economic, social and political life of communities and nations. They explore the political power of local and multinational business organizations and institutions and their influence on government and the state. The perspective of their authors is often one of concern about the elite status of business in modern society and of disquiet over the burgeoning power of big business in international affairs. The issue of social controls over business activity and conduct is central to this perspective.

Academic texts on business and society typically deal with relationships between business and society on an issue-by-issue basis. Issues covered include business and the environment, business and the consumer movement, business and equal employment opportunity, business and individual privacy, business ethics, business and government, business and the arts, business and the community, business and occupational health and safety, and the social responsibilities of business. Most such texts make a conceptual separation of business from society. Business is treated as a system that has its own internal commercial logic. The external, or "not-business," world of society is represented in terms of a series of forces that periodically impinge on business decisions. The texts generally have a managerial focus in that these external constraints on business decisions are seen from a management perspective, usually as unwelcome and negative constraints. The desirability of avoiding social controls on business activity and conduct is central to this perspective. External pressures and the activities and interests of external pressure groups—consumers, governments, environmentalists, women, unions—are to be monitored by managers, and, if possible, dealt with in ways that minimize their impact on commercial decisions. Business, in other words, has to develop a strategy for dealing with society.

Matters related to business and culture, however, have a different focus than sociologies of business and traditional books on business and society. While a division between business and society may be useful analytically, it is nevertheless clear that business is enmeshed with, embedded in, society and culture. The important impact of business on social structures, the development of business-driven market systems for the exchange of goods and services together with the involvement of business in the design and dispersion of new technologies, underscores the central role that business plays in shaping and changing society. The percolation into almost all cultures of business symbols, the language of business, and aspects of business ideology underscores the symbiotic relationship between business and culture.

In a business culture it will be business that dictates the whole way of life of a community. The notion of such a culture can be either confined or extended. Confined to the business community itself, it has a similar focus to that of organizational culture, a relatively restricted set of shared values and ways of doing things understood by a discrete group. Extended beyond the business community, business culture may permeate into all aspects of society and, if pervasive enough, become a suitable label with which to characterize a particular nation or a particular historical era.

What conditions would justify describing a culture as a business culture in this extended sense? First, that business institutions and organizations were the most powerful and influential in the society. Second, that the positions of highest social status and prestige in the society were dominated by business men and women or their representatives, and that key economic, social and political roles were allocated to, or acquired by, the members of this business class. Third, that business had a dominant role to play in the processes of socialization, both in education and in the acquisition of skills and experience. Fourth, that the principal media of socialization and enculturation—that is, the media through which social and cultural values were communicated and reinforced—were under business control. Fifth, that business organizations were primarily responsible for the development, utilization and diffusion of new technologies. Finally, that business symbols, business language, business beliefs and business ideologies pervaded all aspects of the culture, material, intellectual and spiritual.

Similar criteria could be used to describe a traditional familial culture, an aristocratic culture, a religious culture, a military culture, a party political culture or a pastoral agrarian culture. Over a period of time, through the processes of acculturation and cultural diffusion, business may gradually replace the family, the aristocracy, the priesthood, the military, the party hierarchy, or farmers as the fulcrum for cultural development. Equally important in the present context is the question of whether or not, in modern democratic societies, business culture is supplanting or suppressing cultural pluralism. The tensions that arise among the plurality of cultural forces in a society are one of the themes of this book, which explores some of the tensions that develop between business and other forces shaping culture. The chapters that follow examine in detail a few of the component parts of an extended business culture. Attention is paid to the development of the market as an instrument of social control, to the relationship between technology and culture, to the language and symbols of business, to the development of the "consciousness industries," and to the dissemination of business ideologies and values into the broader community, into sport, leisure, the arts and religion. Largely ignored are the equally significant issues of the political influence of business, the impact of business practices on politics, the relationship between business, government and the state, and the place of business men and women in the social structure, all of which have proven fertile fields of inquiry for the social sciences.

NOTES

1. James, C.L.R., 1963: preface.

2. Religious broadcasting and televangelism in the United States was similarly encouraged in the 1960s by a Federal Communications Commission directive allowing paid-for religious broadcasts to be considered part of a licensee's public-service programming quota (see Wilentz 1990: 145).

CHAPTER 3

The Market: From Moral Pariah to Moral Principle

THE GIFT-EXCHANGE ECONOMY

The previous chapter illustrated how, in the Trobriand Islands, the English game of cricket was assimilated into the competitive rituals and symbolism of ceremonial gift giving. The Trobriands were the islands studied by the anthropologist Bronislaw Malinowski between 1915 and 1918 and described in his *Argonauts of the Western Pacific*, published in 1932. The traditional Trobriand Island economy was one based on the exchange of gifts between villagers from the different islands. In some cases the gifts exchanged had purely ceremonial or symbolic value, as for example in exchanges of prized ornaments usually made from shells. Ritual exchanges of gifts of food had a more direct redistributive value in that they might involve exchanges of yam or taro or other vegetables grown by an inland village for fish caught by members of a coastal village. The rituals accompanying all these exchanges emphasized the interdependence of the different island villages and tribes. On other occasions there would be direct barter of produce between villages without the accompanying ceremonial activities.

These structures of reciprocal gift giving and barter created a system for redistributing surplus wealth. The impetus to create surplus wealth stemmed not only from the opportunity to access a broader supply of produce but also from status competition. Both for the individual family and for the village the growth and accumulation of a large stock of food was necessary to acquire prestige in the community. The ceremonial public display of food and other gifts, and the rituals accompanying the exchange and distribution of these gifts, provided communal recognition of this prestige. Occasionally chiefs would demonstrate their status by the conspicuous waste of food that had been stored for display. In general, however, just as in Trobriand cricket it was important not to win by too much, thereby demeaning the opposition, so too in Trobriand gift giving it was important not to cause envy and bitterness by overconspicuous displays of wealth. Gift giving that might establish reciprocal obligations that the other party could not meet was to be avoided. In this way the competitive creation and redistribution of surplus wealth was subject to social controls that minimized the potentially destructive aspects of that competition. Economic activity was also social and cultural activity. It took place within a well-understood cultural context and did not, therefore, threaten to destabilize Trobriand social structure.

Not all economies based upon gift-giving systems of exchange, however, were able to stimulate competition, yet contain its social impacts, so effectively. Cyril Belshaw (1965) described the destructive elements of traditional potlatch competition among the American and Canadian Indians of Vancouver Island and British Columbia. The ceremonial feasting and gift giving of the potlatch provided a mechanism for the accumulation and dispersal of surplus wealth. The giving of food, blankets, canoes and manufactured articles brought status and prestige upon the giver. Such gifts, however, created obligations for the recipient. They could not be refused and in due course had to be reciprocated with interest. This set in train an inflationary spiral of gift and counter-gift as rivals sought to outdo each other in an orgy of conspicuous generosity. A win-at-all-costs psychology entered into status competition, with rivals using the rituals of gift-exchange to show contempt for each other. The ultimate demonstration of wealth and status was the wholesale public destruction of valued products and artifacts, a practice that led Canadian authorities to repress potlatch ceremonies on the grounds that they were wasteful and prevented economic development.

Societies whose economies were exclusively geared to gift giving or to barter and exchange were generally small-scale societies with a common culture. James Redfield (1986: 36) observed that in economies like those of ancient Greece, "goods circulate in restricted networks, and the distribution of land, labor, and commodities are talked of in the language of loyalty and obligation. . . . Commodities, along with authority, are a sign of social status; conversely, the status thus signified constitutes a claim to authority and commodities." Economically self-sufficient village or peasant societies produce primarily for their own use and consumption. Where surpluses are created after subsistence needs are met, then some barter arrangements may be established with nearby communities. Alternatively, those surpluses may be passed to, or acquired by, the households of the leading families in the community, households that control access to land or employ labor. In ancient Greece, and alongside the market economies of medieval Europe, these households, through feasting and gift giving, acted to redistribute surpluses while at the same time entrenching their own prestige, status and position in the social structure. Within the processes of this redistributive network, "commodities change their meaning. What is sent up to the great house as a sign of subservience and deference is returned to the subservient as a sign of the master's generosity. The exchange is thus a form of cooperation which reinforces and at the same time seems to justify the unequal relations between the parties" (Redfield 1986: 36). In cementing the social relationship between the parties, the system of gift exchange also creates obligations on the leading households to provide protection from danger and shortages for the other members of the community:

Many of the payments and offerings that peasants would have no option but to deliver to their lords' homes were for long referred to in contemporary parlance as "presents" (eulogiae). . . . All these offerings had to be matched by open-handedness on the part of those who received them. No rich man could close his doors to petitioners, send away hungry folk seeking alms at his grain-store, or turn down wretched men offering their services in return for food, clothing and protection. . . . It was through seigneurial munificence that early medieval Europe achieved some degree of social justice and reduced total destitution to mere poverty. (Duby 1974: 51)

Gift-exchange and barter were not the only ways in which commodities were redistributed and wealth shared out in pre-market economies. Complementary mechanisms included theft, organized raiding, pillage and warfare. They were complementary in the sense that what was taken through such means still entered into the social framework of gift giving. In the European warrior societies of the Dark Ages, peace between tribes or communities would be cemented by exchanges of gifts. The commodities acquired by theft or conquest would not only be shared out among the comrades-in-arms of a war leader but gifted to churches or monasteries in recognition of divine support of a successful campaign and in anticipation of future protection and prosperity: "In the collective psychology of those times giving was the necessary counterpart of taking" (Duby 1974: 50).

Just as elements of market exchange were present in largely gift-exchange economies, so too elements of gift-exchange survive in the modern market economy. The presentation of gifts and the provision of sumptuous meals accompany major family and communal events—the celebration of births and marriages, giving someone a "good send-off" at their funeral, religious and secular holidays like Christmas, Thanksgiving, and the New Year. Gifts may also be exchanged to cement a business relationship or to mark the successful conclusion of a business negotiation. In the business context the gift becomes a symbol of goodwill between the parties, of their desire to establish or continue a mutually beneficial relationship. As such there may be no expectation of a direct material return from the gift; it is not a payment for specific services rendered or anticipated. The business gift does, however, set up some sense of obligation to reciprocate in kind at some later time. The precise nature of this reciprocal behavior may be unstated or ambiguous. Clearly, however, if a business gift is made in order to create some obligation on the part of the recipient to take some specific action that will advantage the gift-giver, then the fine line between a gift and a bribe may be crossed. It is easy to see how ambiguous gift giving may become in the context of relationships that are primarily commercial and how difficult it may be to determine when a gift is a gift and when a gift is a bribe. In addition, customs vary from country to country. In Japan, for example, gift giving is an integral part of the everyday conduct of business and social life. Subordinates give gifts to superiors and benefactors. Employees, whenever they take a holiday, bring back gifts for the members of their work group. Indeed, they can buy appropriate gifts from all parts of the country at the main railway station in Tokyo. Companies, "the biggest gift-givers in Japan . . . give year-end gifts to 'reward' customers for past patronage, to express gratitude, and to build up obligation for future business" (De Mente 1975: 58). It is therefore not surprising to find that companies involved in international trade provide their staff with information on the protocols of business gift giving in the different countries where they operate and issue precise guidelines for their staff on the giving and receiving of gifts in those countries. The need for such policies was reinforced by the Foreign Corrupt Practices Act (1977). This act, passed after a number of bribery scandals in the mid–1970s, and opposed by the U.S. business community on the grounds that it would give their international competitors an unfair advantage, made it a criminal offense to bribe government officials in order to obtain or retain business.

The competitive element of gift giving in some pre-market economies is also still present. At its simplest level it is the motivational base exploited in much charitable fund-raising activity. In Telethons, for example, it is common for individuals or groups to pledge or donate money with an accompanying challenge to their friends or rivals to match or better their contribution. At fund-raising dinners the atmosphere generated by the public declaration of money gifts encourages conspicuous displays of generosity, displays that provide immediate gratification and prestige for the donors. More destructive and less communally beneficial aspects of gift giving can be seen in periodic displays of conspicuous consumption comparable to the excesses of some potlatch ceremonies. In the United States between 1890 and 1912, a period described by Miriam Beard (1938) as the "Business Baroque" and the "age of arrogance," wealthy industrialists and financiers vied with each other for social status and prestige, often aping the ways of European nobility. The wife of Cornelius Vanderbilt III appeared at the opera wearing a crown that was a replica of Queen Victoria's. A Newport millionaire erected a Tudor mansion at great expense and introduced Tudor words into his vocabulary, commencing every sentence with "prithee." He in turn was upstaged by a coal baron's reproduction of Buckingham Palace at a cost of $5 million. Mason recounts that guests at parties were given $100 bills with which to light their after-dinner cigars, waterfalls were installed in dining rooms for dinner dances, and garden trees were decorated with artificial fruit made of 14-carat gold: "Spending was lavish, always conspicuous and intended solely to achieve social status and recognition" (Mason 1981: 69).

Much of the wealth of this age of arrogance flowed from the plunder and piracy of the new robber barons of nineteenth-century America. The spread of corporate stocks and bonds among a wider investing public during the 1840s and 1850s, and the speculation associated with railway development and the opening up of the West Coast, led to an increasing emphasis on money wealth rather than the ownership of land. In the 1850s, as in the 1980s, money making had become one of the virtues and was no longer subject to any moral code. The financiers, speculators and manipulators of corporate stocks and bonds had displaced the engineers, manufacturers and industrialists in the hierarchy of business and social prestige. The tag of robber baron, used to describe the owners of the new monopolies created by such stock manipulations, originated in the 1860s with *The New York Times'* description of Cornelius Vanderbilt:

If ever there was a man who made his way in the world, it is Mr. Cornelius Vanderbilt. . . . Like those old German barons who, from their eyries along the Rhine, swooped down upon the commerce of the noble river, and wrung tribute from every passenger that floated by, Mr. Cornelius Vanderbilt, with all the steamers of the Accessory Transit Company held in his leash, has insisted that the Pacific company should pay him toll, taken of all America that had business with California and the Southern Sea, and the Pacific Company have submitted to his demand. (Cochran 1959: 174–75)

A further aspect of gift-giving economies with parallels in industrial and contemporary market economies is that aspect that relates to the obligations of the wealthy and powerful. Indeed, when the Industrial Revolution led to the growth of a new manufacturing class in England, one of the complaints of the old landed aristocracy was that the nouveau riche self-made industrial magnates had no sense of noblesse oblige, no understanding that privilege entailed responsibility. They deplored the fact that manufacturers did not extend the kind of paternalistic patronage toward their workers that the great households had traditionally extended to their staff, that the cash nexus between employer and employee was replacing a network of personal and social relationships between masters and servants. Ralph Waldo Emerson described the emerging middle class in England as an "untitled nobility [who] possess all the power without the inconveniences that belong to rank" (Melada 1970: 188–89).[1]

However a number of manufacturers in England, like the socialist Robert Owen in the late eighteenth century and the Quaker chocolate-making companies of Cadbury, Fry and Rowntrees in the nineteenth century, prompted by their own social philosophies and religious beliefs, provided their employees with comprehensive housing and welfare facilities. In the United States the baron of the steel industry, Andrew Carnegie, sought to identify the new industrialists with the patrician practices of the old nobility that he so despised—one of his boyhood dreams had been "to grow up to kill a king"—rather than with the predatory exploits of his robber baron contemporaries. In his essay *The Gospel of Wealth* (1889) Carnegie wrote of the social responsibilities and obligations that attended business success:

This, then, is held to be the duty of the man of wealth: To set an example of modest unostentatious living, shunning display or extravagance; to provide moderately for the legitimate wants of those dependent upon him; and, after doing so, to consider all surplus revenues which come to him simply as trust funds, which he is called upon to administer in the manner which, in his judgment, is best calculated to produce the most beneficial results for the community—the man of wealth thus becoming the mere trustee and agent for his poorer brethren, bringing to their service his superior wisdom, experience, and ability to administer, doing for them better than they would or could do for themselves. (Carnegie 1962: 25)

Although not a religious man, Carnegie was reiterating the doctrine, central to the Protestant ethic, of the stewardship of wealth, a doctrine that expected successful business men and women to use their money to the advantage of the community. It encouraged Carnegie and other millionaires to turn their industrial trusts into philanthropic trusts and led to substantial patronage of schools, libraries, museums, orphanages, hospitals and churches. Initially much of this often very conspicuous philanthropy was directed at the "deserving" poor and working classes in the industrializing economies, those who were "industrious and ambitious," "the best and most aspiring poor of the community . . . who, being most anxious and able to help themselves, deserve and will be benefitted by help from others and by the extension of their opportunities by the aid of the philanthropic rich" (Carnegie 1962: 31).

On the basis of interviews with 140 millionaire philanthropists, Teresa Odendahl has argued that in the contemporary United States the "culture of philanthropy" is a system that services the social elite. Underwritten by the tax advantages of charitable donations and the tax-exempt status of many non-profit organizations, the institutions funded and supported by wealthy philanthropists are primarily institutions of "high culture" patronized by the rich—opera, ballet, symphony, theater, the fine arts. Consequently, other than in the trickle-down form of crumbs from the rich man's table, philanthropic gift giving of this kind no longer serves to substantially redistribute wealth within the community. Rather, suggests Odendahl, it serves to reinforce the power and status of the rich within the community and "assists in the social reproduction of the upper class" (Odendahl 1990: 232):

Through their donations and work for voluntary organizations, the charitable rich exert enormous influence in society. As philanthropists, they acquire status within and outside of their class. Although private wealth is the basis of the hegemony of this group, philanthropy is essential to the maintenance and perpetuation of the upper class in the United States. In this sense, nonprofit activities are the nexus of a modern power elite. (Odendahl 1990: 4)

DEVELOPMENT OF THE MARKET ECONOMY

Many elements of a gift-exchange economy were continued as market economies developed. The early marketplaces were those of peasant or agrarian societies. Producers brought their small surpluses for sale to other members of the community. Consequently market activity took place within a network of personal face-to-face relationships. The approximation of the conditions of pure competition, together with the personalized trading context, provided both market and non-market social controls to constrain exploitation of buyers or sellers. In the marketplace, however, the personal relationship between buyer and seller might be established solely to facilitate the continuity of market transactions between them. In the gift-exchange economy, in contrast, transactions served primarily as a means of sustaining personal and social relationships. The shift from a gift-exchange economy to a market economy marked, then, a gradual change in emphasis in economic and social relations. As market activity expanded, it was a change that would have major consequences in terms of social structure and social control.

The establishment and development of the market required stability and security. "In the absence of secure political institutions, gift-exchange, in which the transaction is in the service of the relation, is rationally preferred to market-exchange, in which the relation is entered into for the sake of the transaction" (Redfield 1986: 37). In part the security of markets was a product of urbanization that, in the case of the Greek city states, for example, provided citizens with an environment relatively secure from piracy and raiding. Urbanization stimulated the development of central marketplaces and brought together in one place a group of people who depended on the market for their basic necessities. At the same time the growth of a non-agricultural labor force located in towns and cities encouraged a greater specialization in production. What was brought to the market was no longer the surplus from production for use; increasingly production for the market became the norm.

The development and dispersion of market activity also required some standardized and acceptable medium of exchange. Joe Cribb (1986) illustrates and describes the variety of objects that different societies have made use of as a medium of exchange: feathers, stones, iron rods, copper rings, salt, cattle and other livestock, as well as coins and banknotes. Cowrie shells, a species of mollusc found in the shallow waters of the Indian Ocean, were used as a form of money in China at least three thousand years ago and later in India, Thailand and East and West Africa. It is a usage reflected in the scientific name of the shells, *cuprea moneta*, or "money cowries." Coins are first found in Greece in the seventh century B.C., and the first known banknotes are from China in the eleventh century A.D. In many societies cult objects, which were already invested with symbolic meaning in the life of the community, became the national medium of exchange. The words *money* and *mint* both had religious links; their origin lies in the establishment of the Roman mint in the temple of the goddess Juno Moneta. Originally in English the word *money* referred exclusively to coinage, only later acquiring its more comprehensive modern meaning as any medium of exchange.

With greater security of markets, concentrations of population and systems of monetary exchange came a consolidation of trade over larger and larger distances. Increasingly this trade was conducted by middlemen and wholesalers rather than directly by the producers of commodities and artifacts. The activities of wholesalers meant that the market became an important vehicle for the storage of products as well as for their immediate redistribution. Gradually there emerged a group of people whose sole livelihood stemmed from trading activities, whether as entrepreneurs, wholesalers or retailers. Gradually, too, whole communities began to depend on the market activities of these people; by the fifth century B.C., for example, Athens was importing three-quarters of her staple food requirements (Redfield 1986: 46).

As market exchange developed, the activities of entrepreneurs, traders and businessmen[2] became a source of social and political tension. Traders and business people naturally sought to establish a social and political place for themselves within their communities, a place commensurate with their growing economic importance. This brought them into conflict with those groups who already enjoyed positions of prestige and status within the social structure. Communities responded in a number of different ways to the increasing power and affluence of the members of the business sector. Some took a largely defensive and conservative posture and sought to protect traditional social structures by insulating them from the commercial world. In ancient Greece, for example, while real money was to be made in trade, landowning and agricultural self-sufficiency continued as the most valued source of social status. The primacy of agriculture over trade was reinforced by epic literature and by elaborate fertility rituals that portrayed agriculture as a transaction with the gods, a divine status never achieved by commerce. The heroes of Homer's *Iliad* and *Odyssey* did not buy and sell commodities: "Commerce is carried on only by the disreputable Phoenicians, 'tricksters, dealing in countless trinkets' . . . ; these are like stereotypical gypsies, mysteriously appearing and disappearing, seducing women and stealing babies" (Redfield 1986: 30).

The suspect social and cultural position of business and trade is a theme running through the history of Western economic development. Georges Duby documents how in the period of the early growth of the European economy, tenacious reinforcement of the ideology and mental attitudes associated with the traditional gift economy was an important constraint on profit making in the market economy. The profit motive and the desire for personal wealth were neither congruent with the traditions of chivalry—of the unselfish, generous nobleman, immersed in debt—nor with the teachings of the Christian Church:

> The Church set before the rich an ideal of perfection: poverty, renunciation of worldly goods, and contempt for money, which twelfth century heresiarchs and orthodox preachers, like the monks of the first millennium, deemed a blemish on the soul. For the men of this age as for their more distant forebears, and all the more readily because their material circumstances kept them secure from want, economic realities were of secondary consideration. They were epiphenomena; the real world was of the spirit, on a supernatural plane. It alone merited attention. Subordination of the economic to the ethical was total, and applicable for a long time to come. (Duby 1974: 259–60)

One of the consequences of this prevailing ideological hostility to money making was that entrepreneurs sought to establish their place within the secular social structure by entering the nobility, and to secure their soul's place within the eternal hierarchy by almsgiving, gifts of piety and service to the destitute.

In the Middle Ages particular controversy surrounded the question of usury, a controversy that Jacques Le Goff describes as the "labor pains of capitalism" (Le Goff 1988: 9). He traces the long Christian tradition condemning usury or the lending of money at interest, a practice forbidden to clerics around A.D. 300 and to Christian laymen in A.D. 626. The Church never censored every form of interest but sought to legitimate lawful profit and differentiate it from unlawful usury. Usury applied to collecting interest on money and arose only "where there is no production or physical transformation of goods" (Le Goff 1988: 18). During the commercial revolution of the twelfth and thirteenth centuries, when a developing money economy was threatening the traditional values and beliefs taught by the Church Fathers, there was growing censure of usury in both secular law and canon law. Thus English law, for example, forbade citizens from establishing themselves in business as private moneylenders. In contrast, prior to their expulsion in 1290 by Edward I, Jews were excluded from all occupations except moneylending; they were the property of the crown and acted as its bankers. Jews were not officially readmitted to England until 1656. The expulsion of Jews from France in 1306, however, was short-lived. They were readmitted in 1315 after popular clamor against the excessive interest rates of Christian moneylenders (see Wills 1990: 22). But for Christians usury was not only a crime, it was a sin, a form of avarice or cupidity. Indeed, argues Le Goff, the bourgeois sin of avarice, the mother of usury, supplanted the feudal sin of pride as the chief of the Seven Deadly Sins. Usurers, along with prostitutes and acrobats, were refused Christian burial and the right to give alms. The usurer, described by Le Goff as a "pre-capitalist Dracula," had an image that makes the modern loan shark look positively benign. Hostility to usurers often spread to merchants generally, particularly merchant bankers. The legal and moral prohibitions and constraints on usury gave banking a disreputable image in medieval times. One of the consequences of Christianity's antipathy to commerce in general and moneylending in particular was that trading and banking was often left to non-Christians. Banking developments, for example, were left mainly in the hands of Jews and Lombards. Indeed, as Leon Poliakov (1977) demonstrated, the Jewish community enjoyed special protection from the Church, a protection that had both economic and theological foundations. Talmudic tradition took a much more utilitarian view of banking and moneylending. Although the pursuit of a craft was preferable to engagement in trade, trading in money was not judged a priori good or evil, but, rather, looked at in terms of its consequences for Judaism and the Jewish community.

Le Goff's work shows how an ideological obstacle such as the Church's teachings about usury "can fetter or delay the development of a new economic system" (Le Goff 1988: 69). It also illustrates the slowness of the transition from one economic system embedded in a maze of social relationships to another. Le Goff in addition analyzes how the Christian Church adapted its teachings in response to the new economic realities of a market economy. He suggests that three complementary forces led to the greater acceptance of the Christian usurer. One was the appearance of new values in the realm of economic activities, particularly ideas related to risk and uncertainty. This facilitated a more sophisticated discrimination between forms of legitimate profit making and usury, a form of riskless profit. Profit from lending at interest was sanctioned if it provided a reasonable return for risk and effort. A second development was in the practices of moneylending, particularly in moderation and control of interest rates. Thus usury came increasingly to mean excessive profit making, an illegitimate and unlawful excess or surplus. Finally, and most importantly in Le Goff's view, the Church refashioned its theology to condemn the usurer to purgatory rather than to hell. This allowed some hope that the usurer's soul could be saved from eternal damnation and that with appropriate restitution of his worldly goods, and prayers, offerings and intercessions on his behalf by his loved ones after his death, his soul could finally enter paradise. However, it was not until 1830 that the Catholic Church formally reversed its opposition to usury and conceded that the charging and taking of interest did not necessarily imperil the soul's salvation.

In general, when social roles are despised, so too are their incumbents.

This was certainly the fate of the Jewish moneylender in European popular culture as moneylending became widespread throughout Europe from the second half of the twelfth century. It was also, though less dramatically and with less disastrous personal and social consequences, the fate of business entrepreneurs and traders generally. As we shall see periodically throughout this book, the portrayal of business and business executives in literature and drama reflects a well established tradition of anti-business sentiment and a continuing suspicion about the role of business within society. It was in literature and drama, too, that the impact of the market culture on notions of the self and of society were explored (Agnew 1986).

A strand of thinking that is critical of money and trade, of the market economy, of the ideology and practice of business, can clearly be seen in Western culture. This has led, argue Maurice Bloch and Jonathan Parry, to an ill-founded set of distinctions between monetary and non-monetary economies. The market economy is presented as the antithesis of the gift-exchange economy, and production for exchange the antithesis of an ideal of self-sufficient production for use. The result has been a highly romanticized idealization of the world of gift-exchange as "non-exploitative, innocent and even transparent." The anthropological literature, however, reveals a vastly more complex picture of enormous cultural variations in the meanings given to monetary and non-monetary transactions. Thus Parry can write about "the poison of the gift" and "the innocence of commerce," illustrating how in many exchange systems the gift can carry moral peril for the recipient and also be expected to yield profit to the donor. It is only in Western culture that the "ideology of the gift . . . has been constructed in antithesis to market exchange" (Bloch and Parry 1989: 9).

Not all pre-capitalist societies, however, sought to constrain the impact of business and trade by subordinating business activities to a superstructure of religious and ideological beliefs and their supporting cultural symbols. Nor was the role of the state exclusively one of protecting the existing social system and social structure from the consequences of economic development. In ancient Carthage, for example, the maligned Phoenicians, a community of traders, found a different way of resolving the tensions between economic power, political power and the social structure. They developed a constitution in which the highest offices were put up for sale (Redfield 1986: 48). The state, the system of government and the social structure became a mirror image of economic life. Other societies accepted the benefits that accrued from the development of trade but sought at the same time to insulate trading activities and markets from the rest of the life of the community. "Free cities" and "ports of trade," for example, were trading posts set up in neutral territory. The port of trade par excellence of the ancient world was Alexandria, a city commissioned by Alexander the Great to stand at the crossroads of trade between the Orient and the Mediterranean via the Red Sea. Autonomous and neutral Alexandria was built by a Greek government on Egyptian soil and then settled by Jews and Egyptians to diminish Greek dominance (Polanyi et al. 1957: 61). Such politically neutral trading places often had special legal protection. In Hittite law, for example, "the killing of a trader amounts to murder, the killing of others, to manslaughter" (Polanyi 1957: 54). In these enclaves the market economy was permitted to flourish without political interference and without the constraints of traditional social mores, religious beliefs and cultural values that might be hostile to unbridled profit making.

THE CULTURE AND MORALITY OF THE MARKET

"The important thing to have is a spiritual environment in this country that will mean we can keep the money we make."
—Nelson Bunker Hunt speaking at an investment seminar for millionaires. (Quoted in Corwin 1986: 119)

The market economy gradually came to permeate all aspects of the economic, political, social and cultural life of many societies. The adjustments and accommodations that societies made, reluctantly or otherwise, to the development of the market economy are indicative of the major impact of the market on culture—on symbols, on language and on beliefs. For example, the symbolism of money changed. In its early forms money had both economic and religious or magical significance. The objects or artifacts or commodities used as mediums of exchange were ones that were sacred in some way (Mauss 1970). They had stories and legends attached to them; they had their own spiritual qualities and personality. Their exchange was often accompanied by elaborate rituals and ceremonies that reinforced the central place that the objects had in the ideological superstructure of the culture. (The signs and symbols of the market economy, as Chapter 5 indicates, carry quite different connotations and ideological messages.) In contrast, in the market economy money loses most of its subjective, personalized properties. In its new abstract, objective form it becomes an important instrument in motivating behavior and a commodity on which people, both as producers and consumers, are increasingly dependent. Within the market economy money is an instrument of social control, directly in that it rewards certain kinds of behavior, and indirectly in that it provides access to the commodities, artifacts and lifestyles that symbolize prestige and status.

Language, a touchstone of cultural change and development, also reflected the transition to a market economy. Sandra Fischer, for example, has traced the impact of economic terminology on English Renaissance drama. She shows how concepts such as exchange value and profit seeking are sprung loose from the traditional morality and customs that tried to constrain them. In the Renaissance period, she argues, economics begins to define, rather than to be defined by, social relationships and individual motivations. Metaphors drawn from the market and from economic transactions are applied to human values and social relations rather than vice versa. In this transition from medieval to mercantilist ethics, the metaphors "indicate first a resistance to the exchange ethic, then a grappling with its operation, and finally an acceptance of its metamorphosed system of economy as the dominant force in society" (Fischer 1985: 18). In Renaissance drama,

plots often treat the growing connection between money and love; courtship and marriage become economic games, legal contracts, exchange transactions. The transference of wealth begins to represent love, the possession of wealth to define social value and status, and human relations to offer themselves primarily as means to profit through exploitation of exchange value rather than appreciation of intrinsic worth. (Fischer 1975: 16)

There are many contemporary parallels in the literature of popular psychology where personal relationships are described with trading metaphors and personality as a commodity to be developed with an eye to its commercial value and marketability. (This commercialization of the self is given further consideration in Chapter 9.)

In modern times the debates about the nature of the market economy and its social and cultural impacts have not focused primarily on comparisons, however inadequately informed, with earlier gift-exchange economic systems. Rather, they have focused on comparisons with the twentieth-century command economies until recently common in Eastern Europe and the Soviet Union. The debate has had a clear ideological component. It has been argued, for example, that the market economy is not simply a more efficient system for the creation of wealth and the distribution of goods and services. It is also a necessary condition for a democratic society. Thus the free market becomes a synonym for personal freedom. Without the free market both individual and political liberties will be severely constrained. Democracy itself is defined in terms of a market analogy. It is the political free market in which individuals and groups can seek to sell their ideological wares. The equation between democracy and the market economy, between economic freedoms and political freedoms, is not a new one. Indeed, it has been suggested that the period during which the Western world, with its associated values of liberty and individualism, became "Western" was the period during which it first developed the free market, a period of two hundred years from the early eighth century to the early sixth century B.C. (Redfield 1986: 29).

It is not difficult to see, therefore, how the market economy, having become divorced from the ideological and moral constraints imposed by vestiges of gift-giving economies, develops around it a new set of beliefs and values. These have been variously described as the ideology of market capitalism, the morality of the market, the market ethic. The invariable focus is on the ways in which the market imposes its values on society and culture rather than the ways in which social and cultural values are imposed upon the market. The market is no longer simply a system of exchange to be evaluated solely in terms of criteria of economic performance:

> In American culture, the market carries additional significance. Whether we acknowledge it consciously or not, the market influences our basic values, helps shape our suppositions about reality, and figures centrally in our tacit assumptions about daily life. We invest the market with moral importance and associate it with many of our most deeply held beliefs. In fact, the market system is so inextricably woven into our view of the world that any threat to the market endangers not only our standard of living but, more important, the very fabric of our society. (Wuthnow 1982: 77)

Robert Wuthnow goes on to identify a number of elements that illustrate the moral characteristics ascribed to market activity. First, participation in the market as a producer or consumer is viewed as a direct form of participation in public life, analogous to voting. Such participation links individuals to each other and to their societies, directly in the exercise of individual choices in the marketplace, and indirectly through Adam Smith's "invisible hand" whereby the collectivity of individually pursued economic interests advances the general social welfare or, to use the terminology of Bernard de Mandeville's satirical *The Fable of the Bees* (1714), "Publick Benefits" flow from "Private Vices." (Adam Smith, it is worth recalling, was a professor moral philosophy.) Second, the market provides individuals with a sense of freedom and dignity and helps to shape moral character. The competitive struggle of the market economy provides a testing ground for the development of talent. It develops self-reliance and self-discipline and fosters the virtues extolled in the self-help manuals of the eighteenth and nineteenth centuries—hard work, frugality, sobriety, perseverance and a general desire for self-improvement. Third, the moral character of the market is evident in that the market is frequently the focus of moral crusades:

> The consumer protection, environmental, antismoking and antinuclear movements, for example—no less than the drives for equal employment, fair housing, accurate advertising, and cleaned-up television—share the assumption that the marketplace is an important focus for moral behavior. Whether to smoke cigarettes, recycle beer cans, and install solar collectors have become decisions of moral as well as economic importance. (Wuthnow 1982: 79)

To Wuthnow's examples can be added such items as fur coats, tuna fish caught without netting dolphins, and a variety of biodegradable and ozone-friendly household products. Thus our purchase decisions can elicit feelings of righteousness or of guilt; the supermarket becomes our confessional.

Fourthly, there is a comparison and implicit corollary between market freedoms and other freedoms. This places the idea of the free market on the same moral plane as freedom of speech, freedom of religion and freedom of thought. Tobacco companies and their supporters, for example, have opposed government regulation and legislative constraints on the promotion and advertising of tobacco products on the grounds, among others, that such actions were undemocratic attacks on a fundamental freedom, the freedom of commercial speech. They have claimed that curtailments of the freedom of commercial speech are an infringement of the United Nations Universal Declaration of Human Rights. The market, then, is seen not only as an arena that maximizes individual freedoms but also an arena in which collective freedoms are to be advanced and protected.

Critics of the market economy are not so bullish about its economic or its moral virtues. The conventional list of its defects is a long one. It includes the market economy's inherent impetus toward monopoly, its failure to produce public goods, its inability to take appropriate account of the social costs of economic activities, the insecurity and instability that it fosters, its focus on the production of trivialities, its wastage of resources, and its generation of vast discrepancies in the ownership of wealth and property (Lindblom 1977). Indeed, the capitalist market economy has had to bear the burden of all society's ills, from crime and racism to sexism, militarism, imperialism, exploitation of people and resources, environmental degradation, drugs, alcoholism, wife beating, infertility and even the state of the nation's teeth (Lindblom 1977; Merritt 1982; Harris 1987): "In the United States . . . great wealth still leaves a segment of the population in a demoralizing welfare system. Its streets and homes are increasingly unsafe. Its expensive legal system is open to the rich, inaccessible to the poor for civil law, and hostile to the poor in criminal law. Its factories, automobiles, and indifferent citizens degrade the environment in countless ways" (Lindblom 1977: 247).

In addition, it has been argued that the market's encouragement to individuals to pursue their economic self-interest, far from stimulating cooperative effort and a sense of community, produces a particular cluster of personality types. Robert Smither (1984), for example, has delineated the origins and development of "the capitalist personality." Through analysis of the experiences of refugees trying to adjust to life in the United States, he seeks to demonstrate how our personality and behavior reflect the economic system, the economic culture, in which we were raised, that economics is "the greatest determinant of personality and behavior." In similar vein, Erich Fromm called one particular character type "the marketing orientation" and placed its origins in the market economy:

The market concept of value, the emphasis on exchange value rather than on use value, has led to a similar concept of value with regard to people and particularly to oneself. The character orientation which is rooted in the experience of oneself as a commodity and of one's value as exchange value I call the marketing orientation.

In our time the marketing orientation has been growing rapidly, together with the development of a new market that is a phenomenon of the last decades—the "personality market"...

The principle of evaluation is the same on both the personality and the commodity markets: on the one, personalities are offered for sale; on the other, commodities. (Fromm 1947: 76)

In the 1980s the yuppie lifestyle reflected a similar obsession with the presentation of images in the personality market. The yuppie became the quintessential characterization of the moral and economic spirit of the times:

He became the collective projection of a moral anxiety. We loaded onto him everything we hated about the times we had been living through—everything we hated about what we suspected we ourselves might have become. We made the Yuppie the effigy of selfishness and self-absorption, of the breakdown of social solidarity, of rampant careerism and obsessive ambition, of the unwholesome love of money, of the delusion that social problems have individual solutions, of callousness and contempt towards "losers," of the empty ideology of winnerism and the uncritical worship of "success." Then we strung the little bastard up. (Hertzberg 1990: 82)

Ambivalence toward profit making and toward individual wealth has been a continuing theme in the discussion about the morality of the market. At one end of this debate were the Christian Church's theological concerns about usury, the stewardship of wealth and the place of business success in the divine order. At the other end were secular ideologies that sanctioned economic individualism, a predatory business mode and ruthless pursuit of wealth in the competitive jungle of the marketplace. In the one, avarice is a deadly sin, the antithesis of godliness:

But the Devil created... the usurers. They do not participate in men's labors, and they will not be punished with men, but with the demons. For the amount of money they receive from usury corresponds to the amount of wood sent to Hell to burn them. The thirst of cupidity impels them to drink filthy water and to acquire filthy money by deceit and usury. Of their thirst Jeremiah [2:25] has said, "Stop parching your throat." And since, in violation of the legal interdict, usurers feed upon cadavers and carcasses when they eat food acquired by usury, this food cannot be sanctified by the sign of the cross or by some other blessing; and so, as Proverbs [4:17] tells us, "They eat the bread of wickedness and drink the wine of violence." (From thirteenth-century model sermon, Le Goff 1988: 56–57)

In the other, as parodied in the character of corporate raider Gordon Gekko addressing the board of the Teldar Paper Company in the 1988 film *Wall Street*, avarice is god and the norms of the competitive market encapsulate social virtue:

Greed, for lack of a better word, is good. Greed is right. Greed works. Greed clarifies, cuts through and captures the essence of the evolutionary spirit. Greed in all of its forms—greed for life, for money, love, knowledge—has marked the upward surge of mankind and greed—you mark my words—will not only save Teldar Paper but that other malfunctioning corporation called the U.S.A.[3]

Between these extreme positions lies a debate that goes to the paradox at the heart of the market economy. The promise of personal or corporate accumulation of capital, wealth and power is the motivating force that stimulates competition and guarantees the investment of individual energy and initiative in profit-seeking activities. But the consequences of successful accumulations of capital, wealth and power may be destructive of the social and cultural fabric within which market activity is embedded. It is from within this paradox that government interventions both to stimulate the market and to constrain its consequences evolve. And it is from within this paradox that the social and cultural values that underpin such interventions are accommodated to the ideology of the market economy.

Bloch and Parry (1989: 24) have argued, on the basis of the anthropological literature, that there are significant cross-cultural regularities and continuities in the moral evaluation of exchange systems, regularities and continuities revealed by the identification of two "related but separate transactional orders: on the one hand transactions concerned with the reproduction of the long-term social or cosmic order; on the other a 'sphere' of short-term transactions concerned with the arena of individual competition." Thus, for example, short-term competitive raiding has to be encompassed within a larger moral framework of redistribution of stolen wealth. Similarly the accumulation of private wealth has to be subordinate to the larger morality of noblesse oblige, the doctrine of stewardship or the culture of philanthropy. They suggest, however, that in the modern market economy the organic relationship between these two transactional systems, in which the morality of the long-term reproduction of the system is more important than the morality of short-term acquisition, may have broken down:

By a remarkable conceptual revolution what has uniquely happened in capitalist ideology, the argument would run, is that the values of the short-term order have become elaborated into a theory of long-term reproduction. What our culture (like others) had previously made room for in a separate and subordinate domain has, in some quarters at least, been turned into a theory of the encompassing order—a theory in which it is *only* unalloyed private vice that can sustain the public benefit. (Bloch and Parry 1989: 29)

The development of the market economy, in changing the practical conditions and everyday experience of life, reshaped societies and remodelled cultures. It changed language and consciousness. It stimulated new conceptions and expressions of personality. It created tension between the economic order and the political and social system. In the processes of social and cultural adjustment to the market economy, moral codes and religious beliefs were revised. In general the changes were in the direction of the replacement of customs, behaviors and ideas that constrained market activity, first with customs, behaviors and ideas that were compatible with it, and then with customs, behaviors and ideas that were generated by market activity itself.

"MARKET RELATIONSHIPS MAY SERIOUSLY DAMAGE YOUR HEALTH"[4]

Consideration of the respective merits of an economy based upon gift-exchange and an economy based upon the commercial market are at the root of contemporary debates on the economics of charity and the provision of health care. In the 1970s this debate focused in particular on the blood business. The question raised was how best to meet the growth in demand for blood and blood by-products. This demand was increasing rapidly as a consequence of the rising number of motor accidents and the development of new surgical techniques such as open-heart surgery. On the one hand were those who argued that the market mechanism—money payment for blood—was the best way to resolve the shortage of supply. On the other were those who advocated the development of voluntary donations of blood, reliance on the altruism of donors rather than on monetary incentives.

The sensitivities raised by this issue, and by extension the issues of organ supply for transplant or the commercial adoption of children, reflect the difficulty we have in detaching some "commodities" from their symbolic meanings, their cultural contexts. Blood, for example, is surrounded with symbols, language and beliefs that make it difficult to consider as a conventional market commodity comparable to bread, cheese or chocolate cake.[5] In most cultures blood has some central part to play in religion, folklore or mythology, and rituals and ceremonies involving blood are customary:

For centuries in all cultures and societies, blood has been regarded as a vital, and often magical, life-sustaining fluid, marking all important events in life, marriage, birth, initiation and death, and its loss has been associated with disgrace, disgust, impotence, sickness and tragedy. Symbolically and functionally, blood is deeply embedded in religious doctrine; in the psychology of human relationships; and in theories and concepts of race, kinship, ancestor worship and the family. From time immemorial it has symbolized qualities of fortitude, vigor, nobility, purity and fertility. (Titmuss 1970: 15–16)

The rejuvenating qualities ascribed to blood are evident in practices such as bathing in blood, or drinking the blood of the young or of defeated warriors. The political symbolism of blood appears in practices where covenants, contracts and treaties are "sealed in blood." Contracts with the devil are also signed in blood. The spiritual symbolism of blood is a central feature of the Christian eucharist: "Whoso eateth my flesh and drinketh my blood hath eternal life; and I will raise him up at the last day." For Orthodox Jews the blood of the animal is the essence of life, and it is only after the blood has been removed that the flesh may be safely eaten. Superstitions about the soul being in the blood still emerge in the hostility of some religious sects to blood transfusions. In some cases such superstitions are married to racial beliefs. During World War II, for example, Plymouth Brethren tried to prevent the Red Cross from pooling the blood of black and white Americans. The racial connotations of blood had an appalling political legacy in Nazi Germany's slogan of Aryan superiority: "Think with your blood."

Animal as well as human blood has been ascribed medicinal qualities. Earle Hackett (1973) relates that in the Greek Herbal of Dioscorides, sunburn was to be cured by anointing the patient with warm hare's blood, and the epileptic cured by drinking the blood of a tortoise. In seventeenth-century Europe, in the belief that blood bore character traits, attempts were made to transfuse animal blood into humans. Thus transfusions of lamb's blood were thought to be an appropriate way of modifying the behavior of the violent and ill-tempered, the blood of the lamb being synonymous with purity and harmlessness. In a similar vein, Hackett records, suggestions were made that marital discord could be remedied by reciprocal transfusions of blood between disputatious partners. The modern engagement ring carries forward old beliefs about blood and health, and blood and the emotions. It is customarily placed on the third finger of the left hand, the leech finger, traditionally believed to be the finger that had a vein in it leading directly to the heart. Contemporary language also continues to reflect the strong symbolic associations of blood, associations that link blood to individual character, as in red-blooded, cold-blooded; to social status, as in blue-blood, noble blood; and to social and familial relationships, as in bad blood, blood feuds, blood relatives, blood brothers.

It is not difficult to see, then, why the development of the commercial market in blood triggered a range of emotional responses and political, religious and racial reactions. It also focused attention on the morality of the motivational basis of market behavior. The protagonists for the money market in blood supply argued for economic rationalism rather than cultural emotionalism in approaching the problem of the scarcity of blood, that it was "criminally irresponsible to permit the supply system of blood to be dependent upon so fickle a source as the public-spiritedness of a section of society" (Cooper and Culyer 1968: 10). As with any scarce commodity the price mechanism was the appropriate guarantor of supply. Paying donors the market value of their blood not only would increase the supply but would also prevent waste, since the recipients, having paid the full cost of the commodity, would have a built-in incentive to make good use of it. Donors were therefore best motivated by direct monetary or indirect non-monetary payments for their blood. Non-monetary payments would include such things as a day off with pay or an extension of holiday entitlement in return for

donations, or forms of blood credit or blood insurance policies where donations were directly linked to some future benefits for the donors and/or
their families. A measurable pecuniary self-interest was the only reliable
motivation for blood supply: "Only healthy money-seeking on the part of
suppliers and healthy profit-seeking by competitive collection and distribution agencies, with health and safety standards imposed by the state, will
ensure the efficient supply of enough blood in the best condition demanded
by users evidenced by what they pay" (Cooper and Culyer 1968: 11). And
if people wanted improvements in the quality of the blood supplied through
the market, then they would simply have to pay a higher price for it.

The case for the voluntary donation of blood, for the exclusion of the
market mechanism and the payment of donors, has rested largely on an
examination of the practices that developed in parts of the commercial blood
supply system. Richard Titmuss documented a number of quality problems
associated with commercial blood supplies. These arose from the practice
of selling outdated blood stocks to Third World countries, from the development of blood-selling rings and rackets in Central and South America,
and from the poor donor pool attracted by money payments. Paid donors
had a financial incentive to lie about their medical histories and about the
time that had elapsed since their last donation. In countries such as India
payment for their blood was the only source of income for many donors who
circumvented the rules on the frequency of donations by registering with
different commercial blood banks. Consequently the quality of commercial
blood was inferior to that of blood voluntarily donated. For example, Titmuss
argued, the risk of contracting serum hepatitis from a blood transfusion was
ten times greater if the blood came from a paid donor than if it came from
a voluntary donor.

Titmuss concluded that the gift relationship[6]—blood voluntarily donated
to an unknown stranger—was not only morally but economically superior
to the market relationship. The commercial blood market produced much
greater health risks for the recipients of its products and was dangerous to
the health of donors. Nor, Titmuss argued, did it perform in terms of purely
economic criteria. In terms of economic efficiency, administrative efficiency,
cost per unit to the patient and quality per unit, the commercial blood market
failed to perform. It was highly wasteful of blood, with chronic and acute
shortages characterizing the demand-and-supply position, making illusory
the concept of equilibrium. The debate about the market versus altruism in
the supply of blood resurfaced in the 1980s as a result of the discovery that
the acquired immunodeficiency syndrome (AIDS) virus could be transmitted
in blood. In reviewing the incidence of the contraction of AIDS and of AIDS
virus infections, Iain McLean concluded that "donor blood is dramatically
safer than paid-for blood. Whereas paid suppliers have an incentive to tell
lies about their health, donors have none. A market system needs truthful-

ness, but it cannot generate it. . . . To tamper with the principle of the gift relationship is to tamper with people's lives" (McLean 1986: 11–12).

NOTES

1. The quote is from Emerson's essay "Aristocracy" in *English Traits* (1856).

2. In many countries the business activities of women were severely curtailed by legal restrictions on their ownership of property.

3. Gekko's speech echoed the 1986 commencement address of Wall Street arbitrager Ivan Boesky at the University of California Business School in Berkeley shortly before his conviction for insider trading (Mills 1990: 20–21).

4. McLean 1986: 10.

5. Even these everyday commodities may, like truffles (see Chapter 4), have intricate cultural connotations, not least of which are their claimed qualities as aphrodisiacs (see Hendrickson 1974).

6. As Mary Douglas (1990) has observed, "gifts" should not be equated with "donations." A gift enhances a sense of solidarity between the giver and the recipient, even when there is no personal relationship between the parties and no precise calculation of the return gift anticipated. In the context of voluntary blood donations, the expression "what goes round, comes round" perhaps best captures the long-term cycle of communal reciprocity involved.

CHAPTER 4

Technology: From Tool to Talisman

"IF YOU CAN'T WIN A NOBEL PRIZE, THE NEXT BEST THING IS TO START YOUR OWN COMPANY."[1]

In the 1970s and early 1980s Santa Clara's Silicon Valley became a focal point for newspaper and magazine stories about a new breed of successful entrepreneurs. These technological entrepreneurs, "adept at harvesting technologies ripe for the marketplace" (Miller and Cote 1985), were aggressively transforming the products of state-of-the-art science and technology into personal and business fortunes. Silicon Valley's high-tech entrepreneur became "the local cultural hero and role model, just as movie directors are in Los Angeles or oil drillers in Houston" (*Time* 1982) or as Wall Street bond-trading "masters of the universe" were to become prior to the crash of October 1987. And the valley at "the heartland of the electronic revolution," with its sense of excitement and adventure, was described as "a metaphor for the American way." The American dream of rags-to-riches on the basis of hard work and private enterprise acquired a newfound high-tech glamor.

Notwithstanding the euphoria about private enterprise, many of these high-tech ventures were dependent upon military and government funding. They developed guidance systems for missiles and communications systems for military intelligence. They were also heavily involved in "the commercial uses of space" (Marsh 1985). There was, however, a downside to this technology-based business utopia. On the personal level it was a workaholic culture that stimulated early burnout, depression and drug abuse, as well as above-average rates of alcoholism and divorce. At the corporate level, the leading-edge (and often secret) nature of much of the production work raised major problems of security against theft, sabotage and industrial espionage.

And at the environmental level in the semiconductor industry major health hazards developed in the use, storage and disposal of chemicals. With the electronics industry, as with so many industries, the boons and mischiefs of the exploitation of technology by business are inextricably mixed. It is a pattern that goes to the root of the love-hate relationship with technology that is so marked in Western European and American culture.

TECHNOLOGY AND CULTURE

The importance of technology in relation to social and cultural change is a major theme in cultural anthropology and in history. Terms such as the "Industrial Revolution," "the nuclear age" and, "the information age" implicitly link historical periods to technological developments. Changes in simple technologies can lead to changes in social etiquette and behavior; the introduction of knives, forks and spoons, for example, changed conceptions about table manners. Developments in transport technology—in shipping, railroads, automobiles, and aircraft—have changed the trading and commercial relationships between communities and nations, the spatial organization of cities, the geographical location and mobility of populations, and the work, leisure and recreational habits of people throughout the world. Changes in communications and information technologies—in print, radio, television, film, and telecommunications—have influenced the ways in which we perceive and interpret the world around us and have played a major part in the transmission of culture and cultural values.

Michael Adas has documented how European and American cultures have used technological sophistication to access the relative merits and development of non-Western societies.[2] Adas's work on sub-Saharan Africa, India and China "examines the ways in which Europeans' perceptions of the material superiority of their own cultures, particularly as manifested in scientific thought and technological innovation, shaped their attitudes toward and interaction with peoples they encountered overseas" (Adas 1989: 4). In the early years of European expansion, other cultures were largely found wanting on religious grounds and European self-confidence was tied to a sense of the superiority of the Christian religion over its pagan alternatives. From the eighteenth century onward, however, religious criteria progressively gave way to scientific and technological criteria in measuring the level of civilization in non-European cultures. This process was accelerated by the spread of industrialization:

European observers came to view science and especially technology as the most objective and unassailable measures of their own civilization's past achievement and present worth. In science and technology their superiority was readily demonstrable, and their advantages over other peoples grew at an ever increasing pace. . . . Prominent social theorists and policymakers drew varying, often conflicting, conclusions from the undeniable fact of Europe's material mastery and its concomitant global hegemony, but few disputed that machines were the most reliable measure of mankind. (Adas 1989: 134)

With technological sophistication so closely linked in the European mind with cultural superiority, it was easy to rationalize European colonialism as bringing civilization to backward peoples. Central to this process was the introduction of the railway, a symbol of "European power and material mastery": "In the speed and regularity of their comings and going, trains (and steamships) proclaimed the Europeans' mastery of time and space and demonstrated their capacity for precision and discipline" (Adas 1989: 224). Indeed, one nineteenth-century British civil servant in India proclaimed that "all signs of civilization disappeared beyond one hundred yards on either side of the railway track" (Adas 1989: 228).[3]

Attitudes toward technology, particularly toward new technologies, have varied markedly. At one extreme have been those who unquestioningly welcomed technological developments as a sign of economic and social progress. These are the technological optimists that E. F. Schumacher (1973) described as the "people of the forward stampede," people who believe in technical solutions to human problems, who believe that "a breakthrough a day keeps the crisis at bay." At the other extreme are those Luddites or neo-Luddites who, in fear of the real or imaginary social dislocations wrought by new tools and machines, have tried to prevent the adoption and spread of new technologies. They take their name from the English artisan followers of the apocryphal Ned Ludd who between 1811 and 1816 destroyed the new machinery being introduced into the lace trade in Nottinghamshire and broke up the shearing gigs that were replacing the labor of shearers in the wool industry of the West Riding of Yorkshire. As a consequence of such activities it was made a capital crime in England to destroy machinery and, in 1813, 17 men were hanged at York for the offense (Pelling 1963: 28–29).

It has not only been the interests of capital and the interests of labor that have clashed over the introduction and dispersion of new technologies. Whole communities and societies have tried to protect or advance their interests by controlling access to the latest technological developments. This is most evident in the case of military technology and in the restrictions placed by the United States, until the late 1980s, on the export of advanced computer systems to the Soviet Union. It is also evident in the practice of industrial espionage, a practice that goes back to the early years of the Industrial Revolution. An elaborate game of technological espionage and counter-espionage was played between the British and the Americans in the 1780s. The British, through strict government regulations, sought to prevent drawings and plans of their new machines from leaving the country. They also prohibited the export of the machines and the emigration of skilled mechanics. Led by Treasury assistant Tench Coxe, the Philadelphia merchant who was spokesman for the country's fledgling manufacturing sector, the Americans advertised in Britain for technicians, offering special bonuses for those who would emigrate, and tried to smuggle embargoed machinery out of the country (Leo Marx 1964: 155–56).

Even in peacetime, technological innovations have become sources of both pride and disquiet, simultaneously promising brave new worlds and threatening apocalyptic disaster. The promise and potential of nuclear energy was offset by the hazards of "incidents," such as that at Three Mile Island in March 1979, and by the Chernobyl disaster of April 1986. Just as certain places and events have become associated with the horrors of wartime use of technology—Hiroshima, Dachau, the use of Agent Orange in Vietnam and of chemical weapons in the Iran–Iraq Gulf War—so too certain names, places and events remind us of technology's peacetime hazards—Thalidomide, Bhopal, the *Exxon Valdez* spill, the ill-fated *Challenger* space mission of 28 January 1986.

Since the early years of the Industrial Revolution, artists, novelists and social commentators, and artists and novelists *as* social commentators, have reflected this tension between optimism and pessimism about technical innovation. The works of the English novelist Thomas Love Peacock (1785–1866) are characteristic of much of the literary reaction to a burgeoning manufacturing industry. Peacock emphasized the depersonalization of the new mechanical society. In his view the rural community and its traditional values was being replaced by a society solely interested in production and material acquisition, a society driven by commercial and market values. One of his characters, Mr. Chainmail in *Crotchet Castle* (1831), longs nostalgically for the imagined color and naturalness of the twelfth century, when men

could come honestly by beef and ale, while they were left to their simple industry. ... Now, we all wear one conventional dress, one conventional face; we have no bond of union but pecuniary interest; we talk anything that comes uppermost, for talking's sake, and without expecting to be believed; we have no nature, no simplicity, no picturesqueness; everything about us is as artificial and as complicated as our steam-machinery.

In Peacock's novel *Headlong Hall* (1816) the debate between the good and evil social consequences of technical change is conducted by Mr. Escot and Mr. Foster. Mr. Escot is a "deteriorationist," seeing only the evils of the emerging factory-based industrial system and sentimentally yearning for the past: "Where is the spinning-wheel now, and every simple and insulated occupation of the industrious cottager?" Mr. Foster, in contrast, is a "perfectabilian" and sees the new economic and industrial system as bringing marked increases in human happiness:

The manufacturing system is not yet purified from some evils which necessarily attend it, but which I conceive are greatly overbalanced by their concomitant advantages. Contemplate the vast sum of human industry to which this system so essentially contributes: . . . employment and existence thus given to innumerable families, and the multiplied comforts and conveniences of life diffused over the whole community.

Another literary work of the same period, Mary Shelley's gothic novel *Frankenstein, or the Modern Prometheus* (1818), has been used by twentieth-century commentators to illustrate this ambivalent love-hate relationship between ourselves and our technological and scientific products. One of the major themes of *Frankenstein* is the notion that we can be enslaved by our own creations. It is a theme reiterated in science fiction, in stories about computers and, as Chapter 6 illustrates, in business cartoons. Langdon Winner, while recognizing the undoubted benefits of technology in terms of improvements in lifestyles, health, material comforts and labor-saving devices, was nevertheless concerned about the "cavalier disregard for consequences" with which powerful technological forces were, like Victor Frankenstein's monster, released into the world. Frankenstein, argued Winner, refused to contemplate the implications of his discovery. He created something new and powerful, something that represented a "quantum jump in the performance capability of a certain kind of technology," and then devoted all his energy to forgetting what he had done:

Victor embodies an artefact with a kind of life previously manifest only in human beings. He then looks on in surprise as it returns to him as an autonomous force, with a structure of its own, with demands upon which it insists absolutely. Provided with no plan for its existence, the technological creation enforces a plan upon its creator. Victor is baffled, fearful, and totally unable to discover a way to repair the disruptions caused by this half completed, imperfect work. He never moves beyond the dreams of progress, the thirst for power, or the unquestioned belief that the products of science and technology are an unqualified blessing for humankind. Although he is aware of the fact that there is something extraordinary at large in the world, it takes a disaster to convince him that the responsibility is his. Unfortunately, by the time he overcomes his passivity, the consequences of his deeds have become irreversible, and he finds himself totally helpless before an unchosen fate. (Winner 1977: 313)

The idea of autonomous technology, of technology out of control and following its own course independently of human direction, has been a central obsession of literature since the time of the Industrial Revolution. Winner's view was that societies should try to anticipate some of the consequences of new technologies and learn to "manage" their social, economic, political and cultural impacts more effectively. This is the perspective that supports the idea of technology assessment and the setting up of organizations such as the Environmental Protection Agency, created in 1970, and the Office of Technology Assessment, set up by Congress in 1972. Other commentators, however, notably Jacques Ellul, have argued that it is already too late to take back control of technology and manage it better. In Ellul's opinion technology has become an uncontrolled and *uncontrollable* sorcerer's apprentice that determines social, political, economic and cultural change: "Technique elicits and conditions social, political and economic change. It is the prime mover of all the rest, in spite of any appearance to the contrary and in spite of human pride, which pretends that man's philosophical theories are still the determining influence and man's political regimes decisive factors in technical evolution" (Ellul 1965: 133).

Albert Borgmann has characterized Ellul's notion of technological determinism as the "demonizing of technology." Technology is seen as a pernicious and irresponsible force that shapes society and social values and "enslaves everything from science to art, from labor to leisure, from economics to politics" (Borgmann 1984: 9). Borgmann calls this the "substantive" theory of technology. He suggests two alternatives to it. One is the "instrumentalist" view in which technology is seen as value neutral. From this perspective tools, machines and techniques are merely instruments that extend human capacities and create new possibilities for social, economic and cultural development. They are, therefore, neither good nor bad in themselves but take on value only in respect of the uses to which they are put. Social and cultural values are paramount in determining and understanding the uses made of technology. Thus technology may be politicized or used as an instrument of domination by one class over another in the community. Whereas the substantive view of technology suggests that technology seeks ends that are consistent with its own logic and rationality, the instrumentalist view sees technology as merely serving the ends defined by its users.

Borgmann, however, favors a third view, which he calls a "pluralist" theory of technology. This allows both for the evolution of technologies in ways that are consistent with their own rationality and for the development and adaptation of technologies in interaction with social and cultural systems. This perspective, he argues, recognizes the complex set of countervailing forces at play in the development and application of any particular technology. It is the perspective adopted by Thomas Hughes in rejecting technological determinism:

The creators of modern technology and the makers of the modern world expressed long-held human values and aspirations. Although the inventors, engineers, industrial scientists, and system builders created order, control and system, in so doing they responded to a fundamental human longing for a world in which these characteristics prevail. They became the instruments of all those, including themselves, who were uneasy in a seemingly chaotic and purposeless world and who searched for compensatory order. In this sense technology was, and is, socially constructed . . . is both shaper of, and is shaped by, values. It is value-laden. (Hughes 1989: 5)

This pluralist perspective is consistent with the model of cultural diffusion described in Chapter 2 and with the general theoretical framework of the present work. It allows recognition of the substantive impact of technology on culture while not ignoring the fact that as in the technology of Trobriand cricket or in the advocacy of appropriate technology for economic development, tools and techniques may themselves be modified and changed in order to accommodate them to particular value systems and cultural contexts.

TECHNOLOGY AND TECHNOLOGY PRACTICE

Arnold Pacey described how the introduction of the snowmobile during the 1960s and 1970s affected life in Sweden, Greenland and the Canadian Arctic. Snowmobiles quickly became part of the equipment many Arctic communities depended upon for their livelihood. Laplanders in Sweden used them for herding reindeer, and eskimo trappers on Canada's Banks Island used them in the winter harvesting of fox furs. At the same time the snowmobile gave a new dimension to winter sports in North America, particularly in the Canadian province of Quebec, where by 1978 several thousand miles of public trails had been established for snowmobiling. The different uses found for the snowmobile by people of different cultures may seem, suggested Pacey, to give credence to the argument that technology is "culturally, morally and politically neutral—that it provides tools independent of local value-systems which can be used impartially to support quite different kinds of lifestyle."[11] At first glance the snowmobile seems to refute Jacques Ellul's ideas of technological determinism and to support the view of those instrumentalists who see technology as good or evil according to use. Thus problems associated with particular technologies, such as chemical pollution, environmental hazards, health risks, and safety, are attributable not to the technology but, rather, to the misuse of that technology by business interests or government or the military or indeed by individuals. The snowmobile, writes Pacey, "seems the perfect illustration of this argument":

The engineering principles involved in its operation are universally valid, whether its users are Lapps or Eskimos, Dene (Indian) hunters, Wisconsin sportsmen, Quebecois vacationists, or prospectors from multinational oil companies. And whereas the snowmobile has certainly had a social impact, altering the organization of work in Lapp communities, for example, it has not necessarily influenced basic cultural values. The technology of the snowmobile may thus appear to be something quite independent of the lifestyles of Lapps or Eskimos or Americans. (Pacey 1983: 2)

However, argues Pacey, the reality is somewhat different. The fake streamlining and flashy colors of the modern snowmobile, and the up-market sexual symbolism used in its advertising, suggest that more than technical performance is at stake:

The Eskimo who takes a snowmobile on a long expedition in the Arctic quickly discovers more significant discrepancies. With his traditional means of transport, the dog-team and sledge, he could refuel as he went along by hunting for his dogs' food. With the snowmobile he must take an ample supply of fuel and spare parts; he must be skilled at doing his own repairs and even then he may take a few dogs with him for emergency use if the machine breaks down. A vehicle designed for leisure trips between well-equipped tourist centers presents a completely different set of servicing problems when used for heavier work in more remote areas. One Eskimo kept his machine in his tent so it could be warmed up before starting in the morning. There are stories of other Eskimos, whose mechanical aptitude is well known, modifying their machines to adapt them better to local use. So is technology culturally neutral? If we look at the construction of the basic machine and its working principles, the answer seems to be yes. But if we look at the web of human activities surrounding the machine, which include its practical uses, its role as a status symbol, the supply of fuel and spare parts, the organized tourist trails, and the skills of its owners, the answer is clearly no. Looked at in this second way, technology is seen as a part of life, not something that can be kept in a separate compartment. If it is to be made of any use, the snowmobile must fit into a pattern of activity which belongs to a particular lifestyle and set of values. (Pacey 1983: 2–3)

Pacey goes on to argue for discrimination between a restricted definition of technology related solely to its technical aspects and a more general conception of technology, "technology practice," that incorporates its cultural and organizational components (see Figure 1). This distinction is similar to that made in medicine between medical science, which is the technical aspects of the subject, and medical practice, a broad and inclusive concept encompassing the organization of medicine, its cultural aspects, the doctor's sense of vocation, and the ethical code of the medical profession. In the remainder of the chapter some of the cultural aspects of technology practice are explored.

SPACE TECHNOLOGY: RECLAIMING THE HUMAN TERRITORY

The twentieth century's most advanced peaceful application of technology and technological systems was the U.S. space program. Highly expensive (the Apollo program of moon landings cost $25 billion in 1976 dollars), controversial in its political and cold war overtones (see McDougall 1985), and with business and military interests integrally involved in its investments and returns, nevertheless the space program tapped the wellspring of technological optimism in American society. It harnessed a large-scale and highly institutionalized technology to the glamor and adventure of exploring new frontiers. The space program also provided a vehicle for exploring the relationship between advanced technology and contemporary American culture. Two narratives that illustrate the dynamics of the technical and cultural

Figure 1
Diagrammatic Definitions of "Technology" and "Technology Practice"

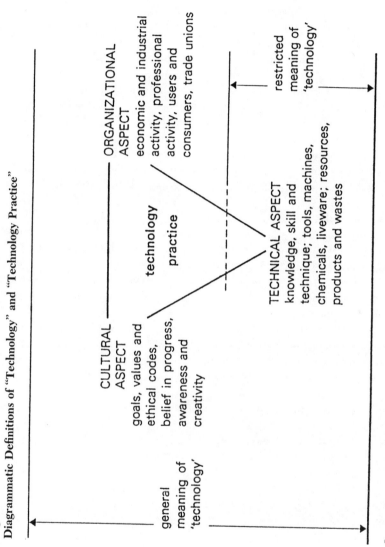

Source: Pacey 1982:6.

aspects of technology practice are Tom Wolfe's *The Right Stuff* (1979), dealing with the seven astronauts of the 1961–63 Mercury program, and Norman Mailer's *Of a Fire on the Moon* (1970), which describes the Apollo 11 flight and first moon landing of July 1969.

An early scene in the 1983 movie version of *The Right Stuff* shows Chuck Yeager, played by Sam Shepherd, horseriding in the Mojave desert. He rides over the brow of a hill and stops. Below him on the desert floor, hissing quietly, is a mysterious, alien-looking rocket plane, isolated and unattended. It is Bell Aircraft Corporation X–1, the plane with which the U.S. Air Force hopes to break the sound barrier. The analogies with Westerns are clear in both book and film. Wolfe's Yeager is the loner, the individualistic pioneer, a test pilot adventurer prepared to buck authority and systems of control, not for fame or personal enrichment but from an independence of spirit and a desire to pit his wits, skill and command of his craft against the unknown—and all for his regular U.S. Army captain's pay of $3,396 per annum. In the evenings Yeager would join the other pilots from Muroc Field at Pancho's Desert Fly Inn: "When the screen door banged and a man walked through the door into the saloon, every eye in the place checked him out. If he wasn't known as somebody who had something to do with flying at Muroc, he would be eyed like some lame god-damned mouseshit sheepherder from *Shane.*" (Wolfe 1979: 51–52).

In *The Right Stuff*'s portrayal of Yeager as "master of the sky," jet pilot and jet plane have a relationship comparable to that of man and horse; they are a modern man-machine system echoing the centaurs of ancient Greek mythology. When the action moves from California to the National Aeronautics and Space Administration (NASA) complex at Cape Canaveral, however, the newly recruited Mercury 7 astronauts—Yeager, significantly, is not among them—confront a large bureaucratic technological system that clearly values technical sophistication and distrusts human judgment. Individual skill and control are to be made redundant, programmed out of space technology wherever possible; the player piano is to replace the player and the piano. But reinforced by the heroic image created for them in the media, Wolfe's astronauts assert themselves against the rigid, precise, mechanical, authoritarian tyranny of the film version's German designers and engineers. They demand a window in the space capsule, the name of the capsule changed to spacecraft, a hatch they can open by themselves, and manual control of the rocket and of the re-entry procedure:

The difference between pilot and passenger in any flying craft came down to one point: control. The boys were able to present some practical, workmanlike arguments on this score. Even if an astronaut were to be a redundant component, an observer and repairman, he should be able to *override* any of the Mercury vehicle's automatic systems *manually*, if only to correct malfunctions. So went the argument. But there was another argument that could not be put into so many words, since one was forbidden to state the premise itself: the right stuff.

After all, the right stuff was not bravery in the simple sense of being willing to risk your life (by riding on top of a Redstone or Atlas rocket). Any fool could do that (and many fools would no doubt volunteer, given the opportunity), just as any fool could throw his life away in the process. No, the idea (as all *pilots* understood) was that a man should have the ability to go up in a hurtling piece of machinery and put his hide on the line and have the moxie, the reflexes, the experience, the coolness, to pull it back at the last yawning moment—but how in the name of God could you either hang it out or haul it back if you were a lab animal seated in a pod? (Wolfe 1979: 186–87)

The assertion of the creative, innovative individual against the technocratic system, of the charismatic entrepreneur against the bureaucracies of big business, of the hand-to-hand combat warrior against the impersonal weapons of mass destruction, these are long-standing themes in American literature, film and popular culture. They reflect a desire to personalize technology and technological systems and to retain or recapture human control of human destinies, to reverse Ralph Waldo Emerson's despairing observation that "things are in the saddle and ride mankind." Even where technology is at its most advanced, the symbolism of human control must be retained. In the imaginative recreation of the Mercury program there is still room for individual heroism and the romance of discovery. These restrain and humanize technology and keep it within the orbit of shared cultural values and everyday human experience, however fictive.

But technology must be constrained on the far side as well as on the near side. There must be realms that technology and science cannot penetrate, mysteries and questions that they cannot resolve. In the film version of *The Right Stuff* much is made of the "fireflies" encountered by John Glenn over Australia when orbiting the earth in Friendship 7. Glenn's mystification and wonder at this experience of the unknown is cut with shots of Aborigines in the Australian outback. The presumption is that mysteries of the cosmos known to an ancient people whose paintings predate the pyramids of Egypt by 20,000 years are beyond the reach of scientific man and the advanced computer technology of Cape Canaveral's space command center. In this episode technology is constrained by a need and desire for transcendence, for a belief in something, anything, beyond the frontiers of rational knowledge. It is the reassertion of what Alvin Kernan (1982: 130) calls the "romantic myth of a vast and mysterious universe, filled with the magic of the unexpected, which is therefore a perpetual source of wonder and joy, never quite to be explained," a universe that "can only be apprehended by intuition, imagination, or powerful sensory excitement—not by reason and logic."

Kernan's elegant and insightful essay on Norman Mailer's book about the Apollo 11 moon landing (the source of much of the material in the remainder of this section) is an exploration of what happens when the literary romantic world comes face-to-face with science and technology. Mailer was commissioned by *Esquire* magazine to write an account of the Apollo 11 mission, a task he apparently took on with some misgivings. However, he brought to it an unusual combination, an initial training as an engineer and a self-image as a literary romantic in the macho brawling, hell-raising tradition of Ernest Hemingway. Thus while both fascinated and repelled by the technical aspects of the Apollo program, he is also determined to reconstruct it as literature. Here, for example, interspersed in the technical commentary from mission control, is Mailer's description of the liftoff of Apollo 11:

The liftoff itself seemed to partake more of a miracle than a mechanical phenomenon, as if all of huge Saturn itself had begun silently to levitate, and was then pursued by flames. . . .
. . . and in the midst of it, white as a ghost, white as the white of Melville's Moby Dick, white as the shrine of the Madonna in half the churches of the world, this slim angelic mysterious ship of stages rose without sound out of its incarnation of flame and began to ascend slowly into the sky, slow as Melville's Leviathan might swim, slowly as we might swim upward in a dream looking for the air. (Mailer 1970: 81)

In his narrator persona, Aquarius, Mailer makes frequent attempts to breathe literary life into the technical marvels of the mission. But he has problems in coming to terms with Apollo 11. The first is the astronauts themselves. Aquarius views them as cloned public relations executives rather than inheritors of the raucous traditions of fighter-pilot jocks:

In fact he could not forgive the astronauts their resolute avoidance of an heroic posture. It was somehow improper for a hero to be without flamboyance as if such modesty deprived his supporters of any large pleasure in his victories. . . . It was as if the astronauts were there to demonstrate that heroism's previous relation to romance had been highly improper—it was technology and the absence of emotion which were the only fit mates for the brave. (Mailer 1970: 88)

Even the moon landing takes on all the impersonal hallmarks of just another scheduled task to be accomplished, "and the famous phrase uttered by Armstrong as he first stepped on the moon, 'That's one small step for a man, one giant leap for mankind,' is so neat, so flatly delivered, so patently manufactured on Madison Avenue for the event that it reverberated with not even the slightest heartfelt spontaneous delight of a man doing something truly extraordinary" (Kernan 1982: 140).

The second problem is the terminology, the language of the technological culture so central to understanding that culture's structure and values. It is a language that Aquarius finds arid, dominated as it is by acronyms, numbers and computerese. For walking on the moon, read EVA, "extra-vehicular activity." For "the first cathedral of the age of technology," the Vehicle

Assembly Building in which the Saturn rocket was prepared for the space launch, read VAB:

VAB—it could be the name of a drink or a deodorant, or it could be suds for the washer. But it was not a name for this warehouse of the gods. The great churches of a religious age had names: the Alhambra, Santa Sofia, Mont Saint-Michel, Chartres, Westminster Abbey, Notre Dame. Now: VAB. Nothing fit anything any longer. The art of communication had become the mechanical function, and the machine was the work of art. What a fall for the ego of the artist. What a climb to capture the language again! (Mailer 1970: 46)

Computerese, argues Kernan (1982: 141), "tends toward abstraction and the stripping away of emotional content, subjective responses, and the historical accretions words have gathered over the centuries as a result of their involvement in the lives of men." And at the heart of computerese, at the core of the language of computer technology, is "that simplest and most reductive of all mathematical forms, the binary system in which all things are ultimately plus or minus, one or zero, yes or no, go or no go, a flash of energy or its absence." For Aquarius the computer is eating away at language, like "some species of higher tapeworm . . . quietly ingesting the vitals of God."

A further problem for Mailer is his sense that the moon landing has no meaning for its participants beyond the demonstration of technical sophistication. While recognizing the huge technological achievement that Apollo 11's success represents, Mailer nevertheless is disturbed by the banality of it all, its lack of magic. He tries to humanize the event. He tries to romanticize it. He tries to restore a sense of mystery and magic by inventing a psychology of machines. He tries to turn the computers, the rockets, the moon rocks collected by the astronauts, the whole technological paraphernalia, into significant cultural symbols. But overall the lead weight of the technological facts overwhelm him. For Mailer, argues Kernan (1982: 134),

the scientific conception of the world has all but triumphed, and the landing on the moon will demonstrate conclusively the enormous power of science, validate its myth, and complete its domination over the minds of men. The world will now become what science makes it, a world of objects moving in relationship to one another in accordance with immutable laws, coming from nowhere and going nowhere, lost in an infinity in which being is only relative. Literature and its humanistic conception of a world corresponding to human desire, organically related and metaphysically purposive, will disappear. As if to make clear its final assault on literature, science has now appropriated the myths of poetry: the mission is named Apollo 11, claiming for a rocket the name of the god of poetry and art, and it will land on and seize the traditional symbol of the poetic imagination, the moon, transforming it into a dead object, another scientific fact, "alien terrain where no life breathed and beneath the ground no bodies were dead."

COMPUTER FETISHISM

It is not only the literary romantics like Norman Mailer who seek to both mystify and humanize technology. The naming of U.S. rockets and space-craft—Mercury, Saturn, Atlas, Titan, Centaur, Gemini—betrays some aspiration within NASA's institutionalized technology to match the heroic and mythical figures of the past. And that machines may have spiritual qualities is a notion shared by computer engineers. Tracy Kidder's *The Soul of a New Machine* (1982) is the Pulitzer prize-winning account of the "titanic" struggle of a team of young Data General computer "wizards" to "dominate a machine," the 32-bit minicomputer, Eagle. The cover blurb of the Penguin edition effuses, "Day-by-day, wire-by-wire, the 'Microkids' traced and re-traced Eagle's labyrinthine arteries, fought back at its tantrums and wooed its obedience." The engineers, as well as the book's author and marketers, share this perception of the personality of machines:

To the two computers that the Eclipse Group used, the engineers had given the names Woodstock and Trixie, after characters in comic strips. They often spoke about these computers as if they had personalities. When especially frustrated, one Microkid would walk into the lab where Trixie resided and yell at the machine. Alsing said: "A lot of people are really tired of anthropomorphizing computers, but it sure is an easy way to talk about them. You can anthropomorphize your car and the analogy works, and then at some level it doesn't. We anthropomorphize big business, the military and so on, as some strange creatures with alien personalities. I think that's sane, I think that's normal. You tend to have to anthropomorphize the computer. It presents a face, a person to me—a person in a thousand different ways." (Kidder 1982: 85)

The messages and symbolism in computer companies' naming of machines fluctuates between a high-tech imagery—the acronyms and numbers of computerese (ENIAC, UNIVAC, TRS–80IIIs), and a down-home folksiness—the user-friendliness of the Pet, the Mac, Lisa. In Silicon Valley, self-proclaimed "world headquarters of the twenty-first century," the naming of the companies themselves went through three distinct eras (Larsen and Rogers 1984). Until 1960 computer firms were generally named after their founders. Hewlett-Packard, for example, was established by Bill Hewlett and Dave Packard. Such names made the companies indistinguishable from grocery shops, furniture stores or dry cleaners. Then followed a period, coinciding with the space program, when acronyms and puns on the words *electronics* and *technology* were common in the naming of new computer firms. This started in 1961 with the founding of Signetics Corporation, Signetics being an abbreviation for "signal network electronics." Other corporate names in this vein were Intel (integrated electronics), Avantek (avant-garde technology) and Zilog (Z, the last word, in integrated logic). Inevitably one corporation was computer named. Its owners fed the name requirements into the computer and chose Acurex from the selection offered.

In the late 1970s space-age science fiction names emphasizing new frontiers of technical wizardry gave way to

more mellow titles implying honesty, truth, and health: Coherent, Verbatim, North Star, and Tandem, for example. Apple Computer Inc. is a good representative of this era. When founder Steve Jobs returned from India he had had a bout of dysentery and became a vegetarian. He decided that people were architected to be fruit eaters and he became especially hooked on apples. He ate a lot of them, becoming a fruitarian for a while. When his new firm was getting underway in the garage in 1976, the U.S. Securities and Exchange Commission required that a form be completed with a company name. Jobs suggested "Apple Computer" because the transposition of the two words would be an intriguing name with high public impact. It also conveyed the friendly, organic image that Jobs wanted. (Larsen and Rogers 1984: 14)

Computer advertising followed a similar pattern of development. Early advertisements, like those for many technologically sophisticated products in their initial years, focused on the technical aspects of performance. They stressed the machines' magical properties in the astringent cold language of the aficionados—the computer literate, the hackers and the "technophiliacs." For the computer-naive, or "paranoid droids," who could make no sense of bits and bytes, of modems and microchips, of RAMS and ROMS, wafers and worms, this insider jargon reinforced a sense of exclusion from the sophisticated consumer gratification offered in the magic technological kingdom. With the development of the personal computer, however, both the machines and their advertising became more user-friendly, taking into account the cultural and organizational contexts of computer usage. In the machine this was symbolized in the development of the "mouse"—a simple little timorous animal that stimulates irrational fears—as interface with the computer. In advertisements it is best illustrated by IBM's use of a Charlie Chaplin lookalike to promote their PC, an ironic transformation of the original Charlie's losing battle with technology in the 1936 Chaplin film Modern Times.

However, the term "user-friendly," applied to a machine, itself betrays the ambiguities in thinking about computer technology. It is the inanimate machine that is actively friendly, the animate user that is the object of this friendliness. As computer languages "breed" from third generation to fourth generation to fifth generation, they too become more user-friendly, embodying a process of natural selection for survival in the mass marketplace. With the advent of speech recognition—the machine will respond to your voice and your voice alone—comes the ultimate user-friendliness, that of the cocooned intimacy of pillow-talk. The attribution of human or spiritual or magical qualities to inanimate objects, so characteristic of the fetish or talisman, is ever-present in the language and images surrounding the computer (Park-Curry and Jiobu 1983). It is little surprise, then, that for 1982 *Time* magazine's "Man of the Year"—"the greatest influence for good or evil"—was not a man at all but a machine, the computer.[4]

TECHNOLOGY AND CONSCIOUSNESS

The masculinity of many computers, and indeed the genderization of science and technology in toto, should not go unremarked. The romantic movement frequently contrasted the hustle, noise and dirt of the machine, particularly the railway locomotive, with the peace and tranquillity of nature. Invariably the machine, a "sudden, shocking intruder upon a fantasy of idyllic satisfaction . . . is associated with crude, masculine aggressiveness in contrast with the tender, feminine and submissive attitudes attached to the landscape" (Marx 1964: 29). Sherry Turkle (1984) found that all children anthropomorphized the computer to some extent and that it was not uncommon for girls to anthropomorphize it as male. Male computers, as heroes and villains, friends and enemies, colleagues, bosses and subordinates, frequent popular culture. The parade includes the power-crazed and untrustworthy Hal in *2001*, the cutesy R2D2 and stuffy C3PO of *Star Wars*, the manic-depressive alienated-worker robot of *A Hitchhiker's Guide to the Galaxy* (a story in which a computer holds the answer to the meaning of life), and the quirky *Max Headroom* with his electronic stutter.

But it is not only encounters with the masculinity, femininity or androgyny of computers and other machines that bring us face to face with the impact of technology on our ways of experiencing and interpreting the world around us. Hugh Kenner (1987) has illustrated the influence of technology on both the content and form of poetry and drama, demonstrating how linotype, the typewriter and the computer altered the way in which writers view and portray the world. Daniel Lerner (1964: 49) considered that the greater geographical mobility made possible by modern transport technologies had its psychological counterpart in a "mobile sensibility so adaptive to change that rearrangement of the self-system is its distinctive mode." Thomas Hughes, in his history of American technology and technological systems, argues that "inventors, industrial scientists, engineers, and system builders have been the makers of modern America. The values of order, system, and control that they embedded in machines, devices, processes, and systems have become the values of modern technological culture. These values are embedded in the artifacts or hardware" (Hughes 1989: 4).

In addition, many of the engineers and technologists and their supporters "believed their methods and values applicable and beneficial when applied to such other realms of social activity as politics, business, architecture and art." On the political front Leo Marx (1964: 165) noted that "the dominant structural metaphor of the American Constitution is that of a self-regulating machine, like the orrery or the steam engine; it establishes a system of 'checks and balances' among three distinct, yet delicately synchronized, branches of government," the legislature, the judicature and the executive. More recently, the development of the post-industrial society and its key industries—that is, information systems, computer sciences, telecommunications, robotics, and biotechnology—has renewed speculation about the benefits of a technocratic society and discussion of the impact of technical and scientific knowledge and expertise on political processes in the democratic state (see Fischer 1990). On a broader plane that included the realms of art and architecture was the cultural revolution known as modernism (c. 1900–1940). Modernism was marked, argues Norman Cantor (1988: 39), by a concern with

how the artist and philosopher should respond to a situation in which mechanization takes command and a revolutionary scientific paradigm has been attained. . . .
    On the one side Modernism was a product of the age of railroad and steamship and was fashioned by the rapid and easy means of transportation and commitment to the urban culture and the trans-Atlantic metropolitan centers. On the other side Modernism was concerned with preservation of rationality, art and learned intelligence in the age of mechanical reproduction and mass culture.

Consciousness of time and space have also been radically altered by technology. Wolfgang Schivelbusch (1986) links changed perceptions of time and space to the development of transport technologies, particularly the railroad developments of the nineteenth century. He illustrates how in England the process of railway development led to the "industrialization of time and space." Time became standardized geographically, concepts of punctuality spread, speed became a new principle in the conduct of business and public affairs, distance was increasingly measured by reference to travelling time, and there was a developing perception of landscape as a swiftly passing panorama. The subjective perceptions and psychology of time and space were, argues Schivelbusch, increasingly dependent on transport technology. In early nineteenth-century England, for example, time was still measured by reference, not always accurately, to the noonday sun. Thus as you travelled west or east, so the time shifted accordingly, the country as a whole being made up of a patchwork of varying local times. In the 1830s Greenwich mean time (GMT) was primarily used by shipping. Each day at 1 P.M. GMT the time-ball on Flamsteed House, part of the Royal Observatory founded in Greenwich in 1675, was dropped, allowing ships on the River Thames that were in view of Flamsteed House to synchronize their timepieces. It was the development of the railways that eventually led to GMT becoming standard time throughout Britain. Initially the independent railway companies standardized time on their own networks. Thus an 1841 timetable of the Great Western Railway Company stated that "LONDON time is kept at all the Stations on the Railway, which is about 4 minutes earlier than

READING time; 5 1/2 minutes before STEVENTON time; 7 1/2 minutes before CIRENCESTER time; 8 minutes before CHIPPENHAM time; and 14 minutes before BRIDGEWATER time" (Wright 1968: 145). Travellers could buy multi-dial watches that showed both railway and local times.

For a while each railway company operated to its own time, but as interconnections between the networks of the different companies increased, GMT was standardized across the country's railways. However, it was not until the Statutes (Definition of Time) Act of 1880 that GMT, then generally known as "railway time," became standard time throughout England. A similar pattern of development took place in the United States, where prior to 1878 some 70 different standards of time were in use, many of them used by the railroad companies. Where companies shared stations, all the company times would be displayed. Thus in Pittsburgh, for example, there were six station clocks each showing the time of a different railroad network. In 1878 the American railroads adopted the present system of five time zones: Atlantic, Eastern, Central, Mountain and Pacific. In 1884, as the result of an international conference in Washington, a similar and compatible world time zone system was introduced based on GMT. This provided for 24 time zones, each of one hour for every 15 degrees of longitude, and set the international dateline 180 degrees from the Greenwich meridian of zero. Political sensitivities did not lead to immediate adoption of this system of British chronographic imperialism. The French would not refer to Greenwich by name but recognized the meridian as a line some degrees west of Paris, and the Irish for some years refused recognition of GMT, keeping Dublin mean time until 1916.

Although the development of the commercial railway networks necessitated a better organization of time, the "nervous system of the railway organism" was the station telegraph office. It was developments in communications technology, particularly the introduction of the electric wire telegraph, that made possible the railways' signalling systems and facilitated the standardization of time over large distances. In 1852 an electric clock at Greenwich was linked to a time-ball in The Strand, London, and in 1853 to a similar time signal in Deal on the Kent coast. From 1865 hourly signals were being sent from Greenwich to the Office of the Electric and International Telegraph and from there to the English railway networks. In 1870, following public dissatisfaction with the inefficiencies of private enterprise telegraph systems, the inland telegraph system was nationalized and the Government Post Office established a countrywide system for the hourly distribution of time. The ubiquitous Government Post Office clock became, until the advent of radio broadcasting, the most commonly utilized reference point for time checks.[5]

Clocks were well established in Europe in the fifteenth and sixteenth centuries, and European explorers of the period frequently commented on the lack of any sense of machine-regulated time in other societies (Adas

1989). In the process of its industrialization, however, time itself became a commodity, something that could be wasted or saved. Wasting time was presumed to be bad independently of the purpose for which the time had been wasted. Saving time was presumed to be good without reference to the use made of the time saved. Punctuality became a virtue and traditions that sustained notions of customary socio-cultural time were derided. In the South Pacific "Island time" and "Maori time" are terms still used to stigmatize what are seen as behaviors showing undue regard for the imperatives of the Protestant work ethic. Whereas in 1839 one English railway company director refused to provide train arrival times for George Bradshaw's *Railway Companion* on the grounds that "it would tend to make punctuality a sort of obligation" (Wright 1968: 143), by 1848 Henry David Thoreau could write of the railroad near Walden Pond:

The startings and arrivals of the cars are now the epochs in the village day. They go and come with such regularity and precision, and their whistle can be heard so far, that the farmers set their clocks by them, and thus one well-conducted institution regulates a whole country. Have not men improved somewhat in punctuality since the railroad was invented? Do they not talk and think faster in the depot than they did in the stage-office?

In colonial India the railway and its timetables were seen as important agents of social change. In the words of one officer in the Indian Civil Service, writing in the 1870s:

Railways are opening the eyes of the people who are within reach of them in a variety of ways. They teach them that time is worth money, and induce them to economize that which they had been in the habit of slighting and wasting; they teach them that speed attained is time, and therefore money, saved or made. They show them that others can produce better crops or finer works of art than themselves, and set them thinking why they should not have sugar cane or brocade equal to those of their neighbors. They introduce them to men of other ideas, and prove to them that much is to be learnt beyond the narrow limits of the little town or village which has hitherto been the world to them. Above all, they induce in them habits of self-dependence, causing them to act for themselves promptly and not lean on others. (Adas 1989: 226)

And by the 1930s Benito Mussolini's fascist dictatorship was being praised for its ability to make Italian trains run strictly to schedule.

In exploring the relationship between perceptions of time and space and the development of transport technologies, Schivelbusch was looking "for evidence of culture at those minute points of contact between new things and old habits" and exploring "the power of things themselves to impress and shape and evoke a response within consciousness" (Schivelbusch 1986: xv). Sherry Turkle had a similar motivation in studying the psychological development of the relationship between children and computers, namely to understand how ideas move out from a sophisticated technical world, "the technical communities around computation" (Turkle 1984: 11), into the culture as a whole and, once there, how they shape the way people think. The focus of her research was on "the subjective computer," on the computer "as it affects the way that we think, especially the way we think about ourselves:—the question is not what will the computer be like in the future but what will *we* be like; what kind of people are we becoming?" (Turkle 1984: 3).

Turkle identifies three stages in the development of the child-computer relationship. The first is the metaphysical stage in which the child seeks to differentiate the "life" of the computer from his or her own life. The second is the mastery stage in which the child seeks to assert control over the machine. And the third is a stage of self-definition and self-creation in which concepts of self and personal identity evolve through interaction with computers. It is the metaphysical stage, particularly the exploration of consciousness, that is most relevant to the present discussion. In that first stage Turkle demonstrates that the child's normal rules for discriminating between the "living" and the "not-living" are on the basis of movement. However, these rules prove inadequate when faced with interactive computers that can talk, teach and play games. Consequently children bring psychological, rather than physical or mechanical, criteria into consideration: "Are their electronic games aware, are they conscious, do they have feelings, do they play fair, or do they cheat?" (Turkle 1984: 35). In these encounters with computers children are forced to think about the differences between their minds and the mind of the machine. In resolving the dilemma many children conclude that it is emotionality rather than rationality that separates human intelligence from artificial intelligence.

As Turkle points out, this is a major shift in the way in which we apprehend the world around us and our place within it. The tradition of the Enlightenment and of rationalist science was to construct a view of human life and consciousness by reference to the natural world. Concepts of natural science, natural law, natural justice, and natural man reflect the primacy of nature as the key reference point for the interpretation of the world and the identification of the special qualities of humankind. What most distinguished the human animal from the rest of the animal kingdom was rationality, the ability to think and to reason. Romanticism too, in its reaction to the cold sterility it saw at the heart of the rational scientific view of the world, emphasized natural feeling, spontaneity, and closeness to nature as the antidote to the logic, mechanism and artifice of the industrializing world. In modern times, suggests Turkle, we increasingly differentiate and interpret ourselves, not by reference to the natural world but by reference to the machine world, the world of our own artifacts. Thus rather than thinking of ourselves as rational animals we begin to look upon ourselves as "emotional machines." Out of this interaction with the machine, claims Turkle, develops "a new psychological culture, a 'computational culture' with new metaphors for thinking about the mind as program and information processor. This culture spreads through the diffusion of computational ideas much as the psychoanalytic culture spread through the diffusion of Freudian ideas" (Turkle 1984: 310–11).

It is perhaps not surprising to find, during the years of the space program and the spreading of this computational culture, a variety of attempts to humanize technology and to escape from the technological world. The space program spun off both traditional fiction and new journalistic "novels of fact." Each strove to constrain large-scale technologies and the vastness of the cosmos within the literary boundaries of storyline, characterization and the personalization of human destinies. The significance of the individual character at the center of his or her own psychological universe, and the insignificance of that same individual in the context of institutionalized technology and of cosmic time and space, provided a fruitful source of dramatic tension. But the attempts to come to grips with the outward explorations of science and technology were paralleled by an increasing interest in exploring the inner world of the self. The "narcissistic preoccupation with the self" (Lasch 1980: xv) characteristic of the 1970s, the Me Decade, manifested itself in a variety of ways. Among them were the nebulae of fundamentalist religious movements and the galaxy of "new consciousness" therapies described by R. D. Rosen (1978) as "Psychobabble"—est, co-counselling, rebirthing, primal therapy, rolfing and, inevitably, computer therapy. For every new black hole discovered by astrophysicists at the outer edge of the physical universe, there was in the psychic universe a corresponding inner "dark wet hole" through which "the egomaniacal, experience-devouring imperial self " passed on its regression "into a grandiose, narcissistic, infantile, empty self " (Lasch 1980: 12). The self, eclipsed by science and technology, reasserted its claim for a place at the center of the universe.

NOTES

1. Graduate technologist quoted in *Time* 1982: 38.
2. A pattern repeated in the 1991 Gulf War.
3. Perhaps this was a particularly British viewpoint. In contrast, a Frenchman in Tahiti in 1847 had a culinary rather than technological measure for the spread of civilization. He considered the Tahitians' acquisition of a taste for truffles the best test of the civilizing influence of French culture (Martin 1981: 98–99). In the twentieth century the presence of a particular soft drink was the litmus test of civilization for an executive of the Coca-Cola company: "When you don't see a Coca-Cola sign, you have passed the borders of civilization" (quoted by Pilger 1984).
4. This was not the first occasion on which *Time* had mounted a machine on this annual pedestal; in 1967 the car was the collective "Man of the Year."
5. The BBC's six-pips time signal was introduced in 1924.

CHAPTER 5

The Languages, Signs and Symbols of the Business World

THE BIZARRE BAZAAR: SEMIOLOGY AND THE LANGUAGE OF ADVERTISING

My lovelies. With Paris and Berlin doing the most angular things with concrete, glass, and metal—so stimulating—one does heave the old bosom just once to find mahoganized, diluvian London shedding the mildew at last! I mean, on the new floor at Jaeger's positively all the fungus has died in the night. My dears, they've gone completely chromium! Tuby chairs, Vulcanite tables, glass walls, plus-ultra pictures, and wholly immediate carpets. A simply gladdening spot, darlings. Utterly 1930 and corpse-reviving! The cerebral background, of course, for the stupefying smartness of the new Jaeger clothes. Tweeds—the most contagious tweeds! Tailored to a slenderizing centimetre. Too plastic! And woollies—millenial patterns, cut with lethal precision but touched with coyest inconsequence. There never were such caressing, emotion-causing clothes! (1930 Jaeger advertisement)

In 1930, aided and abetted by such breathless ad-agency prose, the Jaeger Company achieved a remarkable transformation in its image and clientele. Associated in the 1920s with the "Sanitary Woollen Clothing" of the German Dr. Gustave Jaeger and with the writer Bernard Shaw, "a conspicuous if not ridiculous disciple of the 'Woollen Movement' " (Adburgham 1966: 12), by the end of 1930 Jaeger's London shop had become a mecca of trendy young female fashion. The psychology of consumption is nothing if not strange. That people will buy cans of sunshine, pet rocks, eyelure for cats, doggy jogging suits, belly-button warmers, pickled bottoms, couch potatoes, seeds to make their budgies sing, a combined toothbrush and tongue-scraper, or waterproof cellular phones for use while showering never ceases to amaze me. That *I* will participate in the serious rituals accompanying the swearing of oaths on the adoption of cabbage patch dolls by my stepdaughters strikes me as equally surprising. This is strange behavior; yet normal too. And what are we to make of the gourmet restaurant in Nice, France, that caters exclusively to dogs, or the video therapy marketed in Japan for stressed-out cats, or the Takara corporation's artificial feline, Robocat? Or of John Cage's 4-minute 33-second masterpiece of musical silence, 4'33"? Or of the erotic bakeries initiated in Manhattan in 1978, precipitating, in the United States, the Pornographic Cookie Control Act of 1981 and, in Britain, the impounding by customs of an incoming cargo of sweet but salacious cakes and biscuits?

It is not difficult to see why the languages of advertising, written, aural, and visual, have been a primary source of information about the ideological underpinnings of the business world, a gateway to the exploration of the culture of business. The study of advertising signs and symbols and their social and cultural significance—the semiology of advertising—was in part stimulated by a desire to unravel the processes through which consumers were caught up in the ethics of consumption. The presumption was that an understanding of the subtle mechanisms of "persuasive" advertising would help provide the necessary inoculation for those who wished to increase their consumer resistance. Semiological studies were largely the preserve of sociologists, anthropologists and students of language, literature and the visual arts. More recently, however, the wheel has come full circle. Students of advertising and marketing are being taught about semiotics, not as a basis for cultural analysis but in order to improve the impact of advertising campaigns, brand imaging and point-of-sale displays on consumer purchase decisions (see *International Journal of Research in Marketing* 1988).

In its approach to advertisements, semiology seeks to reveal the meanings of advertising images and how those meanings are embedded in the shared culture of advertiser and potential consumer. The protocols of a semiological analysis, of signifier, sign and signified, the denotative and the connotative, need not concern us here. Suffice to say they are primarily mechanisms for teasing out the relationship between the overt content and images of a particular advertisement and its underlying socio-cultural context. It is from the socio-cultural context that an advertisement derives its meaning:

Diamonds may be marketed by likening them to eternal love, creating a symbolism where the mineral means something not on its own terms, as a rock, but in human terms, as a sign. Thus a diamond comes to "mean" love and endurance for us. Once the connection has been made, we begin to translate the other way and in fact to skip translating altogether: taking the sign for what it signifies, the thing for the feeling (Williamson 1978: 12)

Much advertising operates within this taken-for-granted world of shared symbolic meanings and values. Cosmetic advertisements may emphasize the practical uses of skin cleansers or body deodorants. At the same time, overtly or latently, they sell youthfulness, sexual attractiveness or some other quality that can be "purchased" alongside the purchase of the product itself. As Arthur Asa Berger (1984: x) pointed out, "We are all semioticians, even if we don't recognize it or understand the technicalities of the subject. (We are like the character in the Moliere play who never realized that he always spoke prose.) We all know about status symbols; we all talk about 'images'; and we all read articles in newspapers and magazines about 'body language' and 'dressing for power.' " Semiological analysis exposes this taken-for-granted world to scrutiny. It asks what the taken-for-granted world of an advertisement says about the culture within which that advertisement is placed, accentuating both the advertisement's messages about the product and its messages about the product's purchasers: "Semiology highlights the way that we ourselves take part in the creation of meaning in messages, suggesting that we are not mere bystanders in the advertising process, but participants in a code than unites designer and reader" (Leiss, Kline and Jhally 1986: 159).

Semiological analysis of advertisements and commercial products serves a number of purposes. It reveals how business values and ideologies seep into the collective consciousness and establish and reinforce themselves at the core of Western culture. This is the tradition of Roland Barthes (1973: 11), who "wanted to track down, in the decorative display of *what-goes-without-saying*, the ideological abuse which, in my view, is hidden there." It emphasizes that the taken-for-granted world of advertisements is accepted as the natural order, a reflection of long-standing and unchangeable verities; whereas in reality this taken-for-granted world is an agency of ideology, reinforcing particular beliefs and values and suppressing alternatives.

Evidence of such ideological components in advertising can be seen in the racial, gender and class stereotypes it exploits and reinforces. It is often easier to see these ideological components in hindsight than to unravel the ways in which they are embedded in contemporary culture. In 1991, for example, the Royal Festival Hall in London ran an exhibition of advertisements titled "Black Markets: Images of Black People in Advertising and Marketing in Britain, 1880–1990." Among the most striking of the images presented were a series of Victorian advertisements in which black children are trying to wash themselves white or to shine up their blackness with shoe polish and boot blacking. In soap advertisements of the late nineteenth century whiteness is equated with purity, soap-induced cleanliness is portrayed as next to godliness, and black people from "Darkest Africa" to the Australian outback are invariably presented as inferior and uncivilized. A Pears Soap advertisement of 1889 shows a dying Aboriginal over the caption "Ev'n the Black Australian dying, hope's he shall return a White." And in the *Illustrated London News* of 27 August 1887, a Pears advertisement headed "The Formula of British Conquest" reproduces the following extract from a despatch by the *Daily Telegraph*'s war correspondent in the Sudan:

Even if our invasion of the Soudan has done nothing else it has at any rate left the Arab something to puzzle his fuzzy head over, for the legend

PEARS' SOAP IS THE BEST,

inscribed in huge white characters on the rock which marks the farthest point of our advance towards Berber, will tax all the wits of the Dervishes of the Desert to translate.

In the world of Pears, neither technology nor truffles but the advent of soap marks the onslaught of civilization.

Exposure of the unquestioned ideological presumptions of a culture is one use of a semiological analysis of advertisements. A further use of such an analysis rests upon a recognition that advertisements stand at the crossroads between business and culture, fusing the cultural apparatus of myth making and symbolling to the exchange of goods and services in the marketplace. From this perspective understanding the currency and structure of advertisements is an essential key to understanding one of the processes through which the market economy insinuates its values into the cultural mainstream. Just as political propaganda is most effective when it enters the stream of information in the guise of news, so too cultural propaganda may be most pervasive when it masquerades in the apparently innocent guise of product information and promotion. By illuminating the apparatus for the spread of the ideology of the market, semiological analysis can be used either to facilitate or to constrain the development of the market economy. It also provides a bridge between cultural traditions and contemporary life and a gateway to the analysis of mass communications and popular culture.

There are difficulties, however, with the semiotic analysis of advertisements and products. In particular the identification of shared meanings is problematic. We may readily accept the diamond as a shared symbol of eternal love, or the red rose as a symbol of passion, but we find ourselves uneasy with the latent meanings found in the game Pac Man:

The game takes place in a labyrinth which implies, metaphorically, that we are all trapped, closeted in a claustrophobic situation in which the nature of things is that we must either eat or be eaten. This oral aspect of the game suggests further that there is some kind of diffuse regression taking place and we have moved from the phallic stage (guns, rockets) to the oral stage (eating, biting).

Regression often takes place in people as a means of coping with anxiety and there is good reason to suspect that the popularity of a game like "Pac Man" indicates that our young people, who play the game, are coping with their anxieties by regressing (in the service of their egos). This may be because they are, for some reason, now afraid of taking on responsibilities and feel anxious about long-term relationships and mature interpersonal sexuality. (Berger 1984: 141–42)

Such interpretation is reminiscent of the Freudian interpretation of dreams. The structures of analysis imposed on objects and behaviors tell us more about the analyst than about the objects and behaviors under scrutiny. In such circumstances it is difficult to find a basis for discriminating between alternative interpretations or explanations, for separating a valid interpretation or reading of meanings from an invalid one. Indeed, we tend to be seduced by the richness of a reading, the eloquence of its analysis, and the subversiveness of its insights. In the process we may gloss over its arbitrariness and neglect to closely scrutinize its content. It is this process of seduction, of image over content, that advertisements themselves exploit so successfully. Only when confronted with the more bizarre or absurd claims of semioticians and advertisers do we pause to wonder. For example, a *Wall Street Journal* article titled "Your Suit Is Pressed, Hair Neat, but What Do Your Molars Say?" described how Dr. Jeffrey Morley's Center for Cosmetic Dentistry in San Francisco lured patients. Teeth semiologist and businessman Morley advised potential clients that people consciously or unconsciously "read" one another's teeth for clues to character. "What it comes down to is this: Buck teeth imply people are dumb. Large canines imply aggressiveness. Weak chins imply passivity, while strong chins imply a macho, studly personality. . . . I don't know who made these up, but the fact is, they're cultural standards" (Berger 1984: 98). Dr. Morley stands in a lengthy tradition of promoters of dental health and hygiene. In England in May 1660 the newspaper *Mercurius Publicus* ran this advertising copy for toothpaste: "Most excellent Dentifrices to scour and cleanse the Teeth, making them white as Ivory: Preserves from the Toothach fastens the Teeth, and sweetens the Breath, and preserves the Gums from Cankers and Imposthumes" (Shepard 1973: 115). And in Philadelphia in 1784 a dentist advertised that he could transplant teeth, claiming 123 successful transplants in six months and offering two guineas each to "persons disposed to sell their front teeth or any of them" (Wood 1958: 55).

"LAST YEAR'S WORDS ARE AS DATED AS LAST YEAR'S HATS."[1]

The discrepancy between advertising promise and product delivery is a long-standing theme in the literature about sales and marketing techniques. Part of the critique of advertising is that at the root of this discrepancy lies a careless and destructive approach to language. Since language is so integral to culture, and advertising such an ubiquitous phenomenon, advertising language and practice become useful vehicles for exploring the nature of a business culture and the mechanisms through which such a culture is established and maintained. The presence of hyperbole in advertising language is not new, nor has it gone unremarked in the past. Dr. Samuel Johnson, in his essay "Art of Advertising," published in the journal *The Idler* in 1759, commented that "advertisements are now so numerous that they are very negligently perused, and it is therefore become necessary to gain attention by magnificence of promises and by eloquence sometimes sublime and sometimes pathetic. . . . Promise, large promise, is the soul of an advertisement." In Johnson's time advertising "hype" was known as "puffery." Neil McKendrick, John Brewer and J. H. Plumb (1982: 149) described the puffs of eighteenth- and nineteenth-century England:

There was also the "Puff Ostentatious," the "Puff Concealed" ("so nicely veiled you do not know it is a puff until you have lost your money"), the "Puff Boomerang" ("a weapon which when thrown in one direction, returns with greater force to hit the object in another"), the "Puff Infantile," the "Puff Interjectional," the "Puff Admiring," the "Puff by Reference," the "Puff Authoritative" (Thomas Telford on the quality of a brand of cement), the "Puff Classical," the "Puff Economical," the "Puff Boastful" ("better than any other offered for sale"), the "Puff Superlative" ("the *best* in the world"). There were in addition the "Puff by Emulation" ("By appointment to his, her or their majesties"), the "Puff by Opposition" (inciting, even writing, scurrilous or exaggerated abuse in order to be able to reply, in a dignified and memorable way, which artificially created controversy and could offer, in Wedgwood's words, the opportunity "of advertising away at a very great rate"), the "Puff Mendacious," the "Swindling Puff," the "Puff Familiar," the "Puff Facetious," the "Puff Beguiling" (the "Sure Guide to Wealth and Prosperity" type, encouraging the purchase of Lottery tickets at "the first office in CORNHILL . . . distinguished by its extraordinary Luck in distributing more Capital Prizes, comparatively, than any other office"). There were "Anecdotal Puffs," "Adjectival Puffs," "puffs aphoristic," puffs by proverb and example, puffs through song, verse and puzzles. There were aggressive puffs and defensive puffs. There were high-flown literary puffs and down-to-earth, demotic puffs.

So pervasive was eighteenth-century puffery that it was frequently the subject of comment and satirical review. Sheridan, in his play *The Critic* (1779), has a character called Mr. Puff who advertises himself *viva voce* as "a practitioner in panegyric, or, to speak more plainly, a professor of the heart [art] of puffing." Mr. Puff claims credit for the language of the auctioneers: " 'Twas I first enriched their style—'twas I first taught them to crowd their advertisements with panegyrical superlatives, each epithet rising above the other, like the bidders in their own auction rooms!" He has turned puffery into a science and reduced it to system and order, each principle category of advertisement having its own set of best puffing practices. For promoting a new theatrical production, Mr. Puff uses the "puff direct" in the form of a laudatory review written the day before the first performance. For booksellers and enterprising poets, the "puff collusive" is his newest and best technique. It acts "in the disguise of determined hostility" with an indignant press correspondent observing that a new book or poem "is one of the most unjustifiable performances he ever read. The severity with which certain characters are handled is quite shocking: and as there are many descriptions in it too warmly colored for female delicacy, the shameful avidity with which this piece is bought by all people of fashion is a reproach on the taste of the times, and a disgrace to the delicacy of the age." Here you see the two strongest inducements are held forth; first, that nobody ought to read it; and, secondly, that everybody buys it; on the strength of which the publisher boldly prints the tenth edition, before he had sold ten of the first; and then establishes it by threatening himself with the pillory, or absolutely indicting himself for *scan.mag.*[2] (act 1, scene 2)

No publicity is bad publicity. *Plus ça change!*

In the twentieth century too the language and practices of advertising, and the social values and mores that they are seen to represent, have been subject to frequent satirical comment. In the 1930s the magazine *Ballyhoo* (see Marchand 1985: 312–14) had a character called Elmer Zilch who held the advertising world up to ridicule with such marketing heresies as "if you can build a lousy mousetrap and spend $10,000,000 advertising it the world will beat a path to your door." The third of *Ballyhoo*'s Ten Commandments of Advertising was "Honor thy Father's Day and thy Mother's Day"; and the tenth commandment was "Thou *shalt* covet thy neighbor's car and his radio and his silverware and his refrigerator and everything that is his." The magazine also provided a guide to advertising terminology; its glossary included the following terms (Turner 1965: 218):

Delicate membrane	—any part of the body
Lubricate the skin texture	—put on grease
Pore-deep cleansing	—washing the face
Harsh irritants	—all the ingredients of a competitor's product
Great scientist	—anyone who will sign an endorsement
Lifetime	—until the new model comes out

Used Cadillacs, General Motors decided, should not be described as used but as "cars with previous service" (Baker 1969: 55).

It is not merely euphemisms and superlatives that characterize the language of advertising. There is also linguistic innovation, invention, distortion and devaluation. American advertisers progressively developed a language of their own. In the 1930s, for example, the automobile industry "devised for itself a complete new vocabulary. It offered a levelized ride in a unisteel body, with sound-sorbers, powered by a micropoised engine with an ee-zeedrain sump. There were flashway signals fore'n aft, the steering was permi-firm of safe-t-flex, and fresh air came in through rear-opening ventipanes, or ventiports" (Turner 1965: 221). Turner also observed how food advertisements had generated a whole new baby-talk with words like yummy, tangy, zippy, chewy, krispy, krunchy, all giving "oomph 'n energy"; how the word *eating* had become an adjective: a wonderful "eating" cheese, to be followed in ad-land by "eatingest," as in the "eatingest corn that ever tossed a golden tassel"; and how natural processes were described "in the language of the Song of Solomon," the corn in a Bird's Eye frosted food advertisement having been "picked when the tender kernels are welling with milkiness." But the "most wanton havoc with the English language," he suggested, had been perpetrated by the copywriters employed to boost the sales of lingerie: "Time to consult your bun-eez horoscope for news of size-pruf holeproof and truly whymsy hy-test quality panties. If you are feminine sissy britches or imps sport-eez at heart your best bet in sportswear, twinklette playwear, strutwear is found in the fashion names of nolde and golden nolde" (Baker 1969: 47).

Perhaps the most devalued word in the advertisers' lexicography is *new*. This has bred the bastardized offspring of "newnew," "newnewnew" and "allnew." The washing powder Tide was new every year for a whole generation, and for many years Maxwell House Instant Coffee was advertised as "A New Coffee Discovery." When the Federal Trade Commission advocated a tentative outer limit of six months for newness, an editorial in *Advertising Age* protested that "the newness of the New Year is lost in a matter of seconds; but New England is still called that after nearly 400 years. ... And the New World, geologists say, is probably two billion years old" (Baker 1969: 24). Another hackneyed word commented upon by Baker, who was the president of an advertising agency, is the word *stay*, as in "stay slim," "stay healthy," and "stay young"; the word is used in such a way as to imply that a particular product will *make* you slim, healthy or young. A similar verbal sleight of hand is present in the use made of the word *save*, as in "buy x and save," where saving is equated with spending.

"FICTITIOUS VALUES AS EVANESCENT AS RAINBOW GOLD."

The part played by lingerie, health food products and diet formulas in the advertising fantasies of the twentieth century was in earlier times played by patent medicines. "Famous Drops for Hypocondriak Melancholly," "An Excellent Secret to take away Warts," Scott's Emulsion of Cod-Liver Oil with Hypophosphites "to cure Blood Poverty," Drs. Starkey and Palen's Compound Oxygen Treatment "for diseases incurable by the use of drugs," the Memory Tablet Company of New York's "new physiological discovery Memory Restorative Tablets quickly and permanently increase the memory two or ten-fold and greatly augment intellectual power; difficult studies etc. easily mastered; truly marvelous; highly endorsed"—"BE BRILLIANT AND EMINENT," and miracle cures for consumption populate the pages of newspapers and magazines from the early days of advertisements.[3] In Britain and the United States during the nineteenth century the manufacturers and sellers of patent medicines were the most prominent newspaper advertisers. By the end of the century patent medicine advertisements had given advertising such a bad name that few other manufacturers were willing to advertise on a regular basis. Indeed, many in business thought advertising disreputable, undignified and unethical, as well as being an unnecessary expense. Bankers were reluctant to deal with manufacturers who advertised, feeling such businesses were putting themselves in the same unreliable class as the patent medicine companies. Consequently, reputable manufacturing businesses would conceal their advertising plans and expenditures from their bankers.

Advertising's association with patent medicines gave those who worked in advertising, as copywriters or as advertising agents, an unsavory reputation. But it was through this association that advertising developed its techniques and advertising professionals learned their "craft." If you could sell products that were increasingly being exposed as valueless and harmful, then you developed confidence in your ability to sell anything. The visibility of patent medicine advertising made the patent medicine advertisers and salesmen a natural target for writers trying to come to terms with the growth of commercialism. Emily Watts (1982) has described how the tradition of the Yankee peddler merged, in the nineteenth century, into a literary image of the American businessman as a con man. This was an image portrayed by Charles Dickens in *Martin Chuzzlewit* (1844) and by Herman Melville in *The Confidence-Man: His Masquerade* (1857), a novel that includes a herb doctor peddling "Samaritan Pain Dissuader." It was an image reinforced by real-life characters like P. T. Barnum, whose autobiography was published in 1855. With Barnum there was admiration as well as condemnation of successful sharp practice, admiration particularly for the showmanship and self-promotion of which advertising was a part:

If Americans will good naturedly tolerate shams, applaud the swindler, and admire the duplicity of public figures, provided they are successful at it, it is in large part because Barnum taught them the entertainment value in such things; and taught them, too, that their own credulity and acceptance were amusing and somehow admirable. He defrauded them again and again and let them share in his enjoyment of the joke. . . . They loved him for his bald and boundless effrontery, for his instinctive knowledge of their gullibility, and they pressed their money on him in homage. (Wood 1958: 157)

The antics of P. T. Barnum—the promotion of Jenny Lind, the Swedish operatic and concert soprano, and the exhibition of Tom Thumb, the dwarf Charles Edward Stratton—reinforced in European culture an image of the American businessman as a colorful, crass go-getter. Such salesmen as Barnum with their colorful aphorisms—"A sucker is born every minute"—

were cast in the predatory entrepreneurial mode, surviving by wit and cunning in the commercial jungle. They had long ago rejected the hardworking, God-fearing artisan virtues of piety, honesty and frugality advocated by that untiring promoter and patron saint of American advertising, Benjamin Franklin. However, the now long-standing European belief that commercial crassness, particularly in advertising and sales, flows from American business practices is not supportable historically. Advertising agents set up offices in England and in France in the seventeenth century, yet the first advertising agency in the United States was not established until 1841 (Wood 1958). A fully fledged consumer society had emerged in England by 1800 (McKendrick, Brewer and Plumb 1982). Legislation restricting the use of sky signs on the top of London buildings was consolidated in 1894 and bans placed on balloons and parachutes used for advertising. Before the turn of the century, bylaws had also been introduced in London to curtail electric advertisements. In 1900 one writer complained that "the flashing out-and-in electric advertisements," unknown in New York at that time, were vulgarizing "the august spectacle of the Thames by night" (Turner 1965: 110).

As H. G. Wells's novel *Tono-Bungay* (1909) makes clear, it was not necessary for British writers to travel to the United States to satirize the ways of the advertising world. The novel recounts the rise and fall of patent medicine salesman Edward Ponderevo, manufacturer of Tono-Bungay tonic and a range of complementary products such as Tono-Bungay Hair Stimulant. Ponderevo, as described by his nephew and business helpmate George, starts out as "a busy blackbeetle in a crack in the floor," "a very small shabby little man in a dirty back street, sending off a few hundred bottles of rubbish to foolish buyers." But the Ponderevo formula for success, "that the quickest way to get wealth is to sell the cheapest thing possible in the dearest bottle," assisted by advertising, leads to booming sales:

My uncle had in his inner office a big map of England, and as we took up fresh sections of the local press and our consignments invaded new areas, flags for advertisements and pink underlines for orders showed our progress. "The romance of modern commerce, George!", my uncle would say, rubbing his hands together and drawing in air through his teeth. "The romance of modern commerce, eh? Conquest. Province by province. Like sogers [soldiers]."

For four and a half years the company booms. Ponderevo and George live "a life of mingled substance and moonshine," underlying which lie only "fictitious values as evanescent as rainbow gold." At the height of the Tono-Bungay boom, Ponderevo has a controlling influence over nearly 30 million pounds sterling, a fact that George, whose attitude is shared by many novelists in the face of the apparent absurdities of business success, finds supremely unreasonable:

This irrational muddle of a community in which we live gave him that, paid him at that rate for sitting in a room and scheming and telling it lies. For he created nothing, he invented nothing, he economized nothing. I cannot claim that a single one of the great businesses we organized added any real value to human life at all. . . .

You perceive now, however, the nature of the services for which this fantastic community gave him unmanageable wealth and power and real respect. It was all a monstrous payment for courageous fiction, a gratuity in return for the one reality of human life—illusion. We gave them a feeling of hope and profit; we sent a tidal wave of water and confidence into their stranded affairs. "We mint Faith, George," said my uncle one day. "That's what we do. And by Jove we got to keep minting! We been making human confidence ever since I drove the first cork of Tono-Bungay."

"PECUNIARY TRUTH" AND THE "PERMISSIBLE LIE"

In the United States the poor image of advertising and advertisers created by the patent medicine industry came to a head between 1890 and 1914, a period described by Turner as one of "War on the Quacks." From the end of the Civil War until World War I a growing number of books and articles were published that looked behind the moral facade of American business and exposed the commercial practices of the time. A principal target of this muckraking journalism was the industrial trusts and their creators. Substantial documentation was provided to demonstrate that the greatest of the industrial barons "were robber barons, men who made their way by corrupting legislatures, appropriating resources, organizing monopolies, and crushing competitors" (Wyllie 1954: 146). Another principal target was the patent medicine industry and its advertising practices. Major journals and magazines ran vigorous campaigns to expose the constituent ingredients of some of the industry's products and the health hazards associated with their consumption. In 1892 the *Ladies' Home Journal* stopped carrying advertisements for medicines and from 1902 to 1904 published a series of articles on the "dishonesty and chicanery" of the patent medicine men. In 1905 the magazine *Collier's* joined the crusade with a number of pieces by Samuel Hopkins Adams under the title "The Great American Scandal":

The public learned for the first time that its favorite catarrh powders contained cocaine, that the soothing syrups with which it dosed its children were composed of laudanum and morphine. The Women's Christian Temperance Union was invited to take note of the fact that some medicines were 40 per cent alcohol (it was unlawful to sell a certain widely advertised pick-me-up to [American] Indians, for this reason). One article by Adams began with a list of names and addresses of persons who had died from the effects of a named medicine. (Turner 1965: 159)

The pressure arising from media exposure and public outcry about business practices, particularly meat-handling practices in the Chicago slaughterhouses (documented by Upton Sinclair in his 1905 novel *The Jungle*), led to two outcomes. The first was direct government intervention and regulation through legislation—the passage in the United States of the Food and Drug Act (1906). The 1906 act was supported by the pharmaceutical industry as a means of curtailing the activities of those drug and patent medicine manufacturers whose excessive claims for their products had given the industry as a whole a bad name. In 1914 the Federal Trade Commission was set up to protect consumer interests and to prevent "false and deceptive advertising." And in 1931 the Food and Drug Administration was established with specific responsibility for the safety, effectiveness and labelling of drugs, food and food additives, cosmetics, and medical devices, and for research on toxic chemicals.

The second outcome was increased self-regulation and self-censorship of advertisements by newspaper and magazine publishers and by the advertisers themselves. Initially publishers and advertisers worked independently. Large newspapers quietly censored their advertising pages to cull out offensive copy and extravagant hype. The advertisers, through professional associations like the Advertising Federation of America, developed codes of advertising practice for their members. (Consider the Curtis Advertising Code of 1911, for example; see Wood 1958: 337–38). In 1911 the Associated Advertising Clubs of the World adopted the ambitious slogan Truth in Advertising. It was an impossible and, from the point of view of the advertising industry, a commercially disastrous dream, but it was indicative of the industry's desire to clean up its image if not its practice. Gradually publishers and advertising associations, recognizing their common interests, began to work together. In 1914 the Newspaper Division of the Associated Advertising Clubs of the World produced a new code, Standards of Newspaper Practice, which was endorsed by major newspapers throughout the United States. By joint agreement between the advertisers and the publishers, deceptive or offensive advertising, or advertising that threatened the public welfare, was to be screened out. At the same time newspapers agreed to maintain uniform advertising rates and to sell advertising space on the basis of independently audited circulation figures rather than on the basis of their own inflated claims of readership.

The process of advertising industry self-censorship and self-regulation, set in train in the years immediately preceding World War I, produced new versions of old verities. Previously only the language of advertisements distorted and displaced the traditional meanings of words. Now, as a special branch of ethics—advertising ethics—developed, there was a new moral language to contend with. Here notions of truthfulness are qualified to accommodate the kinds of falsity and half truth ("A half truth is generally the worst half") that are common in advertising copy. Similarly a legal term, *caveat emptor*, "let the buyer beware," explicitly recognizes the misleading nature and intent of much commercial business practice. There are now various codes of advertising conduct that set out to provide guidelines as to what is and is not ethical in advertisements. In the disputes over regulation of tobacco industry advertising, tobacco companies, advertising agencies and publishers have all argued for the freedom of commercial speech. Such a freedom, they suggest, should have the same status as freedom of religious or political speech (Deeks 1992). In all these instances business values and practices are contesting in the public terrain for control of the values and ethics of the broader society. In the process ideas and values that originate in that broader society are imported into the world of business, remodelled in a manner congruent with business interests and values, and then exported back into the larger community in their "new," "improved" versions. Among these casuistries are the "pecuniary truth" and the "permissible lie."

Few modern advertisements make such overtly outrageous promises as those of the manufacturers of Flobar during the cold war of the late 1940s: "Afraid of A-Bomb contamination? In the event of an A-Bomb attack wash contamination away with Flobar. . . . It can be carried about for instant use." Members of consumer societies recognize that advertising claims are not to be taken at face value. When Esso ran its slogan Put a Tiger in Your Tank, we did not take the advice literally. There is clearly a distinction to be made between dangerous and immoral deception in advertising and harmless exaggeration of the qualities of a product. It is precisely *where* this distinction is to be made that is the focus of discussion about advertising ethics. Norman Bowie argues that exaggeration, puffery and hype in advertising are not deceptive because they are expected by consumers. They are a form of harmless bluffing based on the notion of pecuniary truth. Whereas a lie is a deliberate attempt to mislead, a pecuniary truth is a false statement that is not intended to be believed. Advertising falsehoods are permissible lies because consumers all know the nature of the advertising beast and understand the rules of the advertising game. Deceptive advertising, in contrast, "is advertising that is intentionally designed to mislead the rational consumer who knows the rules of the game about the cost, amount or quality of a product" (Bowie 1982: 61).

The notion of pecuniary truth may be fine for those who are familiar with the ways of the consumer culture when confronted with non-technical product information. But it is inadequate protection for vulnerable or unsophisticated consumers, such as young children (by the sixth grade children have acquired a "global distrust" of advertising; see Schudson 1984: 120) or those in Third World countries with little previous exposure to high-pressure advertising. The marketing of infant formula in the Third World, for example, prompted relatively poor and illiterate consumers to substitute bottle feeding for breast feeding of their babies. The results were "commerciogenic malnutrition" and infant deaths as "the tragic consequence of a system of competitive marketing" (Schudson 1984: 125). Ironically by 1991 evidence was emerging that bottle feeding might have a part to play in preventing the spread of the AIDS virus to such infants.

Even in commercially more sophisticated and skeptical communities pecuniary truth has severe limitations. It is little help for the rational consumer confronted with apparently highly technical and scientific advertising claims about the performance or quality of a product. Samm Sinclair Baker, after 30 years' experience in the advertising business, concluded that a permissible lie was "a lie that helps build profits." It was his view that the permissible lie was an immoral concept that pervaded advertising practice even though it was not essential for the improvement of business sales and profits. In addition the all-pervading fakery that the permissible lie sanctioned in advertising, was, Baker argued, "through saturation and repetition, [undermining] the attitudes and ethics of the adult, the child, and the family." Whereas we may not be deceived by the claims of any particular advertisement, we are still "affected by the mist of deception which we continually breathe" (Herbert Agar, quoted in Turner 1965: 11).

JESUS AS AD-MAN

Advertising and commercial business practices have not always been the subjects of such deep suspicion. In the 1920s, with the publication of Bruce Barton's *The Man Nobody Knows: A Discovery of the Real Jesus*, Jesus was incorporated into the pantheon of business heroes and role models. The takeover by business of such a powerful ethical and moral symbol represented a pinnacle in the history of successful accommodation between business ideology and Christian theology. It provided a new, if temporary, resolution of the long-standing tension between spiritual and secular life. The Protestant ethic had sanctioned economic success and placed business high on God's list of approved vocations. Protestant clergymen, like the Rev. Thomas P. Hunt, author of *The Book of Wealth: In Which It Is Proved from the Bible That It Is the Duty of Every Man to Become Rich* (1836), had been leading proponents of the nineteenth century's self-help cult. Married to the doctrine of the stewardship of wealth, it was possible for the business owner to thread the eye of the needle and enter the kingdom of heaven, and for the successful executive to make peace with God. But Barton turned God, in the form of Jesus, into a successful chief executive officer (CEO) and salesman-entrepreneur, the prototypical modern business executive.

Bruce Barton, the Amherst-educated son of a preacher, was a practicing Christian and an advertising agency executive. As Mark Twain illustrated in his satirical short story *The International (Christian) Lightning Trust* (1909), reconciling the necessary half truths of the advertising world with the tenets of the Christian religion was no easy task. Twain's roguish entrepreneurs, having successfully created a fortune by trading "on the assfulness of the human race," become conscience-stricken by some of their advertising and promotional practices. Jasper, one of the partners, realized, with shame, that every new circular he issued contained fresh lies—lies essential to prosperity and expansion in the business, it was true, but lies all the same; he realized that the size of these lies was getting bigger and bigger with every new output, and the thought of it made his cheek burn. He saw clearly that in contriving these unholy inventions he was imperiling his salvation, and he spoke up with decision, and said "I stop it right here! I will no longer soil my soul with it; we must hire a liar."

But whereas Twain's entrepreneurs recast their business practices to fit the demands of an all-seeing Providence, Barton recasts the central icon of religious belief to fit the mold of business. *The Man Nobody Knows*, published in 1924 and America's non-fiction bestseller of 1926, sets out to present an alternative to the Sunday school image of Jesus as the gentle lamb of God, a "man of sorrows acquainted with grief." Barton's Jesus is a charismatic, magnetic leader, "the most popular dinner guest in Jerusalem!," who "picked up twelve men from the bottom ranks of business and forged them into an organization that conquered the world." His story is "the story of the founder of modern business," and it is written so that "every business man will read it and send it to his partners and his salesmen."

Barton's opening chapter, "The Executive," extols Jesus' organizational and leadership skills. Whereas Samson could not organize, Moses was useless until he took Aaron into partnership, and John the Baptist had no follow-up program for those who repented, Jesus has all the hallmarks of the successful CEO. He can command respect; he follows his goals with conviction; and he can select, develop, train and motivate subordinates. In a market already oversupplied with religions, he teaches his staff how to catch the attention of a skeptical and hostile public by translating "a great spiritual conception into terms of practical self-concern":

Surely no one will consider us lacking in reverence if we say that every one of the "principles of modern salesmanship" on which business men so much pride themselves, are brilliantly exemplified in Jesus' talk and work. The first of these and perhaps the most important is the necessity for "putting yourself in step with your prospect." . . . Every one of his conversations, every contact between his mind and others, is worthy of the attentive study of any sales manager.

As a chapter titled "His Advertisements" makes clear, Barton's Jesus had a powerful understanding of the value of publicity and the use of the media to promote his product. He "recognized the basic principle that all good advertising is news" and set out to create news, not through press releases or sermons in the synagogues, but through creating action, happenings, in the city squares, the marketplaces, the Temple Court. To illustrate the newsworthiness of Jesus, Barton constructs the following headlines from Matthew, Chapter 9, for the hypothetical *Capernaum News*:

PALSIED MAN HEALED
JESUS OF NAZARETH CLAIMS RIGHT TO FORGIVE SINS
PROMINENT SCRIBES OBJECT
"BLASPHEMOUS," SAYS LEADING CITIZEN
"BUT ANYWAY, I CAN WALK," HEALED MAN RETORTS

PROMINENT TAX COLLECTOR JOINS NAZARETH FORCES
MATTHEW ABANDONS BUSINESS TO PROMOTE NEW CULT
x x x
GIVES LARGE LUNCHEON

For Barton, the parable of the Good Samaritan "is the greatest advertisement of all time." Indeed, Jesus' parables exemplify all the principles of good advertising copy. They have striking storylines, a clear, unambiguous message and their language is crisp and graphic. "Every advertising man ought to study the parables of Jesus . . . schooling himself in their language and learning these four big elements of their power": first, that they are "marvelously condensed"; second, that their language is "marvelously simple"; third, that they have sincerity; and, lastly, that Jesus "knew the recipe for repetition and practiced it."

From the perspective of the 1990s Barton's work looks like a curious and amusing footnote to business history. It is intelligible in the context of the New Thought movement with its emphasis on personal salesmanship and boosterism, and of a period when church members could be described as salesmen, their pastor as first assistant sales manager and the Holy Spirit as sales manager (Turner 1965: 200). Some academic writing of the period also underlined this tendency to view ideas and beliefs in terms of their marketability. In considering the revolutionary views of Galileo, Edgar J. Swift, chairman of the Psychology Department of Washington University, wrote in his 1925 book *Business Power through Psychology* that

Galileo failed because he was an investigator and not a salesman. Consequently, he could not get his goods marketed. . . . Galileo thought that only facts and arguments were needed to sell goods of guaranteed quality, but he was so greatly mistaken that at the end he was compelled to deny publicly everything which he had said about the value of his wares. His competitors, Aristotle, Moses, and the church fathers, had monopolized the market, and their stockholders would not let them do business. (Baritz 1965: 62)

This sales-oriented view of the world was parodied in Sinclair Lewis's novel *Babbitt* (1922). For Babbitt and his kind,

the romantic hero was no longer the knight, the wandering poet, the cowpuncher, the aviator, nor the brave young district attorney, but the great sales-manager, who had an Analysis of Merchandising Problems on his glass-topped desk, whose title of nobility was "Go-getter," and who devoted himself and all his young samurai to the cosmic purpose of Selling—not of selling anything in particular, but pure Selling.

When one recalls the growth of televangelism in the 1970s and 1980s, the shenanigans of Jim and Tammy Faye Bakker and their Heritage USA theme park, the commercial and religious controversies surrounding the PTL (Praise the Lord) television network, and the direct marketing campaigns and emotional appeals of televangelists like Robert Tilton, then Bruce Barton's macho, publicity-grabbing, socializing, go-getting businessman-Jesus takes on a more contemporary relevance. He, like televangelism, demonstrates the intrusiveness of business language and symbols, business values and business practices into what were traditionally conceived of as non-business areas of society and culture. It is the same intrusiveness that has over the years led to complaints about the commercialization of Christmas, the commercialization of sex, love and affection, the commercialization of the family, of education and of medicine, the commercialization of sport, of politics, of the presidency, and the commercialization of the self. The spirit of Jesus as ad-man and booster did not die with Bruce Barton, nor parodies of it with Sinclair Lewis. Jerry Falwell exhorted his Thomas Road Baptist Church congregation in Lynchburg, Virginia, "to reject the prevailing depiction of Jesus Christ as a meek, diaphanous hippie-type with long hair and a billowing robe: 'Christ wasn't effeminate. . . . The man who lived on this earth was a man with muscles. . . . Christ was a he-man!' " (Wilentz 1990: 147).The evangelist Robert Schuller has called his Garden Grove Church in Los Angeles a "22 acre shopping center for God, part of the service industry," and compared the principles that animated his ministry to those that motivated the builders of drive-ins and shopping malls—"accessibility, service, visibility, possibility thinking and excess parking" (Patton 1986: 208). Edwin Diamond, reviewing the television programs of the electronic church, finds all the glitz and glamor of a Hollywood variety show:

The performers—the star preachers, gospel singers, guest healers, and inspirational figures—are so neatly turned out in their blow-dry hair, capped teeth, thousand-watt smiles, banker's gray suits, and flowing robes; the format is so artfully stage managed . . . the pledge numbers and pay-for-prayer messages so insistently presented, that God's television inevitably evokes images of the charlatan preacher, of the Elmer Gantrys and the Reverend Ikes: I wear $400 suits because the Lord wants me to wear $400 suits. (Diamond 1982: 33)

And in "The Lord's Work," Tom Wolfe's trendily dressed televangelist meshes religious and business language in this speech to camera:

And his lord answered and said unto the servant who had buried his talent, his piece of gold, in the ground: "Thou *wick*ed and *sloth*ful *ser*vant! Thou *knew*est that I reap where I sowed not and gather where I have not strewed. Thou oughtest therefore to have put my money to the exchangers, and *then* at my coming I should have received my *own . . . with interest!*" Now, friends, if you've got your money lying around in a passbook savings account down at the bank . . . *you . . .* are like that *wicked servant! You . . .* have got your *gold . . . stuck* in the *ground!* Wouldn't you rather be able to answer, in the Final Hour, when the Last Questions are asked: 'Oh, *yes*, Lord! I took *my gold . . . out* of the passbook savings account! I put *my gold . . . into* the Gospel Money Market Fund! Fourteen-point-five percent per annum as of June 15! Interest *com*pounded daily! Withdrawals in part or in full . . . at *any* time! Check-writing privileges . . . *of* course! Bank by wire . . . available! Call me tonight, toll free—the Reverend Bob Lee Boyd, Gospel Money Market Fund, *In*corporated— and wake up tomorrow . . . on the *side..*of the *Angels!* This is not an offering, which can be made by formal prospectus only. (Wolfe 1980: 54)

LANGUAGE AND CONSCIOUSNESS

The languages we use reflect modes of thinking about experience and the world around us. If, therefore, the languages of business are used to describe, and reflect on, social and cultural reality, then those business languages become an integral and unquestioned part of our thinking processes and our intellectual life. Business images, symbols and ideas increasingly condition our thinking about a variety of non-business phenomena. And since these business languages are so ubiquitous, so unavoidable in the modern world, it is not difficult to envisage a culture in which they are the primary means through which society and societal values are articulated and interpreted. Business languages become enmeshed in consciousness, at the very root of the processes of thinking, reasoning, and experiencing. Without language, how do we think, and without symbols, how do we visualize? But with *what* language *do* we think and with *what* symbols *do* we visualize?

The culture, like the language that carries it, is first imposed on (or at least offered to) the individual from the outside, but eventually it becomes a part of that person's very self. We do not normally experience the categories of our language as constraints on our ability to think or to express ourselves; on the contrary, they are the very means that enable us to think articulately and to express ourselves. (Bjerke 1986: 2)

Of course, we can stand outside our language too, even while we use it. If we use business languages, it does not necessarily mean that we think with them. They may merely be a useful shorthand, a lingua franca, for communicating, getting alone, making sense, socially constructing knowl- edge, in a culture where other languages have been eroded or marginalized, or have become the exclusive and unintelligible property of intellectual elites, of scientific or technological specialists, or of a self-appointed post- modernist intelligentsia. As we can see in the entry of commercial metaphors into religion and of religious metaphors into business, a dynamic relationship exists between languages and the interpretation and experience of the world, a fluctuating relationship of ebbs and flows in influence.

Nevertheless, unpleasant as it may be to contemplate, business languages are the advancing tide and other languages are on the retreat. Nowhere is this more evident than in the professions of law, medicine and education. Indeed, it is educational specialization, particularly in the universities, that has created the conditions for the languages of business and business management to become the common ground binding together faculties of fine arts, science, architecture, law, literature, and so on, into a common enterprise. In university education the language of the business schools, themselves referred to as industrial service organizations, is increasingly the lingua franca of educational policy making and administration. It is the language of student "inputs" and "throughputs," of the "load factor" on students, of educational "quality control," of "production limits" for particular courses and programs. It speaks of the education "industry," of faculties as the "factory that we run," of concern about producing "what the market demands." It is a language of corporate plans and mission statements and institutional bottom lines. In the increasingly important interface with the business community, business leaders talk about the university's use of resources in terms of "more scholar per dollar," about acquiring "good products of the system," and about the need for business to "utilize this rich resource," the university. For its part the university is exhorted to concentrate on "*turning out* well-rounded individuals" and "to keep marketing themselves and their products" to business. Although now more widespread in its use, the language of production and marketing in the context of university administration is not a new phenomenon. In the 1928 *Transactions of the American Institute of Chemical Engineers* a University of Michigan professor of chemical engineering wrote that

there is some analogy between the college and the manufacturing plant which receives partially fabricated metal, shapes it and refines it somewhat, and turns it over to some other agency for further fabrication. The college receives raw material. . . . It must turn out a product which is saleable. . . . The type of curriculum is in the last analysis not set by the college but by the employer of the college graduate. (Hughes 1989: 245)

Business, through language, transmits cultural values and extends business control of those values. Even Shakespeare has not been immune to the general takeover. Over 20 years ago, Patrick Barwise (1971), with tongue firmly in cheek, advanced the proposition that Shakespeare's plays were really business case studies in disguise. *King Lear*, for example, is the story of an aging CEO who handed the family business over to his daughters, "possibly for tax purposes," but could not adjust to retirement. *Hamlet* is a case study of business decision making. It is about a well-trained young graduate executive who, when faced with the realpolitik of the family business, and conditions of uncertainty, is unable to make a decision. It "culminates in . . . the virtual collapse of the business which is finally taken over by Fortinbras at a knock-down price." *Macbeth* is about a weak executive, with a dominant, unscrupulous and ambitious wife, who places a naive and literal-minded faith in his forecasting unit. And *Othello* is about the manager of a foreign subsidiary who is unable to successfully deal with his subordinates, particularly Iago. Iago, the "archetypal successful salesman," skillfully sells the wrong ideas to his boss, adopting "such a low profile that Othello assumes that he knows more than he is prepared to divulge. Above all, Iago's genius lies in telling people what they want to hear, which is why he is so universally regarded as honest." Patrick Barwise's article is facetious and amusing, certainly, but it is illustrative of how cultural products can be reconstructed in the idioms of the business world.

NOTES

1. Adburgham 1966: 12.

2. *scan.mag* = *scandalum magnatum*, a defamation case against a wealthy or eminent person; in this case, the publisher sues himself for defamation.

3. The term *advertisement* was not used until about 1660; before that advertisements were known as "advices."

CHAPTER 6

Image and Reality in the Cartoon World of the Business Executive

THE CARTOON WORLD

The single panel humor cartoon was an early feature of the British weekly journal *Punch*, founded in 1841. By 1860 it was a distinctive genre, a genre to be distinguished from the longer-standing tradition of the political cartoon and the subsequent development of comic strips or narrative cartoons. The evolution of the single panel humor cartoon has been traced in the pages of *Punch* and of *The New Yorker*, founded in 1925. As Randall Harrison (1981) observed, the early cartoons of this type were heavily illustrated realistic drawings with multi-line jokes that often included stage directions and asides to the reader. It was the words, generally written by someone other than the artist, rather than the tableaux-style drawings that carried the humor.

The New Yorker cartoons of the 1920s and 1930s, however, changed the balance between these visual and verbal elements. Words became fewer (in Charles Addams's cartoons they were absent altogether), the drawings simpler and more expressive, and the humor was largely carried in the situation depicted. To this new expressive shorthand form of drawing, with its emphasis on vitality and movement, and its deliberate utilization of distortion in order to create and convey character, the British cartoonist and one-time editor of *Punch* William Hewison (1977) traces the antecedents of nearly all modern cartoons.

A cartoon is the ultimate in minimalism. The cartoonist strives to create an immediately recognizable situation with a minimum of visual and verbal cues, to conjure up a self-contained world with a few easily understood signs and symbols. The cartoon can work only within the context of a taken-for-granted world shared by the cartoonist and his or her audience. It inevitably, therefore, draws upon and recreates stereotypical characters and stereotypical situations, since it is these that provide the most accessible common domain. Because of the presumed existence of these common reference points, cartoons have proved a fruitful source of data for the analysis of changing cultural stereotypes and of shared public perceptions regarding social, political, religious and technological issues. Studies have concentrated on gender and racial caricatures in cartoons, but they have also covered matters as diverse as religion, aging, computerization and space exploration (Saenger 1955; Winick 1961; Alston and Platt 1969; Greenberg and Kahn 1970; Palmore 1971; Anderson and Friemuth 1975; Anderson and Jolly 1977; Meyer et al. 1980).

The premise of all such studies is that the cartoon can provide insight into, or snapshots of, contemporary life and culture. Sociologists have sought to unravel in cartoons "the deeper meanings of social situations, social injustices, or social trends extending over long periods of time" (Bogardus 1945:147) and to use the cartoon as "an unobtrusive indicator of popular culture in transition" (Anderson and Jolly 1977:454). Ronald Anderson and Elaine Jolly also argued that

humor, especially humorous drawings, reveals insightful, subtle feelings that are difficult to capture in other forms of communication. The nature of the publishing industry, with mechanisms for maintaining close rapport between audience and editorial decisions, tends to insure the usefulness of cartoons as indicators of social phenomena despite the complex industry-audience-product process. (Anderson and Jolly 1977:458)

In addition psychologists and psychoanalysts have used cartoons as experimental devices in the exploration of personality traits, mental adjustment and the processes and techniques of stress reduction (Goldstein and McGhee 1972; Kadis and Winick 1973; McGhee and Goldstein 1983).

That the cartoon can illuminate the nature of changing social trends and social values, can identify role conflicts and ambiguities, and can expose our hidden fears and anxieties is not, however, the exclusive belief of sociologists and psychologists. William Hewison (1977:34) recognized the need for the cartoonist to operate "within the broadest band of common experience" and for the journals that published cartoons to generally "march in step with the main battalions of public taste." He observed that social comment was a primary category of cartoon humor and argued that "the social comment cartoonist is in the way of being something of an historian; he is, after all, a recorder of events, and he reflects a certain attitude to those events." In similar vein, though with a different focus, Garry Trudeau, the creator of *Doonesbury*, suggested that the cartoonist "provides us with the means to look back into ourselves; he's the benign conduit between our self-serious facades and those pockets of vulnerability buried deep within" (Harrison 1981:66). Clearly there are good reasons and a number of precedents for treating humor seriously and for not equating the non-serious with the trivial (Mulkay 1988:1).

There have been a number of studies of the portrayal of business and business executives in literature. Some of these are discussed in the next chapter. To the best of my knowledge, however, the ways in which business and business executives are treated in cartoons has not been explored. Consequently, for the purposes of the present discussion, all the cartoons in *The New Yorker* for the period from January 1985 to December 1989 were screened to establish a population of cartoons in which the main character was a business man or woman or an entrepreneur and/or the punchline of the cartoon related to the practice of business or to the perceived values of the business world. This process yielded a total of 361 cartoons. Each cartoon was then coded in terms of the gender and ethnicity of the main characters, the relationships between them, and the themes of the cartoon. Where a cartoon focused on a particular business practice or value, this was further analyzed in terms of the functional business aspects involved.

Bias inevitably arises from examining only *New Yorker* cartoons. Cartoons reflect the style of a magazine and the presumed interests of its readership. *The New Yorker* has been described by British writers as "rather urbane American, not averse to the pleasures of the flesh, and not unduly obsessed with questions of social class" (Eysenck 1944:49), and its cartoon humor as "suave, sophisticated, literate, witty rather than funny, eastern-seaboard humor that chimes happily with the up-market ads" (Hewison 1977:112). While *The New Yorker* may not have depended traditionally on class stratification as a source of humor to the same degree as its nearest British counterpart, *Punch*, nevertheless it has always had, in American eyes, a "preponderance of jokes, largely satirical, which use "society" and upper class as a target" (Stephenson 1951:570). It continues to carry a large number of cartoons that provide ironic comments on the imagined worlds of top corporate executives, investment bankers, stockbrokers, attorneys, and the metropolitan smart-set.

Some researchers in this field have sought to eliminate bias that may stem from over-representation of the work of individual cartoonists. In the present case no attempt was made to do this. The structure of the commercial relationship between freelance cartoonists and magazine editors suggests that it is editors, rather than cartoonists, who introduce bias into the subject matter and viewpoint of the cartoons published. For each cartoon by a particular artist that is published, a large number may be rejected, even when the cartoonist has a track record of successful submissions to a particular magazine or a contractual commitment to supply a specific number of cartoons per annum. As Randall Harrison pointed out, magazine editors act as gatekeepers, sifting through the floods of cartoons submitted and selecting those that seem best suited to the magazine's target market, that reinforce the concerns and interests of the publishers, or that seem likely to encourage readers to scan the pages where the advertising is located. In the case of *Playboy*, for example, four hundred cartoons may be bought annually from the 200,000 or so submitted (Harrison 1981:42). Finally, it should also be recognized that American cartoonists are typically white males. The male-female ratio, for example, of the Cartoonists' Guild, the organization of freelance magazine cartoonists, is around seven to one (Harrison 1981:38).[1]

BUSINESS RELATIONSHIPS, SEXUAL STEREOTYPES AND OTHER THEMES IN THE CARTOON WORLD OF BUSINESS

The cartoon world of the business executive is also a white male world. In the cartoons studied only 24 (7 percent) portrayed women business managers or entrepreneurs, none of them black women, and none featured black male business executives or entrepreneurs. The dominant relationships in business cartoons (see Table 1) are relationships between white male bosses and white male subordinates (43 percent of all relationships portrayed). Women are nearly always portrayed in subordinate roles, usually as secretaries.

The few exceptions to the pattern of dominant white male/subordinate white female are worth examination. A Frascino cartoon has a male subordinate pleading with his female boss, "Please, RK, stop mothering me." A Stevens cartoon depicts a female executive of "Momco" dressing down a male subordinate: "Now, what's this I hear about you being late for work again, young man?!" A Miller cartoon of the male receptionist to the boss of "Mother Krupkie's Pies and Cakes" shows a nameplate on his desk with the title "Mother's Little Helper" beneath his name. In a Lorenz cartoon a manager, addressing the middle-aged chairwoman of a meeting of executives, says, "Sorry, Chief, but of course I didn't mean 'bimbo' in the pejorative sense." And in a Cullum cartoon a woman CEO is consoling a male subordinate: "We can still be friends, Roger. I just don't want you to be one of my vice-presidents anymore."

The perspective on gender roles is not a critical or radical one. If anything, these cartoons work to reinforce traditional roles for women. They self-consciously play on the strangeness of women in positions of executive authority by making that fact the central theme for the cartoon; the taken-for-granted business world is one of male authority. If cartoons give any indication of social realities, then clearly affirmative action programs and equal opportunity employment policies have not yet penetrated significantly into the top management structures of the corporate world. In the cartoon world of business the patriarchy of the boardroom is alive and well.

There is a long-standing tradition of stereotyping of male and female roles in cartoons. In an analysis of comic strips of the early 1950s, G. Saenger (1955) indicated that single men were depicted in cartoons as larger, more

Table 1
Relationships Portrayed in 361 *New Yorker* Cartoons, 1985–1989 (n = 326)

	n	%
BOSS/SUBORDINATE RELATIONSHIPS	165	50.6
of which,		
(1) Male boss / male subordinate	141	43.3
(2) Male boss / female subordinate	18	5.5
(3) Female boss / male subordinate	5	1.5
(4) Female boss / female subordinate	1	0.3
FAMILY RELATIONSHIPS	38	11.7
of which,		
(1) Executive husband / submissive wife	22	6.7
(2) Dominant wife / submissive executive husband	4	1.2
(3) Other (e.g. parent / child)	12	3.7
PEER RELATIONSHIPS	37	11.3
EXECUTIVE / CLIENT, CUSTOMER RELATIONSHIPS	21	6.4
EXECUTIVE / JOB APPLICANT RELATIONSHIPS	16	4.9
EXECUTIVE / STOCKHOLDER RELATIONSHIPS	4	1.2
Other relationships (e.g. relationships between		
executives and clients, party guests, doctor etc)	45	13.8

Note: Of the 316 cartoons analyzed, 326 portrayed relationships between two or more people.

masterful and more aggressive than single women. Among married cartoon characters, in contrast, the roles were reversed, with the women being masterful, aggressive and physically dominant. Anderson and Jolly identified three general stereotypes of women in cartoons—seductive, incompetent, and angry—each of which had its own specific elaborations. Thus "awful woman driver" is a particular species of the genus "incompetent woman," and "nagging wife" a particular species of "angry female." Overall they found that "cartoon women were stereotyped as vain, seductive, scatter-brained, naive and inexperienced, unintelligent and angry. Cartoon men were not blatantly stereotyped, but were depicted as emotionally uninvolved as evinced by traits such as sadness, boredom, sloppiness, and passivity" (Anderson and Jolly 1977:464–65). They also noted a general rarity of cartoons depicting females only, observing that males were the victims of ridicule more often than females and were often depicted as being stupid, disagreeable or submissive.

However, the stereotypical nagging wife has only a minor role to play in the business cartoons studied here. The worried Thurberesque "little man" type (Yates 1964), bullied in the office and henpecked at home, belongs predominantly in the ranks of the white-collar workers, not in the executive milieu where submissive wives outnumber submissive husbands in a ratio of over five to one (see Table 1). In these cartoons the female role, whether as wife or secretary, is not only a predominantly subordinate one; it is a largely passive and incidental one too. Comments are generally directed at secretaries, for example, without expectation of response, the focus being on the concerns of the executive. In many cases the secretary is not even present but is addressed through the anonymity of the office communications system. A Barsotti cartoon comments on the general dehumanization of executive secretaries. An executive is addressing his secretary in the traditional manner: "Miss Randolph, I need the Stinson file right away, please." The response, however, is not what he expected: She screams at him, "YOU NEED? WHAT ABOUT MY NEEDS?"

Dreams of Power, Nightmares of Impotence[2]

"You'll go far in this organization, Taylor, unless I manage to stop you."

Table 2 shows the major themes of the cartoons studied. The dimensions of the power-impotence theme are nicely caught in two contrasting cartoons, one by Fradon, the other by Lorenz. Fradon depicts a cigar-smoking, three-piece-suited executive behind a large desk, gleefully listening to his secretary read him over the day's appointments: "At ten-thirty, you have an appointment to get even with Ward Ingram. At twelve, you're going to get even with Holns Wentworth at lunch. At three, you're getting even with the Pro-Tech Company at their annual meeting. And at five you're going to get even with Fred Benton over drinks." Lorenz provides a mirror-image of this cartoon in a conscious parody. His executive listens in depression to his secretary: "At eleven Mr. Perkins hits you over the head with the Crowley

Table 2
Themes of 361 *New Yorker* Cartoons, 1985–1989 (n = 558)

	n	%
(1) Power - Impotence	91	25.2
(2) Authority - Subordination	85	23.5
(3) Status	58	16.1
(4) Success - Failure	35	9.7
(5) Security - Insecurity	32	8.9
(6) Domestic Life	22	6.1
(7) Belonging - Exclusion	21	5.8
(8) Riches - Poverty	16	2.8
(9) Business Practices and Values	164	45.4
(10) Other, including Fame - Disgrace, and Leisure - Overwork/Stress	34	9.4

Note: Although the overall pattern of themes is clear, it is not possible to discriminate between categories such as "power" and "authority" with a high degree of reliability. In any particular cartoon both these themes may be interwoven into the relationships depicted. Consequently all themes were included in the coding procedure, thus producing the 558 themes contained in the table. The greatest degree of overlapping of themes arises between the items "power-impotence" and "authority-subordination."

report, at noon your lawyers hit you over the head with the Barlow suit, at three the Board hits you over the head with the Teflow account, and at four-thirty the Durso Brothers hit you over the head with the Melson-Ruppert affair."

The world of business as a competitive jungle is the characteristic assumption for cartoons that reflect the power-impotence theme. J. B. Handelsman shows an executive leaning across his desk and punching another in the face; the caption reads "Violence as a Management Tool." In a later Barsotti cartoon an executive, threatening another with a machine gun, says, "War, J.B., is the continuation of business by other means." Do unto them before they do unto you is the motto of these cartoon executives. Even their wives lend appropriate encouragement: "Take no prisoners, dear" is the parting message of one executive's wife as he leaves for work in the morning. At the boardroom level the battle is sometimes a physical one with a number of cartoons showing fracas as senior executives slug it out on or around the boardroom table. In senior executives' dealings with managers at lower levels in the organizational hierarchy, the dominance made possible by differential power and status is turned to personal psychological advantage: "No, Hoskins, you're not going to do it just because I'm telling you to do it. You're going to do it because you believe in it."

Faced with big boss power "red in tooth and claw," skinny junior executives adopt appropriately protective and self-debasing postures in the hope that perhaps one day they too may prosper in the system: "For the present, Ashland, you'll have to take it, and perhaps someday, if you play your cards right, you'll be in a position to dish it out." Middle managers feed the already large egos of their seniors by appropriately sycophantic and time-serving behavior: "I heartily concur with the others, Mr. Grimby. Expressing your thoughts on America in a full-page ad is a whale of an idea." And eager, aspiring junior executives seek out and cultivate those whom they see as gatekeepers to their fast-track career ambitions: "I don't mean to keep popping in on you, sir, but I just naturally gravitate toward power."

The Executive Desk: Symbol Turns Subject

"This isn't the real me, Miss Tischler. The real me has a bigger desk."

One of the most prevalent symbols of power and status in cartoons depicting the world of business is the executive desk. The imagery is unambiguous. A large desk indicates power and authority, a small desk the relatively inferior place in the corporate hierarchy of the manager who uses it. The higher-ranking executives' desks are generally clutter-free, indicating both mastery of the work to be done and the ability to successfully delegate tasks to lower-ranking staff. Middle and junior management desks in contrast are likely to be full of clutter and paraphernalia, infiles and outfiles. Their occupants are depicted as harassed individuals about to be overwhelmed by paperwork, controlled by their jobs rather than in control of their jobs. For the tyro executive there is the desk with wheels, to be driven until the welcome day when the boss comes in and says: "Big day, Haskins. The training wheels come off."

The executive desk, however, takes on a life of its own in the exaggerated treatment given to it by cartoonists. Thus the size of the desk of a top executive can grow to bizarre proportions. A Barsotti cartoon, for example, has a great elongated desk with the office cleaner walking along the top of it pushing a broom and the executive occupant asking plaintively, "Do you have to do that now?" Other cartoonists draw desks the size of launches or bars, or they draw parallels between the executive desk and the bridge of a ship. In a Mankoff cartoon an executive at his badly listing desk shouts into the intercom: "Attention all hands. Abandon ship!" Among my personal favorites is a Gross cartoon in which the executive is totally dwarfed by a desk all of 25-feet long. To escape from behind this behemoth the worried-looking, balding, bespectacled occupant has to press a button on the desk top. This activates a mechanism that opens up the central portion of the desk like London's Tower Bridge and allows him to walk through to the other side. And a Steiner cartoon turns the executive desk into the desk-executive. Here the executive and the desk are forged into a man-machine system, the executive being grafted to the desktop at the waist like some modern-day centaur, and the whole contraption being opened up by a re-pairman who is searching under the desktop to fix some fault in the mech-anism.

In cartoons such as these the association of status and importance with size of desk is neatly satirized. The symbol of success becomes the central focus of attention, and the executive is accordingly diminished in importance. Indeed, desks come to assume malevolent proportions, threatening or ex-tinguishing the character and personality of their occupants. From beneath the surface tranquility of the office environment emerges the status symbol out of control, the executive equivalent of the well-established theme, dis-cussed in Chapter 4, of the machine-out-of-control. The artefact takes on a life of its own, the would-be human dominator becomes subservient to the instrument of domination. Even the more lowly briefcase may assume com-mand, as in a Wilson cartoon where it instructs its carrier, "Take me home, now!" It has been claimed that a central motif in twentieth-century American humor is the domination of the bewildered, meek, "little man" of the white-collar class. This representative American character is "dwarfed by the mon-sters of industry, science, business and government" and dominated "by gadgets, by his boss, by his associates on the job, by the problems of main-taining a home, by his wife and children" (Yates 1964:355–56). In the business cartoon we have a minor variation on this motif in the form of the struggle of the rich and powerful of the business world to create an identity more imposing than that of their office furniture.

Estrangement and Isolation

In the cartoon world executive desks are also barriers. As well as putting physical distance between the executive and his (or, very occasionally, her) subordinates—and the greater the status, the greater the distance that must be maintained—the desk has a psychologically distancing impact. There are numerous cartoons in which the cliché of the loneliness and isolation of the man at the top of the corporate world is conveyed by the distance that must be crossed to reach him across the vast plains of his desktop. His personal estrangement from others in the organization is further underscored by the practice of depicting him communicating with subordinates by dictaphone, intercom or internal telephone. Even the most personal of communications may take place without face-to-face contact; thus, boss to dictaphone: "Miss Lawler, at the end of next month I am retiring. Please inform the board of directors and the company retirement fund of this decision. Also, send yourself a dozen red roses. Card to read: To Miss Lawler—Sincerest thanks for twenty years of devoted service. Affectionately, Frank W."

This kind of impersonalization of relationships can also enter into the executive's home life. Twohy has a cartoon of an executive dictating to his secretary, "Dear Jean: Confirming our phone conversation of earlier today, I no longer love you, and want a divorce." Martin draws a businessman greeting a woman at the door of her apartment: "How do! I'm Ed Worthington. I'll be substituting for your husband, who has been temporarily transferred to the Minneapolis office." In general the personal emotional life of the executive takes second place to the demands of the job. It is a theme summed up in a cartoon by Hamilton where an executive's secretary, having recounted to him a list of messages, adds as she is about to leave the office, "Oh, and your feelings have been trying to get in touch with you."

Rehumanizing the CEO

Some cartoonists have turned around these common themes of the depersonalization of corporate life and the facelessness of senior executives in large corporate bureaucracies. Thus we find both whimsical and ironic attempts to portray big business with a human face: In a Lorenz cartoon, an executive requests his secretary, "Miss Corcoran, please bring me in my Care Bear." In a Richter cartoon an executive is depicted in his office surrounded by his pets—a cat, a dog, tropical fish in an aquarium on his desktop—with the caption "It's lonely at the top, that's why." A Modell cartoon shows an executive in a party hat sitting at his desk with an ice-cream sundae in front of him and the caption "May I remind you, Miss Bancroft, that today is my birthday?" Wilson draws a smiling executive with the sign "YOUR FRIEND" displayed prominently on his desk, and Stevenson shows an executive sitting at his desk with bunny slippers on his feet.

In the world of the blue-collar worker, the alienating boredom and routine of factor life may be relieved by a variety of stratagems. These are well documented in the sociology of industrial work and range from game playing with production quotas and incentive payment systems to horseplay, sabotage and drug use (Runcie 1980). In the executive suite, however, there is always a presumption of purposeful, motivated activity. It is a presumption that cartoonists, if not sociologists, challenge. A Schoenbaum cartoon, for example, shows a secretary talking on the phone while looking into the boardroom where six male executives are asleep round the board table: "No decision. They're still sleeping on it." In a number of cartoons CEOs engage in powerplays and tycoonery games in order to amuse themselves and stave off the incipient boredom of life on the executive treadmill. At middle management level the opportunity for involvement in such distracting games is less prevalent, but occasionally the office equipment can provide a source of amusement. Stevenson has a cartoon in which a bored-looking manager temporarily amuses himself by playing catching, lassoing and juggling games with the handpiece and cord of his telephone.

Dreams of Authority, Nightmares of Subordination

"I'd thank you Harrison, but, as you well know, yours is a thankless job."

The distribution of power and authority in the corporate hierarchy, together with their attendant status symbols, is a favorite theme of the cartoonist. In the cartoon business world authority can be exercised without restraint. Subordinates are depicted as physically lesser beings and show character traits appropriate to their inferior status—grovelling, anxiety, deference. Arbitrary and absurd decisions can be taken by senior executives without fear of challenge to their authority: thus a balding, bespectacled executive in a three-piece suit, talking on the intercom, "Miss Adamson, pluck someone from nowhere and put him in a position of responsibility." The socialization of executives into the pecking order of the corporate pyramid starts at recruitment. A Harris cartoon shows a personnel officer addressing a job applicant: "I'm sorry, but there's no room at the top, and there's no room in the middle, but there's a little room at the bottom." Job applicants are presented as supplicants, anxious acolytes at the gates of the corporate kingdom, anticipating, and frequently getting, rejection. Those appointed are grateful for the opportunity given them, however meager. In a Cullum cartoon a young executive in a suit and tie, carrying a briefcase and a shepherd's crook, stands in a field addressing a group of sheep: "It's an entry-level position, but I was assured it would just be for a few years." The socialization of successful supplicants into a deferential corporate culture is further reinforced through the imposition of appropriate dress codes ("That tie, Merrick, it's not your friend"; "In this corporation, Mr. Taylor, at this level we do not do shirtsleeves") and through boss-subordinate interactions ("I'm just a number here, like you, Caswell—but a higher number"). Behaviors that violate role expectations are forcefully put down: A Hunt cartoon shows a stubborn-looking manager standing with arms folded in front of the large desk of an older, more senior executive who, with clenched fist and stern expression, is saying, "Being adamant is, I believe, *my* prerogative, Halbersham."

Occasionally the cartoonists also give a hint of resentment among subordinates, demonstrating visually what many lower-level managers may well feel about their inferior status and the general disregard for their views and opinions. "That's it, that's the minority report?" asks a senior executive as two managers in a group thumb their noses at him. Opposition to the authority system by the psychologically downtrodden subordinates of the cartoon business world is depicted as largely pointless. Subordinates' verbal outbursts or acts of aggression are generally futile, ineffective and ill-timed. They may be triggered by a sense of freedom on resignation or retirement from the organization or by the shock of being fired: "I've been fired, Mr. Durslag, but *you* have a nose like a potato."

Business Practices and Values

"It's the S.E.C. How do you plead?"

As Table 2 indicated, 45 percent of the cartoons studied reflected some comment or observation on particular practices or values associated by cartoonists with the world of business. This data is further analyzed in Table 3. Some cartoons commented on the ethics of business practices in a general way. Thus, for example, a Vietor cartoon shows a CEO addressing his all-male board: "This might not be ethical. Is that a problem for anybody?" Other cartoons relate ethical questions to particular business functions (e.g., finance and accounts).

The cartoonists generally see business executives as avoiding too close a scrutiny of the ethical issues raised by their business conduct. In a Richter cartoon, for example, a secretary is standing by with an armful of blindfolds as the chairman announces to his board members, "Miss Johnson will now hand out the moral blinders." The illegal or immoral must be weighed on a commercial set of scales; in the words of a Mankoff CEO, summing up a proposition put before his board, "There you have it, gentlemen—the upside potential is tremendous, but the downside risk is jail." And truthfulness is a high-risk survival strategy, as an executive, returning from work with his box of desk furnishings, makes clear to his wife: "I told the truth and they set me free."

Corporate greed and the personal vanity of top corporate executives are an integral part of the framework of values in the cartoon business world. Having established domination and control within their organization, CEOs treat potential external constraints with disdain. Shareholders, for example, are either bullied or diverted with trivia. A Stevenson director, addressing the annual general meeting, asks aggressively: "That's the report. Now, would anyone like to carp?" A Weber company president says to a note-taking minion: "I've taken to working in my shirtsleeves. We might mention

Table 3
Business Practices and Values (n = 164)

	n	%
(1) ETHICAL ASPECTS OF BUSINESS PRACTICE	22	13.4
(2) FUNCTIONAL ASPECTS OF BUSINESS		
1. Employment and Personnel	29	17.7
2. Marketing, Advertising and Sales	24	14.6
3. Finance, Accounts, Mergers, Takeovers	40	24.4
4. Computers and Information Systems	2	1.2
5. Management and Administration	29	17.7
6. Production and Product Development	11	6.7
(3) OTHER BUSINESS ASPECTS, including role of stockholders, public relations, corporate sponsorship of the arts, the business lunch, business education	23	14.0

Note: Where cartoons relate to both general ethical aspects of business practice and specific business functions, they are included both under category (1) and again under the appropriate functional aspect of category (2) or under category (3).

that in our annual report." And a Martin cartoon has shareholders at the AGM being informed that "in response to numerous requests following last year's annual meeting, you will find ham-and-cheese Croissandwiches and Twinkies in your lunch boxes this year."

Apart from the occasional whimsical touch, and the sense that many corporate executives are trapped in a world that is not of their making, there are few redeeming features in the portrait drawn by cartoonists of executives and their concerns. The remaining part of this chapter explores some possible reasons for the tenacity of such negative stereotyping of business and business executives, and it examines what relationship, if any, cartoon images of business have to the experiential world of business organizations.

THE MEDIUM AND THE MESSENGER

"Humor can be dissected, as a frog can, but the thing dies in the process and the innards are discouraging to any but the pure scientific mind."[3]

There is a complex mix of elements at play in the construction of a publishable cartoon. These elements include the concerns and objectives of the cartoonist; the limitations, possibilities and traditions of the medium; the expectations and perceptions of the presumed audience; the editorial policies of different magazines and journals; and the mechanisms through which editorial policies modify a cartoonist's work so as to make it more acceptable for exposure to a particular magazine's readership. In the wider context of understanding and interpreting the social or psychological workings of the cartoon, and its cultural significance, broader issues arise related to mass communications, to the psychology of humor and to its socio-cultural functions. Understanding and interpreting the cartoonists' view of the world of business is, then, not a straightforward matter. Alongside informative detail of the cartoons themselves, it is necessary to develop some general propositions concerning the cultural, social or psychological significance of their content. Adequate analysis in terms of general propositions and theory, if it is to be at all useful, requires a range of diverse material:

A theory of caricature which would contain interrelated propositions about certain concepts would at least have to tell about caricature itself, its producers (caricaturists), the milieux within which caricatures work, and the audiences to whom caricaturists address themselves. In addition, it appears reasonable to include consideration of the kind of social structure and the historical epoch within which caricature emerges and has a place. (Streicher 1967:431)

The cartoon is a value-neutral medium in the sense that it can portray people, objects and ideas in either a positive or negative manner. However, most of the business cartoons studied have drawn on negative aspects of the business world. While *New Yorker* cartoons lack the often grotesque and savage satirical scorn of much political cartooning, they do gently ridicule some of the more ludicrous practices of the business world and quietly deflate executive pretensions. They have the element of kindliness that Stephen Leacock considered essential to humor: "There must not only be perception of the peculiarities, the contrasts and the shortcomings which lend to any character or circumstance an incongruous aspect, there must also be a tolerance or acceptance of them" (Hewison 1977:138).

Nevertheless as Lawrence Streicher observed, whereas caricature underlies and is present in all cartooning, "in its negative or debunking aspects, there are not many apparent differences between the 'cartoon' and the 'caricature' " (Streicher 1967:431–32). Given the nature of the medium, therefore, it is inevitable that the cartoon world of business is a world filled with caricatures—self-important CEOs, faceless middle managers, aspiring yuppie executives, stone-faced middle-aged secretaries. Caricature indeed presupposes the existence of these relatively immutable character types, each with its economical "tabs of identity"[4] or "hieroglyphs of idiosyncratic characteristics." Without the instant recognition that can be created through caricature, the point of a cartoon would be lost or heavily labored. Streicher compared caricature's use of distortion, its presentation of the object to the spectator "in a whole, in a Gestalt sense, in the form of a *type*, artfully done with an economy of line," to the effective communication of personal idiosyncrasies and expressions by the masks of Kabuki actors (Streicher 1967:436).

In cartoons about business executives and the business world, both the medium itself and the traditional antipathies toward business of the literary and artistic community (see Chapter 7) create an impetus toward negative stereotyping and caricaturing of business. It is an impetus that may be reinforced by the attitudes and experiences of the cartoonists themselves. However, little is known about cartoonists as a group and I have no data on the background, training, work histories or working environments of *New Yorker* cartoonists. S. Fisher and R. L. Fisher (1983), in a study of the background of comedians, suggest that although there is no single "comic personality," comedians tend to come from families of lower socio-economic status and survive parental opposition to their comic ambitions and chosen profession. Their research suggests that comedians have a special concern with the struggle of evil against virtue, that they live in a highly self-centered world, and that in a "pattern common to all sorts of artistic and creative people," they are relatively unhampered by social conventions and are willing to challenge prevailing social mores and assumptions.

Perhaps cartoonists have similar backgrounds and personality traits to comedians. Judging from the comments on his magazine's cartoonists by Harold Ross, editor of *The New Yorker* from 1925 to 1951, they have some unusual characteristics: "They have sinking spells. They can't ride on trains, or drive after dark, or live above the first floor of a building, or eat clams, or stay alone at night. They think that automobiles are coming up on the side-walk to get them, that gangsters are on their trail, that their apartments are being cased, and God knows what else" (Hewison 1977:111).

Hewison, a cartoonist himself, writes of cartoonists' "twitchy life-style," their desperation, persecution mania and panic, and the general absurdity of an existence devoted to the production of four drawings: "a sugar daddy and a dewey blonde; two hoboes sitting on a bench in Central Park; a drunk téte-à-téte with a barman; and a man and his wife getting into their car after a dinner party" (Hewison 1977:111–12). And Jules Feiffer wrote of the emotional drive underlying the political and editorial cartoonist's art: "Cartoons are more likely to be effective when the artist's attitude is hostile, to be even better when his attitude is rage, and when he gets to hate he can really get going" (Harrison 1981:124).

As well as the possibility of anti-authority attitudes among the cartoonists themselves, and the desire they may have to induce their audience to share in ridiculing the institutions, people and ideas that they oppose, there is in much humor a built-in anti-establishment bent. In Mark Twain's opinion humor was "the natural enemy of royalties, nobilities, privileges and all kindred swindles" (Crews 1989:39). Although democratic in sentiment, and the nemesis of hypocrisy and facade, humor is not overly concerned with objectivity. It uses facade to penetrate facade. It may present a mirror to the world, but it will be a distorting mirror. For Henri Bergson (1911:198), taking a less charitable view of humor than Stephen Leacock, "laughter cannot be absolutely just. Nor should it be kind-hearted either. Its function is to intimidate by humiliating. Now it would not succeed in doing this, had not nature implanted for that very purpose, even in the best of men, a spark of spitefulness or, at all events, of mischief." Given the central and privileged position of big business in American society, it should not be a matter of surprise to find a levelling, debunking, pretentiousness-pricking bias in cartoonists' portrayal of the business world.

THE CARTOONIST AS FOOL, SAGE AND PSYCHOANALYST

In many pre-industrial societies the fool or the clown had a protected status that gave license to criticism of authority. Thus among North American Indian tribes, for example, the clown sometimes had a quasi-religious role, carrying out priestly functions while simultaneously mocking religious ceremony (Willeford 1969:84). During the carnival season in fifteenth-century France, students formed fraternities of fools and "claimed the idiot's immunity from recrimination for a temporary attack on evils in society, including notable figures, such as the Pope" (Billington 1984:23). The anthropologist Radcliffe-Brown described the joking relationship in these societies as a relationship with "a peculiar combination of friendliness and antagonism . . . one of permitted disrespect" (Bradney 1957:182). The fool or the clown was allowed to say things and voice criticisms that in other relationships or circumstances might lead to moral condemnation, repression by the authorities of church or state, or physical antagonism and the escalation of conflict and violence. Joking, clowning, fooling became ways of releasing tension and reducing serious hostility between individuals and groups, a pattern that is continued in joking relationships in business (Bradney 1957; Coser 1959).

In addition to the cathartic function of humor in physically or psychologically stressful situations, there is a long-standing tradition of ascribing wisdom to the fool. William Willeford (1969:72) described the Koyemci clowns among the Zuni as both silly and wise, like simpletons and crazy people yet also sages and oracles. In Elizabethan literature and society the court jester could often speak the truth with some measure of impunity, a "sage-fool" whose insights into the human or social condition were often bitter or uncomfortable but were tolerated because they came wrapped in an apparently innocent and artless guise. The fool was licensed to tell you things you would rather not know about yourself and your place in the scheme of things, to prick the bubbles of worldly pretension, expose affectation and confront you with unvarnished realities. Enid Welsford described Feste in Shakespeare's *Twelfth Night* as "a fool who sees the truth and is wiser than his betters" and enjoys the "jester's privilege of licensed criticism." And the "all-licens'd" fool in *King Lear* "is endowed with a penetration deeper and more far-reaching than that superficial sharp-wittedness and gift for smart repartee which went to the making of a successful court-jester. He is in fact the sage-fool who sees the truth" (Welsford 1966:254–56).

The sage-fool character can be traced back to the *vir bonus*, the good plain man, of classical satire. In his American manifestations he comes, suggested Norris Yates (1964), in two varieties. One is the rustic sage, the naif, the simple fellow of clear, direct insights speaking home truths in maxims or yarns. This is the popular Brother Jonathan character of the early American newspapers, "a commonsense philosopher who represented the democratic philosophy that the simple untutored farmer might indeed be the *wise* fool, a laughably unsophisticated but basically honest, shrewd, decent citizen" (Mintz 1983:135). It is a tradition carried forward into more modern times by the character Chauncey the gardener played by Peter Sellers in the film *Being There*. The second variety is the eccentric jester who "slashes his alleged betters with satire that would sting if it didn't come from an apparently stupid or disreputable character" (Yates 1964:13).

Cartoonists clearly have a degree of affinity with some of the traditional roles of the fool. Within certain bounds they are licensed to play the role of social critic. As supposedly impartial observers of, and commentators on, the worlds of business and government, they are free to expose the follies and foibles of those who lay claim to being competent players in those worlds. As artists, men and women of insight and imagination, they are expected to discriminate between image and substance, inner meanings and outer manifestations; to detect the sham from the real, the imitation from the genuine; and to hold up for scrutiny the values of the everyday world. And as both social critics and artists they need not be taken entirely seriously by men and women of action.

The traditional fool, however, had a largely social function and a particular defined status in the social structure. Orrin Klapp (1949) saw the fool as having a number of functions related to the adjustment of, and adjustment to, differences in status between social groups. For those of subordinate status, the license granted to the fool to take comic liberties with people in positions of authority provides both a pressure valve for tension and aggression and a temporary distraction from the routines of organizational life. At the same time, in ridiculing authoritarian leadership behaviors, the fool encourages compliance with alternative behaviors that meet with the approval of lower-status groups. Pamela Bradney, in examining the joking relationship in a large department store, also emphasized the importance of humor in status adjustments:

In general, joking is established more quickly and easily between members of the same status. . . . However, joking also occurs between members of *different* status. The joke may be made by a member of higher status in an attempt to disarm a subordinate member of any antagonism and maintain a good relationship. Joking may also be used in order to give a reprimand without offending—though these methods are not consciously understood by those using them. . . . On the other hand, members of low status may sometimes purposely joke with members of higher status partly because it gives them a sense of bravado and partly perhaps because by means of it they are able to assume at least temporarily an equality of status with those whom they are addressing. (Bradney 1957:184–85)

Cartoonists, operating outside the boundaries of organizational life, have less tightly prescribed roles and functions. They can also move away from social and group concerns as the backdrop for their humor into the realm of the individual psyche. The fact that cartoons have been quite extensively used in psychotherapy is a reflection of the ability of some cartoonists to explore archetypal situations that may trigger neurosis, or at least to cue into the concerns of psychotherapists. A. L. Kadis and C. Winick (1973:108) argued that "the cartoon in psychotherapy has functions similar to those of music: for a certain kind of patient, it seems able to reach through defenses and provide a vocabulary of emotion which is more accessible than words." Among those they identified as being extremely sensitive to psychotherapeutic and psychodynamic concepts was the cartoonist William Steig, who wrote that in his symbolical drawings he tried "to make neurotic behavior more manifest." In the words of one commentator, Steig exposed to conscious view "archaic, irrational, and regressive processes, usually submerged, avoided or denied consciousness by most of us." Robert Barshay described this psychoanalytic role of the cartoonist as "making public that which is ordinarily private through comic confrontation" and "expressing visually that which has been suppressed imaginatively."

The cartoonist . . . is the modern shaman who must perform the magic of exorcism with almost magical finesse. He reveals the precarious situation in which modern man is rooted in a rootless world, exposes the uncontrollable forces against which man is ignorantly pitted, magnifies the impotence of man's will against arbitrary change and concerted hostility, and hopes to exorcise his all too frequent shrinkage from a being with dignity to an insensible object of manipulation. And this he accomplishes with the power of an image packed with meanings and associations. (Barshay 1974:523–24)

THE CARTOONIST AS BUSINESS CRITIC

Cartoonists approaching the world of business may, consciously or unconsciously, be stimulated by a varied mixture of personal motives, artistic traditions and socially and commercially prescribed roles. The mix may include a general anti-authority and anti-establishment mind set, a championing of the little man against those in high-status positions, and a questioning of the ethics and values of the business world. In viewing cartoons, we may admit the cartoonists' sage-fool role because we recognize from our own experience elements of truth in their commentaries on organizational life and their portrayals of executive power games and status competition. And, on occasions, when cartoonists touch a psychic nerve-end of our own, we may ascribe to them some of the more exotic and magical functions suggested by Barshay. But what is the relationship of the cartoon world of business to the real world of business?

It has been argued that cartoons, because they deal so much with stereotypes and stereotypical behavior, are inevitably out of touch with contemporary reality, that there is a time lag between current attitudes and the artistic expression of those attitudes through the medium of the cartoon. A study of a hundred years of the portrayal of women in July 4 cartoons concluded that the cartoons tended to reflect and reinforce the social status quo, that they "demonstrated how the expressive sphere of society often lags behind actual happenings. New norms and structures appeared in cartoons after a lag period from the time when issues had been raised socially" (Meyer et al. 1980:29). In the present study the prevalence of female subordination in the cartoon executive world adds some credence to this time lag argument.

If the cartoon view of the world were essentially a view supportive of the status quo, then one would expect conflicts over values and over issues to be played down. The analytical problem here, and it is one that cannot by its very nature be resolved, is whether the content of cartoons—the overt cartoon agendas—reflects a real social context or denies it: "How can we 'decode' visions of reality that are mythic, distorted by emotional needs, commercial dictates, aesthetic considerations, technical capacities, and other inferences that obscure the motives and functions of the enterprise?" (Mintz 1983:141). If cartoons address a particular social issue, does that indicate some underlying social conflict on that issue? One school of thought argues that when real social conflict on an issue is high, then cartoon coverage of that issue will be low. When racial tension is high, for example, it will become a taboo subject for the cartoon agenda; the increased social conflict arouses fear, and drawing attention to that conflict, even humorously, increases the sense of insecurity (Anderson and Jolly 1977). Thus, a decline in cartoon attention to a particular issue may as likely reflect increased social conflict on that matter as a reduction in conflict: "A theory of caricature must

take both the presence and the *absence* of a given image into consideration"
(Streicher 1967:429; my emphasis).

Perhaps humor requires some retrospective vision when addressing issues
that are personally or socially sensitive, the retrospection of that common
comfort in times of stress and distress that "one day you'll look back on all
this and laugh." Certainly, in the context of the business cartoons studied
here there is no sudden upsurge, following the October 1987 Wall Street
crash, of cartoons about desperate brokers on the window ledges of investment houses contemplating the street life 30 stories below. The gently mocking humorous style of *The New Yorker*, and its sense of propriety, effectively
shuts out sardonic and satirical comment on the world of financial capitalism.

There are other elements in business cartoons, however, that suggest that
cartoonists do more than passively reflect, through variations on long-standing and clichéd themes, the mores and attitudes of a retreating and conservative world. Indeed, William Hewison (1977) credits cartoonists with a
business management innovation, the creation of customer complaints
counters in department stores. These counters, he claims, were drawn by
British cartoonists in the belief that they were a phenomenon of American
stores, and by American cartoonists on the assumption that they were common in Britain. That cartoons reflect some *current* reality, at least within
the confines of a particular audience and its milieux, seems an inescapable
conclusion: "A few cartoonists do not a nation make and caricature may only
be relevant for penetrating restricted milieux and locales and subcultures
or limited ideational systems" (Streicher 1967:429).

Clearly business cartoons do not generally have the immediacy or the
impact of political cartoons. To the best of my knowledge none of these
business critics have suffered the fate of some political cartoonists—prison,
exile, even death. Nevertheless, that cartoons have something insightful to
say about the current world of business and the nature of contemporary
organizations and their culture is attested by two facts. First is the observation that in many organizations, particularly large ones, the posting or
circulation of cartoons is a common occurrence. These cartoons, even though
they may be interpreted differently by the various members of the organization, embrace some shared experience of organizational or professional
life. Hospitals, universities, banks, law practices, computer firms, all have
their own shared subcultures, each with its own jokes and cartoons accessible
to the organization's initiated membership. If, as L. E. Mintz (1983) claimed,
it is absurd to try to explain a society without reference to humor and popular
culture, then it is equally so to neglect the role of humor in the analysis of
organizational and professional subcultures. In a study of humor in a hospital,
for example, Rose Laub Coser (1959) observed that the humor and laughter
of hospital patients could be understood only in terms of their common
concerns and the particular dynamics of their dependent situation: "Jocular
talk and laughter of hospital patients can be understood in reference to three

main characteristics: anxiety about self, submission to a rigid authority structure, and, related to this, adjustment to a rigid routine." In the hospital
environment, Coser argued, humor contributes to the psychic well-being of
individual patients. It provides a collective expression, based on shared
experience, of individual grievances, thereby transforming in the mind of
each patient the undesirable into the harmless and the frightening into
amusement. In that humor also tends to make acceptable what *is* in the
hospital environment, it also contributes to the *social* economy of the organization, reinforcing the efforts of hospital administrations to routinize
emergency.

The second illustration of the abbreviated reality and the contemporaneity
of the cartoon business world is the evidence from our own personal responses to particular cartoons. Idiosyncratic as such responses may be, they
nevertheless flow from a recognition of similarity between the world of the
cartoon and the world of experience. In its minor key the response may be
quiet amusement at an elegant variation on a well-known theme. But the
recognition may equally arise from an unexpected element in the cartoon,
providing "the sort of intense visceral delight which comes from heaving
baseballs at crockery in an amusement park," a reaction recalled by Frederick
Lewis Allen on reading H. L. Mencken for the first time (Yates 1964:142–
43). The emphasis in business cartoons on themes of organizational power
and authority brings into sharp focus the ambiguities that flow from the
contrast, in many enterprises, between the economic reality of organizational
life for most members and the management rhetoric of cooperation and
participation in pursuit of common goals. As an organizational outsider, the
cartoonist can cut away corporate flimflam and disclose, warts and all, the
authoritarianism explicit in the employment status of subordinates.

It has been argued by M. J. Mulkay that "humor is predominantly a
conservative, rather than a liberating or constructive, force in society," that
"it seems in practice overwhelmingly to support and reaffirm the established
patterns of orderly, serious conduct," and that within social contexts "humor
normally comes to be used to conserve the dominant pattern of social relationships" (Mulkay 1988:211–12; 177). Mulkay's studies of humor within
formal social or organizational structures provide him with an empirical base
for rejecting Mary Douglas's alternative view of humor. Douglas argued that
humor and jokes confront and challenge the dominant social patterns, destroy
hierarchy and order, and denigrate and devalue dominant values: "The message of a standard rite is that the ordained patterns of social life are inescapable. The message of a joke is that they are escapable. A joke is by nature
an anti-rite" (Douglas 1975:102).

On the basis of the evidence presented here, business cartoons reflect the
subversive, anarchic disorienting function of humor highlighted by Douglas.
They work to undermine rather than to reinforce prevailing organizational
structures, patterns of managerial behavior and commercial values. Business

cartoons, like jokes, may, in Douglas's words, provide only "a little disturbance," "a temporary suspension of the social structure," but in doing so they give expression to an alternative set of social and organizational values:

> Jokes, being themselves a play upon forms, can well serve to express something about social forms. Recall that the joke connects and disorganizes. It attacks sense and hierarchy. The joke rite then must express a comparable situation. If it devalues social structure, perhaps it celebrates something else instead. It could be saying something about the value of individuals as against the value of the social relations in which they are organized. Or it could be saying something about different levels of social structure; the irrelevance of one obvious level and the relevance of a submerged and unappreciated one. . . .
> A joke confronts one relevant structure by another less clearly relevant, one well-differentiated view by a less coherent one, a system of control by another independent one to which it does not apply. (Douglas 1975:103–4; 105)

Although a cartoon requires a social structure within which to operate, and is inevitably linked into and reflective of that social structure, it can offer critical comments upon it. Business cartoons may not change organizational worlds, but they can ease passages within them. As critics of business, cartoonists have a unique advantage in that they operate simultaneously inside and outside the organizational structures of the business world; inside in the sense that it is their recreation of a recognizable set of organizational relationships that gives their work an air of verisimilitude; outside in the sense that they are free of the constraints imposed by organizational membership. Thus there is no need for their work to meet the requirements of the existing social and organizational structure of the business world, and they are free to direct their humor *up* the organization rather than down it.

Cartoon humor provides a momentary dislocation or fracture in the structure of management authority and undermines the mystique surrounding executive power. In our collective recognition of the underlying realities of the organizational world revealed by business cartoons, we obtain a glimpse of ourselves in our organizational contexts. But, at the same time, in joining that "kind of secret freemasonry, or even complicity, with other laughers, real or imaginary" (Bergson 1911:6) that laughter implies, we share in the temporary subversion of the power, status and authority structures to which we are subordinated. For a brief moment we affirm our psychological freedom from organizational constraints, assert our autonomy and secretly revenge ourselves on those above us in the hierarchy. In their role as business critics, cartoonists introduce an invigorating gust of fresh air into the stifling conformities of much organizational life.

NOTES

My thanks to Hadley Brown for assisting with the analysis of the content of *The New Yorker* cartoons.

1. In November 1991 Barbara Brandon's *Where I'm Coming From* became the first comic strip by a black female cartoonist to be nationally syndicated (*Time*, 25 November 1991:51).

2. For a similar categorization of American dreams and nightmares, see Dettelbach 1976.

3. E. B. White, quoted in Yates 1964:11.

4. "Tabs of identity" are referred to by the cartoonist David Low in his book *Ye Madde Designer* (London: The Studio Ltd., 1935).

CHAPTER 7

The Business of Literature and the Literature of Business

THE CONSCIOUSNESS INDUSTRIES: CULTURE AND THE MEDIUM OF COMMUNICATION

One of the themes of this book is the role of business in shaping consciousness. It has cropped up in considering the development of the market economy and the impact of technological change, and in discussion of the languages, signs and symbols of the world of business. In each case there was an implicit assumption that our ways of encountering and interpreting the world were being shaped by forces that were, in a large measure, beyond our control. This notion of external control of our consciousness, however partial, random or benign, is difficult to accept. We like to believe that the one place where we can build an impregnable fortress against the pressures of society is within the castle walls of our mind. There, at least, we are allowed "a breath, a little scene, To monarchize, be fear'd, and kill with looks."[1] We proudly affirm our ability to "make up our own minds" and presume that the decisions we come to are the product of autonomous independent thinking. In literature and the arts we emphasize the importance of individual creativity, imagination and originality. In philosophy we make our mental activity the fundamental building block for our sense of existence, the starting point from which the rest of life must be explained: "I think, therefore I am."

None of the ideas in the above paragraph is original. Although the organization of the words in which those ideas are expressed is my own, the paragraph overall paraphrases the opening of Hans Magnus Enzensberger's essay "The Industrialization of the Mind." In that essay Enzensberger argues that we would do well, when stubbornly upholding the illusion of the sovereignty of our minds, to contemplate the observation of Karl Marx that "what is going on in our minds has always been, and will always be, a product of society." Indeed, in Enzensberger's view, our notion of mental autonomy is itself a social product: "The idea that men can 'make up their minds' individually and by themselves is essentially derived from the tenets of bourgeois philosophy: second-hand Descartes, run-down Husserl, armchair idealism; and all it amounts to is a sort of metaphysical do-it-yourself" (Enzensberger 1981:98).

Various writers have sought, therefore, to explore the dynamic relationship between what we think—the *content* of thought—and the social, cultural and institutional *context* within which we think. In this relationship between content and context, the medium of communication has a critical role to play. It is through that medium that knowledge and information are transmitted and our perception and understanding of the world are largely structured. As the medium of communication changes, so too does what is valued as knowledge and information. In addition, each communications medium facilitates a particular structuring of perception and cognition. Again, as the medium of communication changes, the favored way of looking at and thinking about the world around us also changes.

Donald Lowe (1982) illustrates these interactions among perception, cognition and communications media by describing four cultures, each of which is defined by its dominant medium of communication: oral culture, chirographic culture, typographic culture and electronic culture. In an oral culture, since there are no written texts or records, knowledge is transmitted entirely through speech. Consequently a high value is placed on oratorical and verbal skills and on memory. Authority and status in the community rests with those elders who can recount the longest and most prestigious genealogy and/or have the greatest command of the spoken word. In a chirographic culture, in contrast, where knowledge can be recorded in a written script, the transmission of knowledge need no longer rely on speech and memory. Script as a medium of communication, argues Lowe, facilitates the development of abstract formal logic. It also creates a special position of authority and status for those in the society who are literate. In both oral and chirographic cultures knowledge resided in the authority of the elders or of the literate members of the community, usually priests or teachers. The few shaped the consciousness of the many through direct verbal face-to-face communication, through talk, instruction, oratory, story telling or through reading aloud from manuscripts.

The advent of printing technology reduced the transparency or directness with which people's minds were being shaped. Typographic culture facilitated the standardization of knowledge and its transmission through the printed text. The availability of recorded information was, argues Lowe, a basic prerequisite for the development of the idea of objective knowledge and, hence, the development of science. It precipitated the Enlightenment of the seventeenth and eighteenth centuries with its emphasis on rationality, systematic thought and the grounding of knowledge in comparison, measurement and analysis. It was also fundamental to the idea of historical knowledge. In typographic culture what is known can be formalized in print and detached from the person who has that knowledge; "authority" becomes vested in the printed word rather than in speech. Control of the printed word becomes a necessary means for the shaping of consciousness. With the spread of typographic culture the attempts of clerics and scholars to sustain their influence and status by claiming exclusive guardianship over the interpretation of authoritative texts, such as the Bible or the works of Aristotle, became increasingly futile.

In an electronic culture a whole new set of communications media provide access to information and knowledge—radio, television, the telephone, film, video, the computer. Consciousness is increasingly shaped through the power of the image, through the picture painting a thousand words. It is also shaped, as we saw in Chapter 4, through interaction with computers. In addition, oral and typographic traditions continue to exist in the modern electronic culture. Consequently it is increasingly difficult to unravel the processes through which our consciousness is being shaped:

Only when the processes which shape our minds became opaque, enigmatic, inscrutable for the common man, only with the advent of industrialization, did the question of how our minds are shaped arise in earnest. The mind-making industry is really a product of the last hundred years. It has developed at such a pace, and assumed such varied forms, that it has outgrown our understanding and control. (Enzensberger 1981:98)

We are subject, then, to a vast number of "messages" from different media. Undoubtedly these shape our ways of thinking and what we think about, our ways of seeing and what we see. How they do this, to what purpose if any, and whether or not the process is controlled or can be controlled, are among the primary concerns of media studies. Various terms have been coined to catch the nature of these processes in the mass culture of modern society: the "mind-making industry," the "consciousness industry," the "education industry," the "culture industries," the "industrialization of the mind," the "commercialization of the self." All these terms suggest the centrality of business and commercial practices and values in our construction and interpretation of the modern world. The United Nations Educational, Scientific, and Cultural Organization (UNESCO) (1982:21), for example, defined a cultural industry as one in which "cultural goods and services are produced, reproduced, stored or distributed on industrial and commercial lines, that is to say on a large scale and in accordance with a strategy based on economic considerations rather than any concern for cultural development."

The centrality of business in the creation of culture raises a number of questions and issues. Does the prevalence of a large number of commercially produced messages and symbols marginalize and eclipse those messages and symbols that are not marketable commodities, thereby impoverishing and trivializing the culture as a whole? Does the commercialization of cultural products lead to their greater standardization or to their greater diversification? Given the central role played by business executives and entrepreneurs in the manufacture of cultural messages and cultural products, how are the roles of artists, writers, filmmakers and other craftspeople changing? What are the cultural consequences of the trends toward concentration, vertical and horizontal integration, and multinational ownership of the media industries? And what are the political consequences, potential and actual, of these trends and of the key role of the consciousness industries in sustaining the nation state?

Whenever an industrially developed country is occupied or liberated today, whenever there is a *coup d'état*, a revolution, or a counter-revolution, the crack police units, the paratroopers, the guerrilla fighters do not any longer descend on the main squares of the city or seize the centers of heavy industry, as in the nineteenth century, or symbolic sites like the royal palace; the new regime will instead take over, first of all, the radio and television stations, the telephone and telex exchanges, and the printing presses. And after having entrenched itself, it will, by and large, leave alone those who manage the public services and the manufacturing industries, at least in the beginning, while all the functionaries who run the mind industry will be immediately replaced. In such extreme situations the industry's key position becomes clear. (Enzensberger 1981:100)

The media have always been a focus of political attention, broadcast media particularly so in recent years. The propaganda value of the control of radio and television has long been appreciated. It was the urge to combat Nazi foreign radio propaganda in the late 1930s that led U.S. networks to broadcast news to Latin America and the British Broadcasting Corporation (the BBC) to add foreign language broadcasts to its Empire Service, radio news services which were greatly expanded during World War II. For many years the Central Intelligence Agency (CIA) ran Radio Free Europe and Radio Liberty. The U.S. Information Agency, an all-purpose press relations, cultural relations, and broadcasting organization, operated the Voice of America radio network. In Communist countries control of the media was generally placed in the hands of the state and the Communist party. Not until the 1960s was Soviet television relieved of predominantly ideological duties and given the freedom to entertain the Soviet people with a diet similar to that of television in Western Europe and the United States; films, quizzes and variety shows became the most popular items, news and current events less popular, and economic, educational and ideological programming least popular (Tunstall 1977).

Television coverage of a political campaign, the degree of television exposure received by candidates in an election, and the editorial-style comment, if any, endorsing particular parties' policies or individual candidates' programs are felt by the politicians themselves to be important, perhaps crucial, features in the success or failure of their attempts to influence voters and win public office. In many countries television time provided to political candidates and their parties is carefully regulated so that exposure is independent of the financial resources available to the candidates or their parties. And in the United States 30- and 60-second television commercials, 5-minute telebiographies and 30-minute campaign-night specials have in recent years become a growing, and very costly, feature of presidential campaigns. The retinue of a candidate for national office now generally includes a media adviser, film and video specialists, a market researcher or public opinion poller, and a person to buy time on network television for the candidate's spot advertisements. Political spots will be placed as adjacent as possible to the programs likely to attract the desired audience, adjacency to news and news magazine programs being much favored positions. These television commercials on behalf of politicians have led to cries that the whole political process is being progressively trivialized. The spots themselves have been described as the art of saying nothing as forcefully as possible, and generally there has been, in the words of Edwin Diamond (1982:176), "renewed public worries about the telegenic emptiness of presidential campaigns," a viewpoint forcefully reiterated by media commentators during the Bush-Dukakis campaign of 1988.

The wisdom underlying the uses and controls of television time during election campaigns is that television is a key element influencing political attitudes and voting behavior and that consequently control of access to television time for political propaganda and persuasion is a matter for public interest and concern. Diamond, however, is cynical about the impact of television on elections, suggesting that political commercials contribute next to nothing to voters' understanding of candidates and issues and little to the overall result of a campaign:

The prevailing wisdom feels the pleasurable paranoia most of us harbor about omnipotent media Rasputins who manipulate our minds, or assuredly, the minds out there, the masses. The actual evidence is less sensational. . . . Back in the 1950s and early 1960s, when the experts started fretting about media manipulation, television was still a fresh experience. It had believability. . . . The first time a viewer saw a sincere candidate with good eye-contact, it might have been effective. By the hundred and first time, it has become an artifice. (Diamond 1982:184–85)

In this respect the treatment of politicians as marketable commodities generates a similar cynicism toward political advertising as the sophisticated consumer directs toward the advertising of other products on television; the political truth of the television spot is given about the same credence as that accorded the pecuniary truth of the normal advertisement.

U.S. television news programs are watched by over 40 million people each evening. For most Americans television, rather than the newspaper, is the major source of credible news information. Following the technological strengths and commercial imperatives of the medium, television news is likely to be more geared to entertainment than print news. TV news aims to reach a mass audience with relatively superficial coverage of a broad range of news issues. Edwin Diamond christened the entertainment-oriented model of news presentation "Disco News." He suggested that television news programs are designed to elicit the sort of response from viewers that the press baron William Randolph Hearst allegedly sought from readers of his paper the *New York American*: "You look at the first page and say, GEE WHIZ! You turn to page two and say, HOLY MOSES! You move to page three and say, GOD ALMIGHTY!" (Diamond 1982:14–15). Diamond accepts that there have traditionally been two distinct models of journalism, the first an informational model that focuses on the reporting of facts and emphasizes the truth value of news, and the second a story model that focuses on entertaining anecdotes and emphasizes the enjoyability of news, the value of style rather than substance. Diamond argues that as newspapers have moved increasingly toward an information-rich factual model of journalism, so the story-telling model has been progressively taken over by the news magazines such as *Time* and *Newsweek* and by television. The main characteristic of television's disco news is hype, the injection of excess or exaggeration into a story to give it an added shot of color, excitement or drama. The hyping up of television news is not

as blatant as the practices of the advertising industry, book publishing, or motion picture makers. These hypes for toothpastes or bad novels, however, are amiable free-enterprise excrescences, involving no more, and no less, than the separation of a few dollars from consumers' wallets. When hype comes to the news, something more is at stake; news hype affects our politics, our public dialogue, our ways of perceiving the world. (Diamond 1982:13–14)

There is nothing new about this sensational story-telling model of news. From the early days of printing in the fifteenth century there was an ever-increasing variety of street literature in Europe. In Britain this literature included broadside ballads sold in the streets for a halfpenny or a penny. These were generally a single printed sheet of verse or prose, often with an illustration, recounting some gruesome story under an arresting headline:

DAMNABLE PRACTISES OF THREE LINCOLN-SHIRE WITCHES. (1619)

MURDER UPON MURDER, COMMITTED BY THOMAS SHERWOOD, ALIAS COUNTREY TOM: AND ELIZABETH EVANS, ALIAS, CANBRYE BESSE. (1635) (Shepard 1973:18;16)

The "kind of musical journalism" of these street ballads provides, suggests Leslie Shepard, a bridge between the folk traditions of the minstrel and the popular newspapers and mass media of the nineteenth and twentieth centuries.

News and profit are time-honored bedmates. Many early newsheets were called "Mercuries," and many newspapers adopted "The Mercury" as their masthead. Mercury was identified by the Romans with the Greek messenger of the gods, Hermes, the god of commerce and theft, the patron of both merchants and thieves. The practices of eighteenth-century newspaper journalism had much in common with those prevalent in the publication of street literature.[2] Bribes were accepted to suppress libelous material or to publish contradictions. "Reviews" of theatrical performances were written by hack Mr. Puffs and colored by money gifts from the theater owners. Such practices were adopted by John Walter, the founder of the *Daily Universal Register* in 1785. John Walter had been a successful British coal merchant who had gone into the business of underwriting merchant shipping. After war with America and hurricanes in the West Indies made him bankrupt in 1784, he established himself as a book publisher. The *Daily Universal Register* was used to advertise his books and to promote the improvements he had made in printing techniques. In 1788, with his book business in decline, John Walter was forced to concentrate on journalism, and the *Register* was renamed *The Times*.

The Times became the respectable voice of the British establishment, a symbol of national pride and, along with the pin-striped suit and the bowler hat, part of the essential dress code for those staking a claim to membership of the English upper class. The fluctuating fortunes of its owners, the conflicts between owners and editors over control of editorial policy, and between management and unions over the introduction of new technology, as well as the paper's loss-making capacities, particularly after 1945, themselves became major news events in Britain. Never was this more so than when ownership passed to "colonials," first in 1966 when *The Times* was sold to the Canadian newspaper magnate Roy Thomson and again in 1981 when it was purchased by the Australian Rupert Murdoch, who became a U.S. citizen.

Murdoch's ownership and control of *The Times* was satirized in the play *Pravda* by English dramatists Howard Brenton and David Hare. The central character of the play is Lambert Le Roux, a South African entrepreneur who is soon to be "100 percent English." Le Roux, wrote one reviewer, "bears no resemblance to any living Fleet Street figure, such as Mr. Rupert Murdoch."[3] Like Thomson and Murdoch,[4] Le Roux adds to his ownership of tabloid dailies the purchase of England's principal newspaper. In the play this is *The Victory* purchased from one-time cabaret booking agency, now multinational conglomerate and manufacturer of the "tail end of the F–16 bomber," the International Song and Dance Company. LeRoux brings to *The Victory* his well-tried formula for success:

Page one, a nice picture of the Prime Minister. Page two, something about actors. Page three, gossip, the veld, what you call the countryside, a rail crash if you're lucky. Four, high technology. Five, sex, sex crimes, court cases. A couple of filler pages then its editorials. Then letters. All pleasingly like-minded, all from Kent. The odd one from Berne, Lucerne, Geneva, Zurich to add weight and variety. An international flavor. Then six pages of sport. Back page, a lot of weather and something nasty about the Opposition. There you are. (*He throws it down.*) The only bit I hate are all those foreign correspondents. They're totally out of your control. They bring you extraneous suffering, complexity. Even now I never look at their little half page. (Brenton and Hare 1985:81–82)

and an entrepreneurial motivation:

I'm still not interested in papers. I like *The Victory*'s name. I'm thinking of concessions. Tea-towels, pillow cases, exploitation. That's what I like. (*He shakes his head.*) Good papers are no good. There's no point in them. All that writing. Why go to the trouble of producing good ones, when bad ones are so much easier? And they sell better too. (Brenton and Hare 1985:118)

In the twentieth century cynicism about the realities of the newspaper business is as great as in the days of Grub Street.[5] It is a business, wrote G. K. Chesterton, that "is conducted as quietly, as sensibly as the office of any moderately fraudulent financier." The frequent claims of owners and entrepreneurs, on purchasing a new paper, that they will preserve its editorial integrity and independence are often merely a smokescreen behind which paid pipers play sycophantic tunes. Ben Bagdikian (1983:88) wrote of "the unholy trinity of newspaper acquisition speeches." First, the owners praise their new acquisition as a splendid paper that they have no intention of changing. Second, they claim that they acquired the paper so that the larger resources of the parent organization could be used by it to provide even greater service to the community. Third, the new owners believe "absolutely, completely, and without mental reservation in Local Autonomy." "And the greatest of these is local autonomy." However, a survey by the American Society of Newspaper Editors found that a third of the editors working for newspaper chains said they would not feel free to run a news story that was damaging to their parent organization (Bagdikian 1983:32). As one British newspaper editor wrote:

It was prudent as a newcomer in the Beaverbrook organization to discover precisely how the policies of the newspapers were decided, but the research occupied only one second of my time. The editors of the *Daily Express*, the *Sunday Express*, the London *Evening Standard* and the *Glasgow Citizen* enjoyed absolute freedom to agree wholeheartedly with their master's voice.

As newspaper ownership has become more concentrated and integrated with ownership of radio and television networks, so the powers of the "press barons" to influence public policy have correspondingly increased. Rupert Murdoch was merely the latest in a long line of newspaper proprietors whose close relationship with political leaders, leaders that his newspapers endorse at election time, has raised comment. It was anticipated, for example, that his 1981 purchase of *The Times* would be automatically referred to Britain's Monopolies Commission:

Since its inception the Commission had examined every major takeover of British newspapers by companies already holding interests in the British press. After discussion at Cabinet level and with the support of Thatcher herself, Murdoch became the exception. In his biography of Murdoch, Thomas Kiernan quotes Charles Douglas-Home, the then editor of *The Times*, as saying, "Rupert and Mrs. Thatcher consult regularly on every important matter of policy, especially as they relate to his economic and political interests. Around here he's often jokingly referred to as Mr. Prime Minister." (Pilger 1990:259)

PUBLISHING: FROM "GENTLEMANLY PROFESSION" TO "REAL BUSINESS"

It is not only news organizations that have become increasingly concentrated during the twentieth century. There has also been a revolution in the book business. For centuries segments of the book trade—those dealing with "serious" works and "literature"—enjoyed a higher status than that of street literature and the popular press. By late Victorian times the "respectable" book publishers had effectively shed their links to grubstreet and established themselves as "an occupation for gentlemen." In this gentlemanly profession the publisher viewed himself as the friend and patron of genius, bringing to public notice "the highest achievements of man's creativity," the publisher himself being "a creator of an unusual and special type" (Warburg 1959:279). Not all authorial geniuses were as rapt in this vision of the publishing profession. Lord Byron's pithy view was that "Barabbas was a publisher," and the novelist H. G. Wells said of publishers that they were "after all, merely men of commerce, honest for the most part, greedy as a matter of course, but wholly unfitted to pick and choose among masterpieces." But some authors did accept that publishers and publishing had a special character. Ernest Hemingway, after the death of his Scribner editor Maxwell Perkins in 1947, wrote, "One of my best and most loyal friends and wisest counselors in life as well as in writing is dead. But Charles Scribner's Sons are my publishers and I intend to publish with them for the rest of my life."[6] Fredric Warburg quoted with approval the tribute of Thomas Mann to his American publisher, Alfred Knopf:

The publisher is not a soloist of spiritual exertion, but the conductor of the orchestra. Whereas the author, in his public loneliness, with only himself to rely on, hemmed in of necessity by his ego, struggles to do his best, the publisher selects from the common effort whatever his instinct and his feeling for the necessary considers as just and beneficial. He takes it over, impresses the stamp of his enterprise upon it, and hurls it in its collective variety into the battle of life, where it must contend with the powers of obstinacy, ignorance and death. . . . What a glorious occupation, this mixture of business sense and strategic friendship with the spirit! What a noble way to gain a livelihood! (Warburg 1959:279)

Warburg certainly cast himself and his publishing house in this heroic mold. He writes of the character and personality of English publishing houses, denigrating in the process the commercialism of their American counterparts. In the "high art" versus "crass commerce" stakes he aligns himself with the artistic angels, one who, "uninterested in the accumulation of wealth, hence became a publisher at an early age."

No doubt my view of a publishing house as having a personality can be regarded as highbrow. It will be said that a publisher is a tradesman who is not in business for his health; his job is to take a book that in his view has a sales potential and boost it to the skies, regardless of its merits or lack of them. This view I understand, respect, and profoundly disagree with. Pushed to its logical conclusion, it produces trash, corrupts the public's taste, and allows the pornographer an unrestricted run for his, or the reader's money. (Warburg 1959:15)

Warburg compares his firm, Secker and Warburg, to a cricket team, with himself as all-rounder and captain. When the firm makes a loss in its early years, he consoles himself with the assurance that it was "a distinguished loss," that prestige was more important than sales, and that "in the long run, the appearance of great books on a new publisher's list does more for it than the easy but insignificant seller." In later years of miserable financial performance, he finds himself admitting that "too many good books and too few sellers are ruining us" and muttering the magic and heretical words "What we need is a best-seller." Nevertheless he claims, proudly, that he was "a fool in handling money and incompetent in dealing with sales." He looks back nostalgically to the days before 1928 when publishing was "a quiet backwater" and publishers "were still gentlemen, pursuing an occupation fit for gentlemen." In those halcyon days publishers were men who could "spend long hours after lunch at the club dozing in the library or playing whist or auction bridge till the late afternoon." It was a time when publishers "published what they liked, and did their weeping in private."

Although Warburg tried to continue in that gentlemanly tradition of the English amateur in business, he recognized that the world of book publishing was changing around him. It was a revolution that he saw as beginning with the foundation of the firm of Victor Gollancz in 1928:

Then we saw the shape of things to come. Instead of the dignified advertisement list of twenty titles set out primly in a modest space, there was the double or triple column, with the title of one book screaming across it in letters three inches high. The forces of modernity had been loosed, the age of shouting, the period of the colossal and the sensational had arrived. (Warburg 1959:118–19)

Now book jackets, which had been optional extras called dust wrappers— there to keep the dust off the books—were covered in dazzling and misleading designs for fascinating the would-be reader. "If," wrote Warburg, "the merit of books was now to be measured by the height of the letters that advertised them, publishing, it could well be said, was no longer an occupation for gentlemen, but a real business, even perhaps a rat-race."

The publishing world that Warburg knew and loved was a world of independently owned and managed publishing houses in which publishers and editors prided themselves on their professional independence. In the United States it was a world perhaps best epitomized by Alfred Knopf. Like Warburg, Alfred Knopf was a devotee of the ritual of the publisher's two- or three-hour business lunch and an advocate for publishing what he considered to be the best literature, even if it incurred a loss; "the books he published were like his personal signature. Everything the house did bore his solid imprint. About the Knopf list clung the aura of great names in world literature" (Tebbel 1987:373). In both Britain and the United States, however, the world of Warburg and Knopf began to disappear in the 1960s. Ownership became increasingly concentrated, and many of the old independent publishing houses merged with, or were purchased by, major conglomerates such as CBS, I.T&T, MCA (which started out as a talent agency booking bands into nightclubs), and Gulf and Western (begun in the 1930s to manufacture rear bumpers for Studebakers). It was a process that continued throughout the 1970s and the "megamergers" of the 1980s. Bertelsmann Verlag of Germany bought RCA Records and the publishers Doubleday and Bantam Books. Collier/Macmillan publishers was taken over by Britain's notorious "Cap 'n Bob," the late Robert Maxwell, who in 1991 "bought"[7] the New York *Daily News* to add it to an empire that included British, German, Hungarian, Israeli and Kenyan newspapers, a number of British football teams, a TV channel, a satellite advertising company, a record company and a language school. Japan's Sony acquired CBS Records and Columbia Pictures. Rupert Murdoch's Australia-based News Corporation bought 20th Century Fox. In 1989 when Time, Inc., acquired Warner Communications (a company that had started out specializing in funeral parlors and parking lots), it established the world's largest information and entertainment company. The new global media giant, Time Warner, Inc., had annual revenues of over $10 billion, a market value of $18 billion, 35,000 employees, and a business that covered book and magazine publishing, cable television, film, TV and video production, and music. Its stable of products ranged from *Time* magazine to Madonna and U2. Officials of the new organization pledged their commitment to journalistic and artistic integrity. In 1990 Matsushita Electric, the world's largest consumer electronics firm, bought MCA, including Universal Pictures, and Matsushita president Akio Tanii assured MCA staff that there would be no interference by the new owners in "creative decisions." Lew Wasserman, who had run MCA for 44 years and was affectionately known in Hollywood as the Godfather, saw greater size as the only way to remain competitive: "We're a 200 lb. gorilla in a game with 1,000 lb. gorillas. We've got to become a 1,000 lb. gorilla or get out of the game" (*Time*, 10 December 1990).

There were a number of economic reasons for the mergers among publishing companies and for the increase in concentration in the book business. The old family-owned publishing houses had in many cases lost their impetus and were poorly and inefficiently managed by aging proprietors. Among the major reasons for their vulnerability were, suggested Thomas Whiteside (1981), their slow editorial and printing processes, their archaic distribution systems, their inadequate finance, and their limited advertising budgets, all leading to cash-flow problems and low profitability. Not surprisingly, when the opportunity presented itself, many of the proprietors grabbed the chance to make a capital gain and to settle their personal estates. The new larger post-merger organizations operated with a far greater emphasis on management and financial controls and introduced a variety of new systems of operation, including central computerized inventory control and centralized book-warehousing systems.

The new management and organizational systems, however, did not always sit easily alongside the old publishing traditions. Personal, idiosyncratic, instinctive styles of publishing and pricing that had to do with "publishers' smell—with what we felt *comfortable* publishing," were replaced by computer analysis and meticulous long-term financial forecasting. Not everyone was happy with the changes. After the merger of Viking and Penguin in 1975, the editorial director of Penguin-Viking, Inc., complained that the expectation that a trade-book publisher could project sales for a five-year period was "absurd. To do so, you would have to count on the work of authors whom you might not even know about, on the output of people who are in the process of being discovered or who are busy writing books whose artistic and commercial worth you couldn't even estimate for another two or three years" (Whiteside 1981:90–91). It was a clash of organizational cultures and value systems that Whiteside characterized as a polarization within the conglomerate publishing companies between the "corporate entrepreneurs" and the "litterateurs." The corporate entrepreneurs rejected the yahoo anti-intellectual image that was being foisted on them. Rather, they saw themselves as "Young Turks fighting against the backwardness of the literary establishment," as "literary populists and innovators" who were using modern merchandising and marketing techniques to bring "books to the people on a previously undreamed-of scale" and to bring publishing into the "mainstream of lively commerce." The litterateurs, in contrast,

tend to see their work as increasingly subjected to the harassments of cost-accounting and cost-benefit calculations, on the one hand, and, on the other, to an ominous emphasis on editors' "performance," which in effect means on their development, promotion, and sale of the big book, of the profit-boosting current best-seller, at the cost of their concerning themselves, as they feel they should, with the discovery and nurturing of perhaps less profitable but artistically more meritorious works. (Whiteside 1981:93)

The emphasis on bestsellers, together with the links provided by conglomerate ownership among books, television and film, brought the publishing business closer to the world of entertainment. Books were lavishly promoted on the grounds that they were "soon to be a major motion picture," and in the reverse process of "novelization," successful movies were turned into books. When *Jaws 2* was published by Bantam Books in 1978, it was advertised as "A Completely New Novel by Hank Searls Based on the Screenplay by Howard Sackler and Dorothy Tristan Inspired by Peter Benchley's *Jaws.*" A book and a movie or TV program could be packaged and marketed as a single product. In some cases of such multimedia deals a book would be sold to a publisher on the basis of a concept generated at a conference table and a writer hired later. Authors were also affected by the emphasis on marketing and entertainment values. The pattern was set by the successful promotion through TV talk shows in the 1960s of Harold Robbins's blockbuster novel *Valley of the Dolls*. The book spent a year and a half on the bestseller list and sold over 22 million copies in paperback. By the mid–1970s the promotion of authors through television shows was an essential ingredient in book-publishing economics, the emphasis being on selling the author as a personality rather than on the quality of the work itself. McGraw-Hill, for example, instructed its authors on how to handle themselves on a TV talk show:

Always bring a copy of your book with you. They may not have it on hand, it may have been filched—safe is safe. Assume that your interviewer has NOT looked through the book; be prepared to give a quick capsule-summary of its contents. Radio and TV commercials can be put to good use, as during that time you can quietly mention to the host what topics you would like to hit next.

A measure of showmanship is definitely in order. By agreeing to appear before a TV camera or behind a radio mike, you have temporarily assumed the obligations of a show-biz personality. You must radiate self-confidence, charm, charisma. Keep in mind that your normal hand and head gestures will lose all impact when reduced to a TV screen: do not fear to over-gesticulate within reason. . . . Also practice to vary the pitch, tonal qualities and volume of your voice—the purpose is to add strength, punch and interest to your delivery. . . .

For every point you make, have two or three stock examples that *illustrate your statement quickly and memorably*. Be armed with a supply of well thought out, brief personal anecdotes, and pertinent, relevant aphorisms which will sound as if they had just occurred to you and are being ad-libbed on the spur of the moment. . . .

Do not hesitate to mention the title of your book from time to time, and your publisher at least once. . . . Never refer to "my book"—always mention the title, were it only for the benefit of that part of the audience which always tunes in late. (Whiteside 1981:27–28)

THE LITERARY REACTION TO FICTION AS COMMERCE

The new regime of conglomerate-dominated publishing raised a number of concerns among authors. In the United States the Authors' Guild feared that the greater concentration of ownership would reduce the opportunities that authors had to get their work into print. They expressed fears that only books that had immediate commercial appeal would be published, and that books with literary merit but less marketability would be neglected. Authors regretted the depersonalization of the author-editor relationship, and they decried the emphasis in book promotion on bestseller lists[8] and the Academy Award–style hoopla attached to the "popularity contest" of the annual American Book Awards. For their part the publishers argued that mergers had not reduced the total number of competitive publishing businesses and that authors had never had more outlets for their work or been better rewarded.

Many of the authors' fears were ungrounded. A common pattern in many industries of large firms growing larger and small firms more numerous was repeated in publishing. Small entrepreneurial publishing houses catering for specialist markets have survived and in some cases flourished. In Britain, for example, the degree of concentration in book publishing is less marked than in the United States and the majority of publishers are still small entrepreneurial organizations. Through the 1960s and 1970s a steadily expanding number of new books was published each year, and of these, fiction output remained consistently between 50 percent and 60 percent (Curwen 1981:19). Nor has the electronic revolution led to the once-feared demise of fiction and the disappearance of the printed book. Christopher Evans (1979) predicted the death of the printed word and the replacement of the printed book by small, cheap and portable electronic book readers. Indeed, the electronic book is both technologically and economically feasible, but it has yet to prove acceptable to the majority of readers.

Although the output of fiction may not have declined as a result of the changing structures and economics of publishing, some of the litterateurs maintained that the character of fiction has been significantly changed. Albert Van Nostrand, for example, argued that the treatment of fiction as first and foremost a commercial product led to the "denaturing" of the novel. His proposition rested on a particular view of the nature of fiction, a view based on historical justifications of the novel as being educational, morally uplifting, useful—above all "serious." Whereas serious literary fiction was an art form, popular or commercial fiction was merely business. Fiction, for Van Nostrand "is everyone's continuing preoccupation. Being small and fallible, every human being compensates with fiction, inventing a world that will acknowledge him according to his own desires. He spends his life keeping that world in repair" (Van Nostrand, 1960:33–34). In Van Nostrand's view, the fiction-is-merchandise approach of the book trade denatures the novel by encouraging its stylization and by emphasizing the development and resolution of the storyline at the expense of complexity, psychological dilemma and unresolved conflict. Nowhere are these processes more evident than in the formula writing of various popular genres—the Mills and Boon romance, the science fiction novel, the heroic fantasy, the detective story, the thriller, the war story, the Western.

For the litterateurs, book and magazine fiction driven by commercial considerations treats customers as consumers rather than readers. In magazines,

the fiction the editor prints serves the need of his sponsors, the advertisers, to the extent that it must capture and hold as many readers as possible. This is a restraining influence. The fiction may not offend business in general or in particular, or American government of any variety, or any religious, civic or military organization. The fiction may not contradict the mores of the average consumer-reader without punishing the offender. These well-known prohibitions are similar to the ones levied on motion pictures; most of them also apply to the inexpensive paperback books. The prohibitions and the devious ways around them belong not to art but to manufacture. (Van Nostrand 1960:86–87)

The books and magazines as merchandise school emphasizes giving the readers what they want, which is usually taken to mean more of the same, people generally wanting what they already know and are comfortable with. Thus commercially successful books and magazines stimulate a demand for a host of imitators and clones. (The same principle informs the film and popular music industries.) It is a process reinforced by the bestseller lists that turn book purchasing into a matter of fashion. And it is the purchasing rather than the reading that is important. Books like Umberto Eco's *Foucault's Pendulum* and Stephen Hawkins's *History of Time* become major sellers that, surveys indicate, remain unread by the majority of their purchasers.

It is generally only magazine editors outside the confines of conglomerate ownership who can resist the pressures to produce for target markets, the right demographic niches or profiles to attract advertising revenues. William Shawn, when editor of *The New Yorker*, thought it was unthinkable that advertising and business people should tell him that the journal's editorial content was attracting readers with the wrong demographics:

We never talk about "the readers.". . . I won't permit that—if I may put it so arrogantly, I don't want to speak about our readers as a "market." I don't want them to feel that they are just consumers to us. I find that obnoxious. . . .

Now the whole idea is that you edit for a market and if possible design a magazine with that in mind. Now magazines aren't started with a desire for someone to express what he believes. I think the whole trend is so destructive and so unpromising so far as journalism is concerned that it is very worrisome. Younger editors and writers are growing up in that atmosphere. "We want to edit the magazine to give the audience what they want. What do we give them?"

There is a fallacy in that calculation. . . . The fallacy is if you edit that way, to give back to the readers only what they think they want, you'll never give them something new they didn't know about. You stagnate. It's just the back-and-forth and you end up with the networks, TV and the movies. The whole thing begins to be circular. Creativity and originality and spontaneity goes out of it. The new tendency is to discourage this creative process and kill originality. (quoted in Bagdikian 1983:113–14)

THE BUSINESSMAN AS ANTI-HERO

Hostility from writers toward the world of business goes back a long way in both Europe and the United States. In Britain it was part of a general hostility to industrial society, to the environment of "dark satanic mills" in the industrial cities, and to the emergence of a new class of merchants and manufacturers. Whereas there was some admiration among writers for the mechanic and the inventor, the granting of knighthoods to nouveau-riche self-made business entrepreneurs was generally an excuse for a scornful epithet—the Lords of the Loom, the Cotton Lords, "My LORDS SEIGNEURS of the Twist, sovereigns of the Spinning Jenny," the "iron gentlemen" (see McKendrick 1978:xxix). Indeed, one prospective baronet, brewery entrepreneur Bass of Bass's Ale, refused the honor on the grounds that he thought it better to be "first in the beerage than last in the peerage" (Beard 1938 v.2:238). Part of this hostility stemmed from humanitarian concerns with working conditions in the new factories. But part of it was undoubtedly triggered by writers themselves losing money through speculative investment, particularly on railroad stocks, during the slump of 1839–42; "it is in the great depression of 1839–42 that the British industrialist first really earned the black literary reputation that has stuck to him to this day" (McKendrick 1978:xxx).

Disdain for the nouveau riche businessman was a favorite posture of European writers, contemplating the commercial wonders of the New World. For example, the English writer Mrs. Trollope, mother of Anthony Trollope, visited the United States in the 1830s. She was astonished at the pride taken by leading Americans in the fact that they were self-taught, self-made men and women. She acidly and condescendingly remarked that in her opinion such men were merely badly taught and badly made (Cawelti 1965:3). It was an attitude adopted in part by American writers, some of whom shared the perception of Europe as a haven where the cultured and sensitive could try to escape the crassness of American commercialism and the philistinism of H. L. Mencken's "Boobus Americanus." Henry James, born in New York in 1843, settled in Europe in 1875 and died in England in 1916 a naturalized Englishman. The clash between European and American culture and values, and the contrasts between European and American character, are major themes of his novels. The central figure of *The American* (1877) is Christopher Newman, who having been "odiously successful" in business travels to Paris in the certainty that there must be more to life than continually adding "dollars to dollars."

It must be admitted, rather nakedly, that Christopher Newman's sole aim in life had been to make money; what he had been placed in the world for was, to his own perception, simply to wrest a fortune, the bigger the better, from defiant opportunity. This idea completely filled his horizon and satisfied his imagination. Upon the uses of money, upon what one might do with a life into which one had succeeded in injecting the golden stream, he had up to his thirty fifth year very scantily reflected. Life had been for him an open game, and he had played for high stakes. He had won at last and carried off his winnings; and now what was he to do with them? (James 1978:32)

Christopher Newman wants to redress his own perceived cultural shortcomings, shortcomings born of a life of action that has swamped any life of feeling. He describes himself as "a sort of animal that has had no idea in life but to make money and drive sharp bargains," caring not so much for the money as for the money making. He views the world as "a great bazaar where one might stroll about and purchase handsome things." And among the many cultured things that can be plundered from the corrupt and status-ridden Old World by this "great Western Barbarian, stepping forth in his innocence and might," is a wife:

"Well," he said at last, "I want a great woman. I stick to that. That's one thing I *can* treat myself to, and if it is to be had I mean to have it. What else have I toiled and struggled for all these years? I have succeeded, and now what am I to do with my success? To make it perfect, as I see it, there must be a beautiful woman perched on the pile, like a statue on a monument. She must be as good as she is beautiful and as clever as she is good. I can give my wife a good deal, so I am not afraid to ask a good deal myself. She shall have everything a woman can desire; I shall not even object to her being too good for me; she may be cleverer and wiser than I can understand, and I shall only be the better pleased. I want to possess, in a word, the best article in the market." (James 1978:44)

It is not only in cartoons that business men and women have been caricatured. Caricature is also a well-established tradition in the portrayal of business executives in literature and in film and television. As Anderson and Jolly (1977:467) observed, "The images and meanings contained in popular humorous drawings are not especially unique, but rather an elaboration of role socialization found in other literature." The dramatis personae of the fictional world of business contains a contrasting mix of stock characters. Among them are old-style tycoons—boorish, egotistical entrepreneurs and robber barons dominating and exploiting their corporations. There are puffed-up self-made men like Charles Dickens's Mr. Josiah Bounderby of Coketown, "a remarkable man, and a self-made man, and a commercial wonder more admirable than Venus, who had risen out of the mud instead of the sea" (Hard Times, 1854). There are bright, upwardly mobile executives desperately climbing the corporate ladder in endless competition for new images of success. There are plodding, frightened organizational yes-men with escapist fantasies of life beyond the clutches of bosses and mortgage payments. There are cynical middle managers, like Joseph Heller's Andy Kagle, trapped in the routines and predatory sexuality of office politics:

In the office in which I work there are five people of whom I am afraid. Each of these five people is afraid of four people (excluding overlaps), for a total of twenty, and each of these twenty people is afraid of six people, making a total of one hundred and twenty people who are feared by at least one person. Each of these one hundred and twenty people is afraid of the other one hundred and nineteen, and all of these one hundred and forty-five people are afraid of the twelve men at the top who helped found and build the company and now own and direct it. . . .
    The thought occurs to me often that there must be mail clerks, office boys and girls, stock boys, messengers, and assistants of all kinds and ages who are afraid of everyone in the company; and there is one typist in our department who is going crazy slowly and has all of us afraid of her. Her name is Martha. Our biggest fear is that she will go crazy on a weekday between nine and five. We hope she'll go crazy on a weekend, when we aren't with her. (Something Happened 1974:13;17)

And there are the modern self-made billionaire villains of Ben Elton's Stark (1989), men who, with the "social conscience of a dog on a croquet lawn," conspire to abandon the economy they have so successfully sabotaged and to desert the planet they have polluted. Foremost among them is "the Aussie street kid made good," Silvester (Sly) Moorcock. This rude, brusque and handsome entrepreneur, who regards women as "things to be used and discarded," makes a fortune through insider trading and asset stripping. He is lauded in the press as a role model for the young and presented with the Australian Businessman of the Year Award in recognition, say his business rivals, "for being disgusting and immoral morning, noon and night."
    Attempts in novels to present the business man or woman in a positive light are few and far between. Henry Nash Smith, in his search for a capitalist hero in American fiction, concluded that writers saw the businessman as an alien and unwelcome intruder into the world of literature and treated him

as a scapegoat for the dislocations brought about by rapid economic expansion:

In contrast with the familiar protagonists of sentimental love stories, he seemed both crude and immoral. Yet he was acknowledged to be immensely powerful. He controlled the energies of economic, social, and political change; the future belonged to him; and no matter how many times the novelists might condemn the businessman to social rebuffs, rejection by the heroine, bankruptcy, public exposure for his crimes, or even suicide, they recognized at bottom that traditional manners and morals were doomed by the growing dominance of the business system. (Smith 1964:85)

When authors did present businessmen as positive role models, the literary critics were less than enthusiastic. The Cheeryble brothers, the benevolent employers in Charles Dickens's *Nicholas Nickleby* (1838–39), were carefully modelled on two brothers who owned and managed a Manchester calico-printing company. The critics denounced them as "stupid," "gruesome," "nauseous," "thoroughly tiresome" and "incredible" "monstrosities of benevolence," and they declared that no such "babies could ever have been successful in business" (McKendrick 1978:xxxiii).

Studies of the portrayal of business in literature demonstrate that fiction writers have some fascination for, but little sympathy with, the personal, moral, social and commercial predicaments of their executive creations. Antipathy to business was particularly strong in Victorian England, where "the businessman's image became so tarnished that his appearance in fiction, like the demon king on the stage, was usually the cue for public hostility" (McKendrick 1978:xxxiv). Even in the United States, where admiration for the successful struggles of the self-made entrepreneur can be traced back to Benjamin Franklin, there have been complaints that "a distilled malevolence, a cold and frightening spite, went into the painting of practically every fictional businessman" (Chamberlain 1948:138). Emily Watts located the initial distrust of the American businessman with the Pilgrim and Puritan Fathers; she found in the late eighteenth and early nineteenth centuries "a broad kind of anticapitalist and antibusiness sentiment floating along at the intellectual and creative top of our literature" (Watts 1982:35).

The question that arises is whether or not novelists and writers create such stereotypes about business and business entrepreneurs and executives, or simply reflect prevailing attitudes within the community. In exploring this question, Neil McKendrick suggested different patterns existed in Britain and the United States. In Britain, he argues, life has imitated art. The prevailing hostility of the literary and intellectual world toward business has produced a "managerial schizophrenia" or "psychological absenteeism" in many business executives. The executives come to regard their business careers in purely instrumental terms, as a distasteful, necessary evil through which they can generate sufficient income to pursue their real goals, goals that are realized in their private, non-work lives. In the United States, in contrast, there is little evidence of such managerial or executive alienation other than in literary works about business. The prestige attached to a business education, the lack of envy of successful business people, and the prevalence of a more positive literature about business—the business-success books in particular—have provided, suggests McKendrick, an effective antidote to the attacks of the literary Luddites:

whether the subject of bitter attack as merciless robber baron, of subtle send up as "the bland leading the bland," or of hilarious satire, the American businessman has retained much of his status: "a stream of unfavorable portraits from Charlie Anderson to Babbitt has not made any noticeable effect on American youth. They have swallowed both the success books and the novels of protest, and gone on to business school."

... the fact is that in America the novels of protest and satire are running against a fundamental American belief that "business remains, by and large, the American way of life and private enterprise the right system for God's own country." (McKendrick 1978:xxxix/x1)[9]

ELECTRONIC CULTURE: TELEVISION AS SOCIO-CULTURAL AGENCY

Ben Stein saw a similar pattern of hostility in the portrayal of businessmen on American television. Indeed, if media owners and entrepreneurs were more interested in the detailed content of television programs than in the audience share the programs command, then they might be concerned about the way in which television depicts people like themselves. One of the curiosities of commercial television entertainment is the largely negative view it portrays of commerce in general and business people in particular. Ben Stein examined the way a number of different groups and institutions were portrayed on television: the police, the military, the government, small towns and big cities, the rich and the poor, the clergy, and businessmen. One of the clearest messages of television, wrote Stein, was that businessmen "are bad, evil people, and that big businessmen are the worst of all," hard, vicious, conscienceless people with the morality of the jungle who torture and kill any of the weak and powerless who may stand in their way. Even in television comedies businessmen play unflattering roles as con men or pompous fools. In adventure shows their three-piece pinstripe suits point to their criminal intent and depravity, respectable stock brokers head up dope empires, art dealers use their connections to import and sell heroin, and candy store owners fence stolen goods.

The well-dressed businessman who pays for the kids' orthodontia by selling heroin to teenagers and the manufacturer who has murdered his go-go dance girlfriend are staples of TV adventure shows. . . . The murderous, duplicitous, cynical businessman is about the only kind of businessman there is on TV adventure shows, just as the cunning, trickster businessman shares the stage with the pompous buffoon businessman in situation comedies. (Stein 1979:18–19)

The Media Institute, an organization funded by business corporations, came to very similar conclusions in a survey of the portrayal of businessmen in prime-time programming, a survey published under the title "Crooks, Con-men and Clowns" (Theberge 1981).

Although there is hostility in other media to the rich and successful, particularly the rich and successful in business, such hostility is generally united with a mixture of admiration and fascination. Only on television, it would appear, are businessmen depicted almost exclusively as murderers, drug dealers and fools, a view that would not be shared by most viewers. Why is it, asks Ben Stein, that writers and producers who celebrate the American way—the opportunities for success, the freedom under the Constitution, the energy and zest that are among the best qualities of American life—and who themselves are beneficiaries of a free-enterprise system and the economic rewards of success within that system, should be so venomous in their apparent distaste for business, businessmen and the market economy generally: "What has any executive of General Motors ever done to a $5000-a-week writer?" Why do so many writers and producers believe that business controls people's lives in subtle and unseen ways, that most business is amoral, that big business dictates to government and is in league with the Mafia? "If you don't believe that the Mafia is running big business," said one producer, "you must be blind." Stein proffers a number of explanations for the animosity. He suggests that the unpredictability and randomness of success and failure in Hollywood makes television writers particularly prone to conspiracy theories of events, that the direct experience such writers have of selling their labor to a business is generally painful and unpleasant, and that businessmen are often felt to belong to a different class from that of television writers and producers, the businessmen from AT&T or IBM being perceived as having gentile Ivy League backgrounds in sharp contrast to the "school-of-hard-knocks" backgrounds of the writers and producers. He believes that writers and producers perceive themselves to be outside the establishment, alienated from and at war with the power centers of American life. The TV production community is portrayed as part of a small but extremely energetic and militant class that has a vested interest in attacking, denigrating and humiliating the top people it wishes to displace.

Television is strategically placed to be the number one consciousness industry. 98 percent of all U.S. households contain a television set, and only the hours spent working and sleeping exceed the average hours spent in front of television each week. Television news is Americans' principle source of information about the world; newspapers, as providers of news, fell to second place in 1970. Over 5 million hours of television programming are broadcast annually in the United States, and in any one week the U.S. television networks carry over 1,000 commercial spots, these advertisements taking up about 15 percent of all broadcast time. It is not surprising to find ascribed to television a variety of influential roles as creator of consciousness, disseminator of cultural values, educational medium, and socialization agent, "without question the single most economically and politically powerful industry in our nation's history" (Johnson 1970:6). Claims regarding the power of television to influence political events and to stimulate social change were dramatically reinforced by the collapse of Soviet hegemony in Eastern Europe. Complementing such Brave New World views of television lie fears of the dangers of the medium, especially of its allegedly addictive and hypnotic qualities. Television has been described as the "new opium-of-the-people," the "plug-in-drug," the "boob tube," the "idiot box" and, by Frank Lloyd Wright, as "chewing gum for the eyes."

The television industry provides another important arena for analyzing the intricate strands of the relationship between business and consciousness. The impact of television on culture and the business of television itself are linked. If television's impact on the way in which we, as viewers, perceive the world, on our models of reality, our values and beliefs, our political and social consciousness, is minimal, then questions about the ownership and control of the television industry and about changes and developments in the structure of that ownership and control—while of interest in themselves in terms of understanding the economics and organization of television production—are merely peripheral to any broad discussion of the impact of business on culture. Conversely, if it can be demonstrated that television is an important influence in the development of social attitudes, in the construction of social reality, in the dissemination of cultural values and in the determination of social behaviors, then the powers and responsibilities of those who control television content and programming are powers and responsibilities that justify close examination and critical review.

Television has received considerable public criticism. Comments have been made about the poor quality of children's programming, about the exploitation of sex and violence, about gender and ethnic stereotyping, about the trivialization of political debate, about turning the courtrooms into theater and soap opera, about hyped-up news and sports coverage, about the crass materialism of television advertising, and about the insipid banality of much of the entertainment transmitted. Others have emphasized the positive features and benefits of television: its entertainment qualities and associated therapeutic values, its educational benefits, its ability to focus public attention on matters of political, economic and social importance, and, occasionally, to draw the world together, however briefly, in the way that the 1985 Live-Aid concert for famine relief in Ethiopia did so successfully. But whether the issues are parochial or global, the shared perspective of both the negative and positive commentators is that television is a medium that matters, that television shapes public consciousness. The perspective is that all television programs—whether soap operas or situation comedies, quiz shows, sports programs, commercials, party political broadcasts, news coverage, old movies, chat shows, police dramas or weather forecasts—convey, to a greater or lesser degree, a view of the world, a "televised reality," and that this "televised reality" conditions people's attitudes and behaviors in important if not readily measurable ways.[10] This perspective of television as socio-cultural agency is a thesis that covers a number of areas of enquiry and research. The large amount of violence on television, a level of violence disproportionate to that in the community generally, has for long raised fears of television's anti-social impacts. Questions have been raised about the effects of advertising upon children. In addition, since the budgets for television commercials often make up the largest single item in any political candidate's campaign for national office, issues arise as to the ways in which television influences political attitudes and voting behavior. The reliance on television as a primary source of news raises matters regarding the concept of news itself, the selection of items as newsworthy, the independence, impartiality and balance of the news presented, and the extent to which news can be managed and manipulated, matters that came into particular focus in the television coverage of the 1991 Gulf War.

Finally, there is the question of television's cultural imperialism. The export of television programs from the United States and from major European countries like Britain and France leads to charges that countries whose programs are primarily imported are finding their own indigenous cultures swamped by the all-pervasive nature of foreign television–transmitted culture. Authentic, traditional and local culture in recipient nations is seen as being overwhelmed by the large quantities of foreign, particularly American, programs put to air on local networks or available through satellite transmission. A homogenized American commercial culture is imported, a culture that comes to dominate leisure patterns, education, language and consciousness in the recipient society.

In its more extreme forms, then, the television as socio-cultural agency thesis asserts that television violence causes increased crime and anti-social behavior, that television advertising is creating a world of avaricious children, that politicians can buy political power through control of the media, that television news coverage inculcates a hopelessly prejudiced view of the world, and that the export of American television programs is destroying the cultural heritage of developing countries. The sweeping assertions of this general thesis make it difficult to test in any very satisfactory way. Refutations take a number of forms. Jib Fowles, for example, represents the position that the power of television to form attitudes and influence behaviors is grossly exaggerated in the first place, that television deals largely in fantasies and not in information or instruction, and that since they generally watch it with their critical and conscious faculties largely dormant, people learn little from the medium. Fowles rubbishes those media critics—media snobs, in his terminology—who conceive of the television industry as some mythological, all-powerful Machiavellian force insidiously selling subliminal cultural messages to an innocent public on behalf of advertisers, businessmen, government or the American way. He sets aside claims such that "the power to dominate a culture's symbol-producing apparatus is the power to created the ambiance that forms consciousness itself." He cites studies on viewer comprehension carried out for the American Association of Advertising Agencies that demonstrated that over 90 percent of viewers misperceive at least part of whatever kind of programming they watch, routinely misinterpreting between a quarter and a third of any broadcast, whether entertainment, news or commercials. From this viewpoint, the cultural imperialism thesis is largely a non-starter, since the basic premise of television's impact on culture is itself seriously questioned.

A less extreme position is that adopted by Jeremy Tunstall, who argues in general for a media impact on culture while not necessarily sharing fears of a developing pattern of cultural dominance and submission. Tunstall compares concerns about the export of American culture via television with the export of American culture via film in the 1930s. At that time some countries saw the import of Hollywood films in political as well as cultural terms. Among these countries the governments in the Soviet Union, Japan and Germany were willing to make the substantial economic investments necessary to develop their own domestic film industries and to successfully resist domination by imported products. Nevertheless the influence of Hollywood films was very marked:

Since the beginnings of Hollywood even the most serious of European writers have been influenced by media portrayals of American social reality. Bertolt Brecht was continually returning to Chicago gang warfare as a metaphor for capitalism, and although Brecht did spend some time in the U.S. his knowledge of Chicago gangs seems to have been derived from press and film coverage. Franz Kafka's gothic novel, *Amerika*, is a parable of social success in the New World and full of visual melodrama straight out of Hollywood. (Tunstall 1977:82)

On the question of cultural imperialism Tunstall observes that some countries have imported little U.S. technology and much U.S. programming while others have done the reverse. In addition, many countries now own space satellites, which they can use for their domestic needs, especially for literacy campaigns and educational programs. He argues that overall the thesis that television is a medium of American or Anglo-American cultural imperialism is both too strong and too weak. Too strong in that the high point of American television exports was in the mid-1960s, a time when in poor countries only the wealthy could purchase television sets. Too weak in that studies of the imported component of television programming in different countries failed to recognize that the proportion of foreign material broadcast on television in prime-time hours appeared to be considerably greater than at other times. The data available to test the media imperialism thesis clearly have a number of weaknesses, and no factual common ground on which to base the arguments for and against the thesis has been agreed upon.

NOTES

1. *Richard II*, act 3, scene 2, 164–65.

2. In England weekly newspapers date from 1622, but the first daily newspaper, the *Daily Courant*, was not published until 1702. The first successful daily newspaper in America was the *Boston News-Letter*, which started to appear in April 1704.

3. Michael Davie in *The Times Literary Supplement*, May 17, 1985:551. In the original National Theater production in London, Le Roux was played by Welsh actor Anthony Hopkins. At the time of the production the National Theater had a number of newspaper organizations among its patrons, including Rupert Murdoch's News International.

4. They were not alone in this respect. When Lord Northcliffe purchased *The Times* in 1908, he already owned the *Daily Mail*, *The Observer*, *Weekly Despatch*, *Evening News* and *Daily Mirror*.

5. Grub Street, according to Samuel Johnson, was "originally the name of a street near Moorfields in London, much inhabited by writers of small histories, dictionaries, and temporary poems, whence any mean production is called *grubstreet*."

6. Charles Scribner's Sons was established in 1846. It was merged with Macmillans, founded in 1869, in 1984. Scribner's, the bookstore on Manhattan's Fifth Avenue, remained in the family.

7. Part of the deal was payment of $60 million to Maxwell by the Tribune Company to take the loss-making paper off their hands.

8. In the United States the first national survey of best-selling books was compiled by the journal *Bookman* in November 1897.

9. The quotes are from Lewis and Stewart 1958:214–15.

10. How to measure the impact of television on public attitudes, behaviors and beliefs is an ongoing issue in media studies, as is the meaning of the findings of such research. "Active audience" theorists maintain that individual television viewers have considerable power and control over the medium, interpreting program "texts" in different and sometimes subversive ways. Their critics argue that although television is clearly not "an evil demon manipulating the viewers as if they were programmable robots or marionettes," nevertheless it does severely constrain the information, views and images available to viewers and, in doing so, influences viewers' attitudes, behaviors and beliefs: "The problem is not with audience interpreting practices, but with what is available for interpretation" (Seaman 1992).

CHAPTER 8

Fashion and Society

THE LANGUAGE AND IMAGES OF FASHION

If we didn't believe in fashion, where would we be? We'd be sitting at the racetrack in powder blue nylon stretch pants without a scrap of makeup on our faces. There's no dignity in that. Without fashion, there'd be no waiting at the Magazine Rack at three in the morning for the latest edition of *Vogue* to be dropped in the gutter, there'd be no scrambling through it for the newest things in the shops, there'd be no ripping out of pages to stick to our walls and frantic raiding of our piggybanks to see if we can afford any of it. There'd be no mooning over Thierry Muglers in Barney's windows and no fun in spending a whole afternoon in the changing room trying on heavenly things we could never afford but that make us look a million and a half dollars for a minute anyway. There'd be no thrill whatsoever in discovering an old Mary Quant mini at the back of some thrift shop in a suburb where they don't know the value of these things and buying it for a song and taking it home and sliding into it slowly, the zipper going up and up, and watching the jealousy grow on our friends' faces when they see us in it for the first time. No, without fashion, we might as well all be dead. As far as I'm concerned, fashion is like *oxygen*. You can't breathe without it. (Tulloch 1990:77–78)

In Samuel Butler's utopian novel *Erewhon* (1872) students were encouraged to study Unreason under the tutelage of Professors of Inconsistency and Evasion. The syllabus for the course would surely have included a session on fashion, an area where irrationality and images of irrationality abound. In 1830, for example, a man in Massachusetts was pilloried by members of his local community. He was physically assaulted in the street, rocks were hurled through the windows of his home, and he was refused communion at his local church. His offense was to sport a beard at a time when beards were not fashionable. Dwight E. Robinson (1976) traced the cyclical changes in beard-trimming practices among Englishmen from 1842 to 1972. He was unable to offer any rational explanation for these changes and demonstrated that the major technological innovation during the period—the invention of the safety razor—had little effect on beard fashions. In the world of fashion even practices that were once quite rational live on beyond their functional usefulness. It was allegedly Napoleon who decreed that buttons should be placed on the cuffs of men's jackets. He was irritated by his soldiers' wiping their noses on the cuffs of their uniforms and insisted that the cuffs be ornamented, first with braid, later with buttons, to discourage the behavior. Modern suits have redundant buttons on the cuffs, and pockets for a handkerchief.

The language of fashion suggests that many fashion practices not only have no reasonable basis but are directly contrary to reason. Fashion is described as fickle, capricious, full of mystery and absurdity. The word *fashion* has become synonymous with change, impermanence, the new and the novel. "I cannot keep track of all the vagaries of fashion. Every day, so it seems, brings in a different style," wrote Ovid in the *Art of Love* in A.D. 8. And in the words of Shakespeare, in *Much Ado About Nothing*, "The fashion wears out more apparel than the man." In the eighteenth century the vicissitudes of fashion posed particular problems for portrait painters; their clients often insisted on being painted in whatever dress was most modish, the mode often changing before the sittings were completed.

Nowhere have the "follies of fashion" been more evident than in the willingness of people to damage their health for the sake of appearing fashionable. The nineteenth-century corset, at the height of its popularity, required a wasp-waist as the voguish form of female beauty. For a young woman in her late teens or early twenties, this meant a waist of 16 inches. The tight-laced corset, advertised as a health aid, was both damaging to health and a physical torment to wear. It disfigured the body, severely restricted the breathing and circulation, displaced the liver and kidneys, compressed the lungs and could destroy the support from the muscles and the spine. Corsets were criticized as contributing to miscarriages and the birth of deformed children. The romantic swooning and fainting tendencies of the stereotypical Victorian heroine reflected the fact that the restrictions and debilitating pressures on the internal organs arising from the wearing of corsets made fainting common.

Another nineteenth-century style that had no utilitarian value whatsoever from the wearer's point of view, and was also a health hazard, was the crinoline skirt. This skirt, which at the peak of the "crinolinomania" of the 1850s might contain 20 yards of fabric, weigh over ten pounds and measure six feet across at ground level, could so completely immobilize the wearer that boating accidents frequently led to drownings. "Women and children first" was not so much an expression of male chivalry as a reflection of a fashion that rendered women helpless in the face of danger. There was criticism in high places. Queen Victoria never wore a crinoline and was a fervent opponent, describing it as an "indelicate, expensive, dangerous, and hideous article." Florence Nightingale, the most worshipped woman in England, was also an opponent of the crinoline. But in spite of its critics, and in spite of the repetition of coroners' verdicts of deaths by fire caused by crinolines, the fashion survived for many years. It was a period when dressing "in the breadth of fashion" supplanted dressing "in the height of fashion." The pavements and ballrooms were clogged with crinolines, even if fewer guests could be invited to social functions and dancing partners had to be held at arm's length. Husbands were advised to insure their wives at fire insurance offices; "dressed to kill" had taken on a literal meaning. The British magazine *Punch*, in reporting the death by burning of a young wife, aged 18, said that the coroner's verdict should not have been accidental death but, rather, "suicide committed in a fit of fashionable insanity" (Adburgham 1961:58). In Britain there was even an alternative national anthem, the "Fashionable Anthem":

> Long live our gracious Queen,
> Who won't wear Crinoline,
>   Long live the Queen!
> May her example spread,
> Broad skirts be narrowed,
> Long trains be shortened;
>   Long live the Queen!
>
> O storm of scorn arise,
> Scatter French fooleries,
>   And make them pall.
> Confound those hoops and things,
> Frustrate those horrid springs,
> And India rubber rings,
>   Deuce take them all!
>
> May dresses flaunting wide
> Fine figures cease to hide;
>   Let feet be seen;
> Girls to good taste return,
> Paris flash modes unlearn,
> No more catch fire and burn
>   Thanks to the Queen!
>
>   (Adburgham 1961:72)

As well as metaphors emphasizing irrational and non-rational elements in fashion behavior, the language of fashion is full of metaphors of social control. Alongside images of the mystery and unreasonableness of fashion lie images that suggest that the impact of fashion is inescapable. Fashion is "all-embracing" and "casts its spell" even over those who have no intention of yielding to it. Fashion "dictates" particular dress codes and practices, and whether we like it or not, one way or another we conform, even in our nonconformity. In the words of J. C. Flugel (1966:137), fashion is "a mysterious goddess, whose decrees it is our duty to obey rather than to understand." The "demands" of fashion, the "dictates" of fashion, the "rules" of fashion, make of fashion a "tyranny" that is forceful and absolute, a tyranny in which the consumer subjects are "dedicated followers of fashion," "slaves of fashion," "subservient to fashion." Fashion, wrote Ambrose Bierce in The Devil's Dictionary (1881–1911), is "a despot whom the wise ridicule and obey." And so, whether it be state banquet and obligatory "black tie," punkrock parade and safety-pinned nose, Madonna look-alike contest, or Hell's Angels' convention and gang insignia or patch, we "dress for the occasion."

These images of novelty, change and folly in the world of fashion, and of fashion as an inescapable form of social control, immediately raise some key questions as to the practice of business in such a world and the relationship between business activity and the development of social values. For example, are fashion enterprises subject in the marketplace to unpredictable changes in customer preferences, or do the enterprises themselves create and exploit a culture of change and impermanence in order to sell more fashion merchandise? Are the entrepreneurs of the fashion industry puppeteers skillfully controlling planned and choreographed performances by fashion dolls costumed to their designs, or are they themselves puppets pulled hither and thither by the vagaries of public taste? Are they the gods or are they the toys of the gods? And are the entrepreneurs and managers of the fashion world instruments, wittingly or unwittingly, of subtle and indirect forms of social control, reinforcing, through the imposition of dress codes, particular social values and social structures?

FASHION AND SOCIAL CONTROL

The most direct form in which attempts have been made to impose social control over the population by the regulation of their dress has been through government regulation and statute. For example, Charlemagne, the king of the Franks crowned emperor in Rome in A.D. 800, decreed that peasants' clothes might be made only of coarse fabrics in dull colors and that peasants should keep their hair short, cut in a line with the middle of the forehead. The simplest form of dress laws were those that reserved certain clothing colors for particular groups—the imperial purple, for example, reserved for the exclusive use of the Roman emperors and their immediate family, or the yellow reserved for the Sons of Heaven, the Chinese emperors. Similarly, sumptuary laws were enacted in Europe during the Middle Ages regulating purchase decisions along class or caste lines. In fourteenth-century England, tradesmen and artisans were forbidden to wear expensive cloth and restrictions were placed on the types of fur people might use in their garments.

Such laws were motivated, suggest Stuart and Elizabeth Ewen (1982), by three general concerns. One was "to preserve class distinctions, so that any could tell by merely looking at a man's dress to what rank in society he belonged." In 1530 in Augsburg, for example, ermine and sable could be worn only by princes and aristocrats; simple townspeople could wear furs of fox and polecat; goat and lamb skins were the approved peasant attire. A second concern was "to check practices which were regarded as deleterious in their effects, due to the feeling that luxury and extravagance were in themselves wicked and harmful to people." Initially the rich and powerful wanted to curb what they saw as the profligacy and waste of the lower orders of society. Later, with the ascendancy of Puritanism, it was the conspicuous consumption of the Christian Church and the nobility that were the most frequent targets of legal constraint. A third concern was to protect and promote home-based industries at the expense of imported luxuries and finery. This economic aspect of sumptuary laws was often linked with the objective of encouraging more thrifty habits among the lower classes and tapping their savings to support the political, military or social glories pursued by their rulers. Many of the sumptuary laws were not enforced directly. There was little need to do so in most cases, since inequalities in the distribution of wealth guaranteed that economics rather than law dictated the kind of clothing that people would wear; "cloth of gold," ermine and sable were generally beyond the purchasing power of the poor.

There have been less coercive ways, however, in which fashion has acted as a status-placing mechanism within society. Clothes have been used to indicate rank, wealth and power, and both individuals and groups have used fashion as an element in their competition for social prestige. In 1661, for example, Lady Wright declared that the great happiness of being in the fashion was to show scorn for those who were not, such as citizens' wives and country gentlewomen. Imitation of the dress of those in prestigious positions in the social hierarchy has long been an important element in the development of fashion trends—thus the emphasis on the clothes worn by such people as the Queen of England, Diana, Princess of Wales, and the stars of the entertainment world.[1] Robert and Jeanette Lauer (1981) describe this process of imitation as the "trickle-down theory of fashion." They suggest that the motives for imitating the dress worn by "top" people are a mixture of reverence for those people and what they represent and a desire to assert equality with prestigious people in the social hierarchy. The trickle-down theory of fashion explains changes in fashion, and the diffusion of those changes among a wider proportion of the population, in terms of a top elite of fashion leaders who are constantly seeking new and distinctive clothes in order to reassert their social superiority over the hosts of reverential but egalitarian imitators in the social strata below. "Fashion," wrote William Hazlitt in 1830, "is gentility running away from vulgarity and afraid of being overtaken."[2]

Social status and economic affluence can be asserted through fashion by wearing clothes that are both expensive and dysfunctional. Thorsten Veblen in *The Theory of the Leisure Class* (1899) argued that expenditure on dress was one of the clearest expressions of conspicuous consumption, demonstrating both conspicuous waste and conspicuous leisure:

It goes without saying that no apparel can be considered elegant, or even decent, if it shows the effect of manual labor on the part of the wearer, in the way of soil or wear. . . . Much of the charm that invests the patent-leather shoe, the stainless linen, the lustrous cylindrical hat, and the walking stick, which so greatly enhance the native dignity of a gentleman, comes of their pointedly suggesting that the wearer cannot when so attired bear a hand in any employment that is directly and immediately of any human use. Elegant dress serves its purpose of elegance not only in that it is expensive, but also because it is the insignia of leisure. It not only shows that the wearer is able to consume a relatively large value, but it argues at the same time that he consumes without producing. (Veblen 1953:120–21)

Indulgence in wasteful and fashionable consumption and emulative spending to underline social status later came to be called the Veblen effect. It was the kind of consumption behavior characteristic of a society in which women were expected to reflect the position and wealth of their husbands. In Victorian England ladies planning to spend a week in a stately country home were advised by the magazine *Punch* to take with them a minimum of three dresses for each day of their visit, and it was not uncommon for a woman in society to change her clothes as many as five or six times a day. The "need" for such fashionable behavior arose from marital duty, the new clothes and expensive accessories being a silent but necessary advertisement of the husband's status. Some understanding of the expense involved in keeping up such appearances can be gleaned from the fact that in the 1860s the simplest day dress purchased from a top couturier like Worth would cost around 60 pounds sterling; at this time 500 pounds a year would have been a good salary for a professional man or a merchant, and a working man would have thought himself fortunate to earn more than 50 pounds a year. In 1910 the price of a fur coat by Lucile, the first Englishwoman to become internationally famous as a dress designer, represented an estimated 85 years' work for a working woman.

Some of the status-placing and status-enhancing aspects of fashion are extremely subtle and scarcely visible to those uninitiated in the rites and mysteries of the fashion world. Tom Wolfe wrote of "the secret vice" of real buttonholes on men's suits:

Real buttonholes. That's it! A man can take his thumb and forefinger and unbutton his sleeve at the wrist because this type of suit has real buttonholes there. Tom, boy, it's terrible. Once you know about it, you start seeing it. All the time! There are just two classes of men in the world, men with suits whose buttons are just sewn onto the sleeve, just some kind of cheaper decoration, or—yes!—men who can unbutton the sleeve at the wrist because they have real buttonholes and the sleeve really buttons up. Fascinating!

. . . Practically all the most powerful men in New York, especially on Wall Street, the people in investment houses, banks and law firms, the politicians, especially Brooklyn Democrats, for some reason, outstanding dandies, those fellows, the blue-chip culturati, the major museum directors and publishers, the kind who sit in offices with antique textile shades—practically all of these men are fanatical about the marginal differences that go into custom tailoring. They are almost like a secret club insignia for them. And yet it is a taboo subject. They won't talk about it. They don't want it known that they even care about it. But all the time they have this fanatical eye, more fanatical than a woman's, about the whole thing and even grade men by it. . . .

The whole thing is in the marginal differences—things that show that you spent more money and had servitors in there cutting and sewing like madmen and working away for you. Status! Yes! (Wolfe 1965:192–93;196)

DRESS CODES

It is clear that there are precise expectations in society and in groups within society as to appropriate and inappropriate dress. The first notice pinned in 1870 to the notice board of the All England Croquet Club at Wimbledon, soon to become the All England Croquet and Lawn Tennis Club, referred to a matter of dress: "Gentlemen are requested not to play in their shirt-sleeves when ladies are present." In fashion behavior the individual confronts social norms; these norms are society's values and conventions concerning proper modes of dress, proper dress being accepted as a likely outward and visible sign of proper conduct and behavior. When these social norms dominate individual desires, then fashion becomes a coercive social force. In some cases, as has been indicated, social norms are codified in law. In other cases they are institutionalized as custom and practice. In the 1960s, for example, many restaurants would not admit women in tailored or formal slacks; nowadays jeans, sandals, bare feet, boots, gang patches, insignia or emblems may be sufficient to guarantee a similar exclusion. Society's fashion norms are expressed in dress codes, codes aimed at all members of society or codes for particular occupational groups or members of particular organizations. General social dress codes may be written down in books of etiquette, books that have a long tradition behind them. The *Galateo*, for example, a book of manners by Giovanni Della Casa first published in 1558, had a section on "How to Dress without Disrespect to Others":

Everyone should dress well, according to his age and his position in society. If he does not, it will be taken as a mark of contempt for other people. . . . Not only should a man's clothes be made of fine cloth, but he should also do his best to follow the prevailing fashion and conform with local customs, even though he may find, or think he finds, them less comfortable and becoming than the ones he is used to. If everyone in town has short hair, it is wrong to grow long tresses, just as it is wrong to go clean-shaven if everyone else has a beard, because this implies contradiction of others, which is a thing never to be done except in case of necessity. . . .

Clothes should also fit well and suit the wearer. People who have fine and elegant garments, but wear them so untidily that they look as if they were made for someone else, show either that they are indifferent whether they please other people or not, or that they lack taste and discrimination. Their manner of dress leads the people with whom they associate to suppose that they have no respect for them, and for this reason they are unwelcome and unpopular in most circles. (Della Casa 1958:33–34)

Although practicality rather than fashion dictates most working clothing, certain occupations have developed their own special attire and dress codes (see Williams-Mitchell 1982). Servants frequently had uniforms prescribed for them by their employers. In Europe, by the middle of the fourteenth century, male servants, who were also potential fighting men, wore the livery of their masters. The livery usually bore an insignia of some kind that the servant, when not dressed in his master's uniform, would display on his ordinary dress. An allowance of clothes was often part of a servant's wage, and royal retainers might receive two sets of costume each year, one for summer and one for winter. Ostentation in the liveries and clothes provided for servants was one way in which the rich displayed their wealth. In large households ladies-in-waiting and female servants tended to dress in the prevailing fashion because they received hand-me-downs of fashionable garments from their mistresses.

Servants' livery and uniforms were originally introduced as a means of identification. They were later provided to encourage smartness and to develop a sense of community with the employer and his or her business or household. Occupational costumes are also a form of advertising, thus the butcher's traditional blue and white striped apron and straw boater hat. In other cases, as with lawyers, judges and university academics, archaic dress styles have been deliberately preserved as a means of conferring dignity on the occupation. In some occupations, such as hairdressing, fashionable clothing may be almost a prerequisite for employment. In the eighteenth century many shop proprietors insisted that their male shop assistants powdered and curled their hair in the latest fashionable style. In other occupations fashionable clothing may be prohibited, as, for example, in the nineteenth century when certain factories forbade the wearing of crinolines at work because the dresses were liable to catch in the machinery, with potentially fatal results. In the 1960s the elite New York department store Bergdorf Goodman expected its employees to avoid looking overly stylish: "Committed to upholding an air of mystery, magic, and originality for their clientele, Bergdorf's instructed its employees: 'We don't want our sales people mistaken for customers.' " (Ewen and Ewen 1982:217).

Company dress codes are the modern counterpart of the medieval livery. Failure to recognize or observe them may lead to various sanctions and disadvantages for the unwary or the nonconforming. In Joseph Heller's novel *Something Happened* (1974), the narrator describes the insecurities of Andy Kagle, head of the sales department, who is afraid of losing his powerful position in the company. Not only is Kagle's name suspect but he shows poor dress sense. He is offered some advice:

"Play more golf. Talk to Red Parker and buy a blue blazer. Buy better suits. Wear a jacket in the office and keep your shirt collar buttoned and your necktie up tight around your neck where it belongs. Jesus, look at you right now. You're supposed to be a distinguished executive."
"Don't take the name of the Lord in vain," he jokes.
"Don't you."
"I've got a good sales record," he argues.
"Have you got a good sports jacket?" I demand.
"Jesus Christ, what does a good sports jacket matter?"
"More than your good sales record."

Such pressures do not merely belong to the world of fiction. In his book *Think: A Biography of the Watsons and IBM*, "written with the active non-co-operation of the company," William Rodgers described some of the methods, informal yet unambiguous, through which the founder of IBM, Thomas Watson, established modes of conduct and dress in the company:

Some new office staff member, or a service man obliged to deliver equipment to customers, might somehow have slipped through the employment screening process and, after reporting to work, begin to appear in a despised colored, or striped, shirt. If his boss had assimilated the Watson style properly, he would not summarily dismiss the offender but rather keep an eye on him for a few days. If the offence was repeated, the supervisor would go to him with a gift of perhaps a half-dozen white shirts, and suggest calmly that he was considered a good man to have in the company and that the shirts were intended to make his work more satisfactory to all concerned.

It was not necessary to put into writing the rules for grooming, clean white shirts, neckties, and conservative attire. . . . It was said that Watson himself communicated his insistence on dark suits and white shirts by standing at a podium at one of the early sales conventions and, looking at the forward rows of attentive salesmen, their stiff collars and shirt fronts gleaming in the morning light in contrast to their dark suits, said pointedly to the executives gathered about him, "My, but those men look nice; I am proud to have them represent the company." It was quite enough, and the expression of approval instituted a universal, undeviating policy. (Rodgers 1971:104–5)

Male business attire, especially the business suit, has traditionally been a badge of probity and conservatism. In his *Autobiography*, Benjamin Franklin, who in so many ways personified Max Weber's "Protestant ethic and the spirit of capitalism," wrote that "in order to secure my credit and character as a tradesman, I took care not only to be in reality industrious and frugal, but to avoid all appearances to the contrary. I drest plainly." Ewen and Ewen (1982:131) point out that commercial dress is the clothing of diligence, not idleness, and also, in America by the late eighteenth century, a hallmark of morality and Christian virtue. Philadelphia's Quaker businessmen "forged a powerful unity between commerce and Christianity" and the simple "plain style" of dress that they adopted was a visible sign of their commitment to hard work, just dealing and moral uprightness. Their "plain style" of clothing, "the cloak of morality," was a style, nevertheless, and incorporated simply cut elegant coats made of fine and expensive cloth. It established a trend in commercial dress that continued through the twentieth-century gray-flannel or pin-stripe business suit, a uniform signifying industry, a dedication to family and society, and the denial of individual spontaneity.

SEX ROLES AND EROTISM

Although on the face of it the imperative that "pink is for girls and blue is for boys" is one of the fashion world's many irrationalities, it is, as Alison Lurie observes, the start of sex-typing in dress:

Sex-typing in dress begins at birth with the assignment of pale-pink layettes, toys, bedding and furniture to girl babies, and pale blue ones to boy babies. Pink, in this culture, is associated with sentiment; blue with service. The implication is that the little girl's future concern will be the life of the affections; the boy's earning a living. (Lurie 1981:214)

Sex stereotypes in society have consistently been reflected in clothing. Most clothing styles have reflected role expectations rather than gender differences. For example, there have been acrid and acrimonious conflicts over women wearing trousers, "who wears the trousers?" becoming a synonym for questions of male-female dominance and submission. Fashion has frequently maintained sex-role differences, and fashion norms have traditionally reflected the belief that fashion should maintain such differences. The architects and beneficiaries of this normative system have generally been men in that men historically have been able to impose certain roles on women through the instrument of fashionable dress. For women in particular, therefore, fashion has often been a coercive mechanism in their control by men and by male-dominated institutions.

Attempts by women to change the accepted definition of their roles by changing what they wear have a long and controversial history. The most celebrated case is that of Mrs. Amelia Jenks Bloomer, who in the nineteenth century was part of an attack upon the whole structure of female fashion. Born in New York State in 1818, Amelia Bloomer was the wife of the proprietor and editor of a weekly journal. Drawn into journalism herself as a result of working for the temperance movement, in 1849 she founded a small paper, *The Lily*, as a voice for women in the temperance crusade. The paper soon became a vehicle for female rights generally and bore the legend "devoted to the interests of women." In 1851 when her husband's paper, probably tongue-in-cheek, published an article ridiculing the long skirts and heavy petticoats and crinolines fashionable at the time and suggesting the greater practicality of the ankle-length trousers and short skirts worn by Turkish women, Mrs. Bloomer's paper took up the gauntlet, agreeing that such a costume would be eminently sensible for women. Mrs. Bloomer was among the first to wear the new dress, which was a compromise between fashionable taste and practical needs.

Nevertheless, the very suggestion of women wearing anything resembling trousers was anathema to Western man. The majority of women themselves were amused by the suggestion, but they were too conditioned by conventional views to dare to do anything "indelicate" or "too forward." . . .

The New York press latched on to the story and turned it into a sensation—women in trousers! Demand for *The Lily* soared, and requests for patterns poured in from American women, while Mrs. Bloomer as editor of the women's paper was seen as the prophet of a new concept of clothing. She was invited to go on lecture tours, and went wearing the new costume, finding it most convenient for travel, although the subjects she spoke on were not dress but temperance and women's suffrage.

The news crossed the Atlantic very quickly, and *Punch* and the London music-halls had a field day, ridiculing the costume and asserting that women were now trying to take over the established role of men. This, of course, was not true. Mrs. Bloomer simply wanted votes for women and a more practical costume, and not the total reversal of social roles. (de Marly 1980:65)

Bloomerism was a short-lived movement, however. "If Mrs. Bloomer had been La Duchesse de Bloomer," observed Alison Adburgham (1961:42), "it might have gone otherwise; but Mrs. Bloomer was middle class and came from America, whence no fashions had ever been known to come. Bloomerism was, therefore, not a fashion, but a freak."

Most of the support for the clothes reform movement came from adherents of women's rights. By the end of the 1850s Mrs. Bloomer had decided that the press publicity and sensationalism attaching to the question of reformed costume was interfering with the more important issue of votes for women. The campaign for rational dress was revived periodically during the rest of the nineteenth century. In England, for example, a Rational Dress Society was founded in 1881 advocating some sort of trouser-skirt for women. The society was opposed to any attempts by the fashion industry to impose unhealthy and unnatural garments upon women and campaigned on the basis that any form of dress that restricted movement, prevented proper exercise and deformed the body was to be vigorously resisted. In 1882 in England the society ran a Hygienic Wearing Apparel Exhibition. In 1890 another society, the Healthy and Artistic Dress Union, was formed advocating classical styles of dress for women. But it was changes in leisure activities and in the technologies associated with leisure, particularly the advent of the bicycle and of bicycle riding as a popular pastime for women in the 1890s, that finally began to effectively break down the traditional forms of female dress.

In addition to the sexist elements in fashion, fashion and dress have long been associated with erotism (Steele 1985). Clothing, as well as providing a basis for status competition and satisfying utilitarian needs for warmth and protection, provides an arena for sexual competition. Both male and female fashions provide opportunities for sexual display, becoming a medium, in an almost theatrical manner, of sexual attraction and seduction. The fashionable codpieces of Renaissance costume, for example, were a very explicit form of male display. (One idiosyncratic sixteenth-century tailor used his codpiece as a pincushion.) Victorian pornography focused on displays of lace-trimmed underclothes, customarily thought of as the garments of prostitutes, and the French cancan was allegedly invented to show off the dancers' lacy underwear. In contrast to such abandoned, unchaste and immoral displays, the fashionable and approved restrictions of the corset implied a woman of taste and propriety while at the same time providing sexual titillation. Havelock Ellis, author of *Studies in the Psychology of Sex* (published between 1896 and 1928 in seven volumes) observed that corsets tended to make breathing "thoracic instead of abdominal, thereby keeping the bosom in a constant, and presumably sexually attractive, state of movement."[3] A similar mixture of tastefulness, romanticism and coy erotism can be found in some of the delightful dress names the Edwardian designer Lucile gave to her creations: Give Me Your Hearts; When Passion's Thrall Is O'er; Do You Love Me?; The Meaning of Life Is Clear; The Sighing Sound of Lips Unsatisfied; A Frenzied Song of Amorous Things; Red Mouth of a Venomous Flower.

The rationale of erotism in fashion is that modesty and immodesty, morality and immorality, rest on ways of dressing. Modesty and morality are defined through cultural symbols and judgments of persons based on judgments of clothes. Writing about the ethics of dress, J. C. Flugel observed that

most men of the upper social classes experience a curious feeling of guilt and embarrassment if surprised by a woman without a collar and tie or in their shirt-sleeves. On analysis, this feeling seems to be composed of three principal elements: (a) a disagreeable suspicion of having been detected in a condition of moral relaxation; (b) the feeling that the man is somehow insulting the woman by appearing without the panoply of chivalry; (c) a feeling of being sexually inadequate to the demands of a female presence—in other words, the feeling that the man is impotent or castrated. (Flugel 1966:209–10)

Such judgments of modesty and morality have been largely made in terms of the dressing of the female anatomy. Bare legs, bare ankles, bare shoulders and bare breasts, as revealed by the rise and fall of skirt lengths or of the décolletage, have all in various historical periods been considered immodest and indecent and at other times the height of respectable fashion. Since the part of the body defined as erotic changes from time to time, erotism itself has to be seen as subject to its own changes in fashion and taste. This phenomenon has been labelled the "shifting erogenous zone theory of fashion."

FASHION AND THE ZEITGEIST

Just as individuals may be defined in terms of the clothes they choose to wear, so too the characteristic ethos of particular historical periods has been described by reference to prevailing fashion styles. If clothing can reflect an era, then changes in fashion may indicate something about changes in society generally. "Fashion," argue Robert and Jeanette Lauer, "like every facet of culture, is a reflection of the Zeitgeist, the spirit of the times." A similar notion is contained in James Laver's "Time Spirit Theory," the idea that the forms of dress, apparently so haphazard, so dependent upon the whims of designers, nevertheless have an extraordinary relevance to the spirit of an age. Thus the flapper look of the 1920s has been viewed as a visible manifestation of a general breaking away from the constraints and conventions of Victorian society, particularly the constraints and conventions imposed upon women. Ewen and Ewen point out that in 1913 an average woman's outfit required 19 ¼ yards of fabric in its production compared with only 7 yards by 1928. Wage-earning city women needed styles that gave them mobility for sporting and leisure pursuits but were also serviceable for working wear. The lean and sinewy flapper style also reflected, they suggest, the impact on fashion of the movies, a powerful agency for changing tastes in the mass market. They accept that the reduction in volume of women's clothes was partly due "to the visual need for the completely clothed body to be seen *in motion.* . . . Movies taught everyone how ways of walking and dancing, of using the hands and moving the head and shoulders, could be incorporated into the conscious ways of wearing clothes."[4] In the pre–World War I days of *La Belle Époque* the fashion leaders had been royalty, high society, opera stars and the newly rich. By the 1930s the film star had taken center stage for the mass of the population as the epitome of glamorous fashion, more influential and widely known than any society lady had ever been. Since films were in black and white, black and white became fashionable dress colors, and since movie stars were thin and mobile, so too their imitators (Ewen and Ewen 1982:201).

Similarly the mood of the 1960s is caught in the youth-led fashions of the period, an Anglo-American teenage revolt in which young people broke away from the conservative dictates of the mass fashion industry and sought their own forms of individual expression. It was a revolt led by young British designers unconcerned about what Paris might have to say on appropriate dress styles, but focusing, rather, on the needs of themselves and their contemporaries. The era spawned the boutique, where individual designs were produced for the ready-to-wear market, and a coterie of designers who rejected the haute couture tradition of luxurious salons and expensive custom-made clothes. The greatest of all haute couture houses, Maison Worth, founded in 1858, taken over by Paquin in 1954, had closed in 1956. 1956 was the year that Mary Quant set up a shop, Bazaar, in Chelsea, London, and, unsatisfied with the clothes available from the large manufacturers, began to make her own. In 1959 John Stephan opened in Carnaby Street, London—soon to become the mecca of 1960s' clothing fashions—and started selling colorful clothes for young men in place of traditional gray suits and white shirts. In 1962 two graduates from London's Royal College of Art opened the first boutique within a department store—the 21 Shop at Woollands. With London now the leading center of young fashion and the purchasing power of the youth market far greater in value than the sales of haute couture, Paris had to follow suit. In 1964, Courreges and Pierre Cardin joined in the flood of instant designs aimed at the fashion-conscious young. Describing the breakdown of the fashion mainstream in the 1960s, Diana Vreeland, editor of *Vogue*, said:

A youthquake was starting. High society had disintegrated incredibly. . . . Suddenly it seemed everyone had gravitated to his own private world and the center was lost. Meanwhile, the young did things their way without regard to the old world. And anyone who wasn't with them made no difference at all. (quoted in Ewen and Ewen 1982:245)

Both the flapper style of the 1920s and the Chelsea Look and Carnaby Street clothes of the 1960s were fashions led and sponsored by young people and the youth market, in rebellion against the perceived restrictions imposed by the adult establishment. Taking a much broader view of the relationship between fashion leadership and the zeitgeist, Ewen and Ewen suggest that the growing dominance of the young in fashion leadership reflects the long-term transition from a *customary* society, where the young learn from their elders, to a *consumer* society in which older people look to youth for guidance, a process reinforced by the way in which contemporary fashion goods are advertised and marketed. The modern fashion industry, they argue, is one where people wear what they like rather than what they are told to like, where "doing one's own thing" is the norm, where the old rules have disappeared and no decipherable new ones have emerged, where there has been "a shift of creative initiative, from the design rooms of industry to the emancipated intuition of people in search of autonomy and personhood" (Ewen and Ewen 1982:245). In consequence in the 1980s diversity and choice were seen as the prevailing ethos of the fashion world and of society generally: "Today there is no fashion; there are only fashions." It was a point of view, however, considered passé by other writers on fashion. Thus Alison Lurie argued that by the end of the 1970s this period of individualism, of doing your own thing, was already over, that it had been redefined as narcissism, that counter-cultural lifestyles were now dismissed as irrelevant, and that free sexual experiment was now viewed as reflecting a neurotic incapacity for emotional commitment. In her opinion the romantic dress styles of the 1970s were replaced in the 1980s by expensive and conservative clothes, the clothes of responsible adults.

Fashion, then, has a number of distinctive social elements, and business activities form an integral part of all these elements. For example, fashion advertisements and fashion magazines have played an important role in underscoring the status placement and status enhancement aspects of fashion purchase decisions. They have also promoted all manner of physically healthy and unhealthy dress practices as the height of fashion. Over the years fashion industry entrepreneurs have exploited sexual competition and erotism as major themes in their marketing strategies. They have emphasized and profited from the relationship, in the mind of the consumer, between clothing purchase decisions, mental well-being and the expression and development of personality. Business organizations in many different industries have "enforced" dress codes among both their own employees and their customers or clients. These approved dress codes have often reinforced traditional sexual stereotypes about gender roles. In the world of fashion, social values and business practices are inextricably mixed. Clearly, the notion of business in society, a key theme of this book, is an apt one in the context of the fashion world. The next chapter seeks to examine more thoroughly the implications of this for the practice of business by contrasting in particular the business world of haute couture with that of mass fashion enterprises. This allows some further illumination of the relationship between social values and business practices and an opportunity to discriminate among patterns of business behavior in the fashion industry.

NOTES

1. Even royal limps have been imitated. When rheumatic fever left Princess Alexandra, wife of Edward VII, lame in one leg, the "Alexandra limp" was adopted by some ladies as a fashionable affection (Hibbert 1982:87).
2. A similar pattern is evident in "fashionable" holiday resorts: "As soon as the

railroad reached the seaside towns of southern England that had been strongholds of the aristocracy far into the nineteenth century, the middle classes took them over. Then the aristocracy retired to remote localities such as Scotland, Ireland, and the Lake District" (Schivelbusch 1986:42).

3. Quoted in Ewen and Ewen 1982:139.
4. Anne Hollander (1975) quoted in Ewen and Ewen 1982:200.

CHAPTER 9

"There's No Fashion If Nobody Buys It"[1]

HAUTE COUTURE AND THE ARISTOCRACY OF FASHION

Until the late seventeenth century in Europe the professional business of making clothes was in male hands. Court gowns, fashionable townwear and riding habits were made by male tailors for a clientele of upper-class ladies. Women lower down the social scale made their own clothes, while the poor relied on the second-hand and old clothes markets. This pattern was changed significantly by a law passed in Paris in 1675. Women were allowed to enter three-year apprenticeships in cutting and dressmaking at the conclusion of which they could go into business as couturiers. As a result, more and more women became professional dressmakers until, initially in France but then in neighboring countries too, the business of making clothes for ladies virtually became a female monopoly. (Male tailors continued to make riding habits and, later, many became corsetmakers.) Since fashions were launched at court, the court dressmakers, like Rose Bertin, dressmaker to Queen Marie-Antoinette and the court of Versailles in the 1780s, themselves often became well-known and socially prominent people.

Curiously, the man who broke this female monopoly was not a Frenchman but an Englishman, Charles Frederick Worth (1825–1895), "the first of the great fashion dictators." Worth completely changed the nature and status of the fashion business. He started his business under the patronage of the French court but eventually became sufficiently established to survive the disappearance of that court and to become a totally independent fashion authority in his own right. Worth's career is an instructive example of the development of a business catering to a small, elite group of fashion leaders and exemplifies some of the business practices associated with the trickle-down theory of fashion described in the previous chapter. He is a major entrepreneurial figure in fashion history.

Worth was born into a professional family that was ruined when he was still a child. When he was 13, his mother took him to London, where he was apprenticed for seven years to the drapers Swan and Edgar, in Piccadilly Circus. There he gained experience in handling textiles, judging their qualities and assessing their suitability for particular kinds and styles of dress, and in advising lady customers on the purchase of fabrics to be made into gowns by their dressmakers. After his apprenticeship was completed, Worth went to Paris, arriving there at the age of 20 with five pounds sterling in his possession. He struggled in a number of jobs while learning to speak French until, in 1847, he became a sales assistant for Gagelin, the most famous mercers in Paris. He worked with Gagelin for nearly 12 years, initially selling fabrics, shawls and mantles, later rising to the position of *premier commis*, or leading salesman. At Gagelin he met Marie Vernet, one of the shop's models, and since he had to sell the shawls that Marie modelled, Worth started to make dresses for her that would display the shawls to the best advantage. Lady customers noticed these plain but elegant creations, and after initial hostility from his employers, Worth was permitted in 1850 to set up a small dressmaking department within the firm.

Worth's creations, wrote Diana de Marly (1980:17), "set a new standard for dressmaking. Their fit was perfection, their finish unparalleled. Here was the foundation of a new art, the creation of clothes which were perfect in every way, clothes which were haute couture." Impressed by the appeal of Worth's dresses Gagelin included some of them in their exhibit at the 1851 Great Exhibition in London and again at the Exposition Universelle in Paris in 1855. Railway expansion and tourist excursions by train and boat made both these exhibitions extremely popular events, and regular transatlantic steamship crossings brought American buyers to the fashionable streets of Europe. For Worth this all added up to greatly expanded opportunities. His clothes for export were of a quality equal to those he sold to his French customers, and foreign buyers went to Worth knowing that they were purchasing the best. Insufficiently encouraged by Gagelin, Worth, supported by Marie Vernet, whom he had married in 1851, went into a dressmaking partnership in 1858 with a Swedish salesman friend, Otto Bobergh.

In 1858 Napoleon III was on the throne of the French Second Empire, setting a pattern of splendor in Paris that

made other European capitals appear dull and staid. Entertaining became a veritable industry, with state balls, ministerial and ambassadorial functions, imperial receptions, military parades, state visits, and gala performances of opera and ballet. At the summit of this glittering assemblage was the beautiful Empress Eugénie, whose elegance and style gave a new impetus to French fashion. What she wore, other women copied. (de Marly 1980:19)

It was necessary, if a couture house such as Worth et Bobergh were to flourish as a business, that it find a customer of great social importance who could provide regular aristocratic patronage. Consequently, early in 1860 Worth and Bobergh decided to approach Princess Metternich, the wife of the newly arrived Austrian ambassador, and Marie Worth was sent to her with an album of dresses. The princess liked what she saw, ordered a morning and evening dress and wore the evening dress of white silk tulle woven with silver to the next ball at the Palais des Tuileries, where it received favorable comment from the Empress Eugénie. The outcome was that after some initial hiccups, Worth became the imperial dressmaker, making dresses for the Empress Eugénie to her own taste and at the same time, with the help of Napoleon III, persuading her to wear dresses that would help the French textile trade, gowns she dubbed her "political dresses." The corresponding efforts of manufacturers to persuade Worth to promote their products at court gave him a great deal of influence within the trade. Worth's prices became the highest in Paris, and princesses and duchesses flocked to his salon. From a business point of view the built-in obsolescence in the customary practice of only wearing a highly fashionable evening dress on one occasion gave a guarantee of repeat orders to the successful couturier. The customers of Maison Worth soon included a wide range of the richest people in the world: Russian nobility, American millionaires, the old European aristocracy and the nouveau riche wives of bankers and industrialists, people who in the 1870s might spend from four hundred to four thousand pounds sterling a year on Worth dresses alone. Although royal marriages were a specialty, Worth also dressed successful actresses and some of the leading courtesans of the time, ability to pay being the only criterion by which he judged his clientele. One of Worth's favorite places for launching new fashions was the racecourse at Longchamp, opened in 1859. For example, he persuaded women to lighten their shawls by sending his wife and Princess Metternich to the races with only gauze and lace over their shoulders: "Such simplicity made all the other women appear overdressed, and by the next opening of the races no shawls were to be seen on the fashionable set" (de Marly 1980:29–30). In using the racecourse as a location at which to introduce new fashions, Worth "established a tradition which couturiers were to follow for nearly a hundred years," a tradition that lives on in the fashionable race day parades of Ascot in England, Melbourne in Australia and Kentucky in the United States.

Writing in his weekly journal, *All the Year Round*, Charles Dickens described Worth as "a perfect gentleman, always fresh shaved, always frizzled. Black coat, white cravat, and batiste shirt-cuffs fastened at the wrists with golden buttons, he officiates with all the gravity of a diplomatist." Indeed, this "gentleman of business" established himself in the social milieu of his clientele. He built himself a luxury villa outside Paris and was visited by Princess Metternich and members of the French court and nobility. Worth came to view himself as an artist. His dresses were artistic creations through which he imposed his will on his customers rather than responded to their tastes. Diana de Marly describes how a lady visiting Maison Worth would find that her own dress ideas counted for nothing:

Worth would study her, note her coloring, her hair, her jewels, her style, and then he would design a gown which he thought would suit her. . . . Such dictatorship from a dressmaker was unprecedented. Some attributed it to arrogance on Worth's part, but the philosophy behind such dictation to the customer was to create a house style and a standard of excellence. If Worth controlled the final product, no woman could ruin his design by wearing the wrong hat or the wrong shawl; thus the reputation of his house was sustained. This control was so absolute that before a state ball Princess Metternich and other ladies would report to Worth at 10 P.M. They would wait in a drawing room with *pâté de foie* and madeira for refreshment and one by one be ushered into the presence of the great designer, so that he might make the finishing touches. The princess declared that his last inspection was essential for she would not have felt dressed without it. (de Marly 1980:22)

Worth became "the supreme arbiter of taste in dress." He turned dress-making into big business and transformed the role of the dress designer into one of power and status: "He found Paris with a craft and left it with an industry."

THE DENIM DEMOCRACY

Although Worth's business was firmly grounded in the design and making of expensive garments for a small, elite clientele, its growth necessitated the development within it of some of the characteristics of a mass production industry. This was particularly evident during the era of the crinoline. In fact, Worth was credited with, or blamed for, the introduction of the crinoline, it being alleged that in 1856 a pregnant Empress Eugénie first put on a large crinoline "to conceal her interesting situation." The crinoline was the first industrial fashion. *The Times* of London reported on 18 July 1857 that 40,000 tons of Swedish iron had been imported for the manufacture of crinolines, and in 1865 Henry Mayhew wrote that "crinoline had become a special and distinct branch of trade. It is no longer a mere accessory of the milliner's or haberdasher's shop. There are great factories where nothing else is made but crinoline wires and hoops; there are warehouses where nothing else is stored, shops where no other commodity is sold." Even a business like Worth's, custom-making dresses for the aristocracy, reflected some of the processes of the burgeoning manufacturing industries of the mid-nineteenth century. With a staff of 1,200 and the technological improvements of the sewing machine, first patented in the United States in 1846, Maison Worth turned out hundreds of ball gowns a week. But it was in the development of ready-to-wear clothing that mass production methods came into their own.

One explanation for the rise of mass fashion examined by Ewen and Ewen is the mechanical or technological one, in which the development of ready-to-wear clothes for the mass market is seen as a consequence of technological advancement. Thus in 1733 the invention of the flying shuttle allowed broad pieces of cloth to be woven at a much faster rate than previously. In 1764 the invention of the spinning jenny improved the production of yarn and thread. Later in the eighteenth century power looms replaced the old weaving frame, and the new cotton gin separated cotton seeds from bolls at a rate that allowed for the mass production of cotton cloth. In England factory production methods were developed in the "dark Satanic mills" of Lancashire, and in the United States the slave system of plantation labor produced great quantities of cotton at low prices. In the nineteenth century sewing machines, lace-making machines (the targets of Ned Ludd's men in Nottinghamshire, England), machinery for riveting boots and sewing leather, all contributed to the growing mechanization of the clothing industry. In this technology-driven model of change, innovative geniuses with new inventions are promoted and exploited by industrialists striving for profit.

However, it is not, argued Ewen and Ewen, a sufficient explanation for the rise of a mass clothing market, that is, for the fact that by early in the twentieth century most working people bought rather than made their own clothes. Rather, they suggest, the roots of the ready-made clothing industry lay largely in social and economic changes, not technological ones: "While today's ready-made clothing industry is enveloped by the propaganda of aesthetic transcendence, its roots were neither aesthetic nor transcendent, but a part of the banal misery of nineteenth-century working-class life" (Ewen and Ewen 1982:168).

The clientele for most of the earliest forms of ready-to-wear clothing were mobile workers and laborers who had no stable home base in which to make their own clothes. Whalers, fishermen and sailors patronized wharfside shops where the clothing sold "stood in stark contrast to the tailored garments of gentlemen; it was woefully crude in terms of both workmanship and material used. Clothing was generally produced in only one size, to be tied, tucked, or cut by its wearer to achieve the approximation of comfort, if not of 'fit'" (Ewen and Ewen 1982:163). In the United States, from the 1800s to the 1870s, such shops were known as "slop shops" and the clothing they sold as "slop clothes," the analogy being with the slops put out for pigs. (The famous American haberdashers Brooks Brothers began as a slop shop in 1810.) Following the California gold rush of 1849, the market for functional and uniform clothing for working men moved to the West Coast. The gold diggers, miners and lumbermen who arrived in San Francisco to make their fortunes or simply to find work were outfitted in the durable clothing produced by manufacturers such as Levi Strauss. The denims of the 1850s were clothes designed to withstand the wear and tear of hard labor, and their riveted seam construction was borrowed from technology used in the manufacture of horse blankets. Like the other ready-to-wear garments of the period, they were mass produced, loose and ill-fitting.

Another major segment of the ready-to-wear market in the 1850s was the black slave workforce of the southern plantations. In a period when the Singer sewing machine company advertised a "new, improved sewing machine especially adapted to the making up of Negro clothing," it was common for ready-to-wear clothing to be referred to as "slops and Negro clothing." Further expansion of the industry came with the Civil War and the demand for mass-produced military uniforms. The Civil War gave a particular boost to the garment industry in New York and led to some limited attempt to provide ready-to-wear clothes in a wider range of sizes with better standards of fit. After the war many of the factories that had been producing military uniforms turned their energies to the production of low-priced men's suits; at the same time, in response to the increased mobility of women in a developing urban and industrial world, women's clothing also began to be mass-produced. The manufacturers now sought to replicate tailor-made or custom-made garments in mass-produced form and concentrated on quality and fit as well as economy. This was the era of the sweatshops, of an industry described by Ewen and Ewen as "promoting dreams and propounding misery." Initially organized by German-Jewish immigrants who entered the men's clothing industry in the 1850s, the mass market in styled clothing was later greatly influenced by the influx of Russian-Jewish entrepreneurs who thronged into New York between 1882 and 1915 to escape the savage pogroms of czarist Russia. Stephen Birmingham describes the impact of these entrepreneurs:

The tailors and seamstresses of the old country were going into the fashion business. What could be riskier or more unpredictable than the whims of fashion? Yet it was apparent that some East Side cloak-and-suiters were prospering. It made no sense. (What was overlooked was that the former Russian tailors had brought with them the concept of sizing, which was already revolutionizing the garment industry; before the Eastern Europeans, all men's or women's ready-to-wear was sold in one or two, or at the most three sizes.) . . . Once they had mastered the mechanics of the garment industry—the machines that had been unavailable in the old country—they were able to introduce to it literally thousands of innovations, to perfect and revolutionize the industry. With the new techniques of mass production, they were able to offer women stylish, well-fitting clothes off the racks at low prices, and by 1920 fashion was available to even the lowliest waitress or shopgirl. They had invented American fashion. (Birmingham 1984:76–77)

Innovations in the marketing and distribution of ready-to-wear garments were also led by Jewish entrepreneurs. Julius Rosenwald, an early wholesaler of sweatshop suits, eventually became president of Sears Roebuck. By the

1920s fashion goods for women were a major feature of mail-order catalogues, and the Sears Roebuck catalogue, "America's Dream Book," was the leader in its field. In addition, ready-to-wear departments had, by the start of World War I, become standard in all the big department stores, and advertising of ready-to-wear clothes was a common feature of mass circulation newspapers. Mass fashion was now an established aspect of a burgeoning mass production, mass consumption society, and fashion, once the prerogative of a leisured aristocratic elite and of an economically privileged middle class, became available to all. As early as 1902 the social worker, reformer and peace activist Jane Addams was asking, "Have we worked out our democracy further in regard to clothes than anything else?"[2]

FASHION AND CONSUMER SOVEREIGNTY

The trickle-down theory of fashion is based on haute couture traditions of fashion leadership among a small elite, an elite that in turn may be considerably influenced by the dictates of top designers in London, Paris, New York or Tokyo. It is a model of the fashion world that suggests that most consumers have little influence or control over the prevailing fashions of the time, a model where fashion sovereignty rests predominantly with designers and couturiers who have access to influential fashion leaders. With the development of the mass fashion market, however, comes a suggestion that the fashion world is democratic and responds to the needs and tastes of the population or segments of the population, a suggestion that in some respects, at least, the consumer is sovereign in the world of fashion. The development of ready-to-wear fashions has been seen as a prime example of the responsiveness of the fashion world to the needs of consumers and as indicative of a shift in the fashion industry away from dictating clothing styles toward responding to public tastes, a move from authoritarianism to democracy.

Fashion history provides many examples of both "top-down" and "bottom-up" modes of fashion change. On occasions the dictates of Paris have been ignored or rejected by consumers. In 1921, for example, veils suddenly and dramatically lost popularity. Notwithstanding the attempts of indignant and fearful veil manufacturers to convince women that Paris approved of veils, the veil business collapsed overnight. In 1970 the midi skirt, a Paris-led fashion change, was a fiasco, earning the midi the epithet "the Edsel of fashion." A year earlier the maxi skirt had proved a similar disaster, in spite of the tremendous fanfare and considerable deception that heralded its launching—magazines and newspapers printed photographs of New York and London street scenes populated with maxi-clad models disguised as passersby. In the early 1980s knickerbockers were similarly short-lived, leaving many manufacturers and retailers with embarrassingly large unsold stocks. At other times, as with Amelia Bloomer, consumer needs and demands have been unable to turn the dictates of Paris-led fashion houses.

And in some cases Paris-led fashions have been accepted in spite of strident public opposition. In 1947, for example, the first collection of designer Christian Dior, which introduced the New Look, created a sensation in the fashion world and a furor in the political one.

When Paris was liberated in August 1944, the British and Americans, whose clothing was rationed and restricted under wartime regulations, were astonished to find that haute couture had survived under German occupation. There was an outcry at the extravagant styles and luxury on show in the Paris fashion houses at a time when the French government was appealing for foreign aid to help clothe the ordinary population. The result was that by the autumn of 1945 Paris fashions were less flamboyant and wasteful and the amount of material in a dress was limited to three meters. Christian Dior's New Look of 1947, however, launched during the austerity of post-war reconstruction, renewed the controversy:

What was shocking after so many years of shortages was the amount of material used in Dior's skirt. One day dress with an 18-inch waist had 50 yards of stuff in the skirt. Others had 20 to 30 yards of flute-pleated tweed. Evening gowns were even fuller. How could a woman with a limited number of clothing coupons afford such creations? Such extravagance could not be copied exactly, but by the end of the year even ready-to-wear manufacturers were adopting an impression of style, with longer skirts, although using very much less material. (de Marly 1980:201–2)

For many in the fashion business the New Look seemed to mark the end of the drabness of the immediate post-war years and the reinstatement of Paris as the authoritative world fashion leader. Femininity returned to women's clothes, replacing the utilitarian wartime styles. In Britain, however, the president of the Board of Trade, Sir Stafford Cripps, denounced the New Look and argued that there should be a law to stop it. A Labour member of Parliament, Bessie Braddock, said that the longer skirt of the New Look was "the ridiculous whim of idle people" who should be doing something more useful with their time than worrying about the length of their skirts. An article in the British magazine Picture Post, under the headline "Paris Forgets This Is 1947," argued that Dior's New Look marked a return to Edwardian days "when fashion was the prerogative of the leisured wealthy woman, and not the everyday concern of typist, saleswoman or housewife." Nevertheless, in spite of such opposition in Britain, Norman Hartnell, dress designer to the Royal Family, presented a special private showing of the Dior collection to the Queen, Princess Margaret and the Duchess of Kent at the French embassy. The British royals were captivated and soon Princess Margaret was wearing the New Look. With the French government promoting the new fashion with showings at its embassies around the globe, other influential fashion leaders, including Eva Peron in Argentina, were also quickly won over to the look that dominated women's fashion for the next ten years. Maison Dior became the most important haute couture house of the period much to the satisfaction of Marcel Boussac, the textile magnate who financed Christian Dior.

The topsy-turvy world of fashion, with its interplay of elite and street fashions, of aristocratic and popular trend-setting, is nicely caught by Ewen and Ewen in tracing the changing role of blue denim jeans from the 1850s to modern times. In the 1850s, when blue jeans were a symbol of deprivation and sweat, it would have been inconceivable that the fashionable would consider wearing these proletarian and peasant dungarees. By the 1930s the movies were beginning to establish for jeans an image of rugged individualism as the clothing of cowboys, "icons of a noble, rural simplicity": "Blue jeans were conspicuous within the moral landscape of media Americana. On the screen these pants taunted the imaginations of city folk as emblems of a simpler uncorrupted life." It became acceptable for affluent consumers to wear such clothes at home or in the garden. In the 1950s blue denim jeans, once a piece of Americana, became a symbol of rejection of American values, particularly the conservative values of a burgeoning consumer society. In the mid–1960s student activists and anti–Vietnam War demonstrators adopted denim as a symbol of protest, as anti-fashion and anti-uniform. Later in the 1960s feminists adopted blue jeans as a weapon in their fight against the passive femininity imposed upon them by the fashion world, the "cloth of actions and labor" becoming an "emblem of liberation." By 1980, in contrast, jeans were a $5 billion industry and a fashion mainstay, and the status-conscious designer jeans of Gloria Vanderbilt, Jordache, Calvin Klein, Bon Jour and others, available in a variety of colors, textures, fabrics and fit were far removed from the proletarian origins and counterculture uses of their forebears. In such garments, wrote Ewen and Ewen, women were "hobbled in the finery of freedom."

Jeans are the facsimile of freedom; brought to us by models who are tucked—painfully—into a skin-tight fit. They are the universal symbol of individualism and western democracy; mass produced clothing of workers, embellished by the imprimatur of Paris, the home of haute couture since the time of Louis XIV. They are the vestments of liberated women, cut to impose the postures of Victorianism: corsets with the *look* of freedom and motion. (Ewen and Ewen 1982:114–15)

In the world of fashion, then, changes may originate in quite opposite worlds, develop and mesh or collide in unexpected ways. Mass ready-to-wear fashions may derive from trend-setting displays by prominent figures in the social or entertainment world, and the labels of top couturiers be attached to the once-unfashionable garb of working men and women. And even blue denim jeans, that most American of garments, finds it linguistic origins in Europe, in the cloth imported into America in the early 1800s known as "jene fustian" (from the French word *Genes* for Genoa, the Italian city where it was manufactured) and later, when it was manufactured in Nimes, France, as "serge de Nimes."

Increasing affluence and leisure gradually brought fashion garments to a wider segment of the population. In the post-war period the bulk of the income of even the haute couture salons began to be derived from mass sales rather than from servicing a wealthy or aristocratic clientele. However, fashions available to all are inevitably dependent upon mass production and mass marketing methods so that, ironically, a growing freedom of choice, and increasing democratization and consumer sovereignty in the fashion world, is dependent upon a substantial degree of uniformity in materials and styling. The success of the fashion industry in catering to the needs of consumers, suggest Ewen and Ewen, has rested in the capacity of the industry to produce and distribute standardized goods under the guise of satisfying demands for self-expression and individual choice:

Fashion, perhaps more than any other area of consumption, was a piece of the marketplace that displayed an interaction between spontaneous choice and mass-produced goods. The process by which social desire was translated into commodified forms was more present within the realm of fashion—on the surface of things—than anywhere else in the unfolding consumer society. This is why the term "manipulative" is inadequate to describe fashion merchandising, although the corporate profit motive certainly plays its part in the drama. The capitalist process of producing fashion on a mass scale, rather, was a fusion of expressed, popular desire and the powerful ability to replicate that materialization in a mass-produced, mass-marketed form. (Ewen and Ewen 1982:229)

Ewen and Ewen cite the development of boutique styles of merchandising in large department stores as an effective example of this process. By creating the aura of a small shop within a mass-selling location, the retailer is striving to individualize every sale, for "if clothing is a symbolic route to individual freedom, all connections to the mass are best denied." The dynamic of mass fashion, they argue, lies in the tension and interaction between fashion's images of individual freedom and spontaneity and the uniformity imposed by mass production ready-to-wear garments; it is a dynamic that highlights a condition of contemporary life: "The tensions between spontaneity and uniformity speak to the issue of what it means to be a person, living in the shadows of commercial enterprise, striving for the democratic objective of self-determination for all."

THE COMMERCIALIZATION OF THE SELF

Fashion is a medium through which individuals and groups establish an identity for themselves in society. Blue jeans, flower power, radical chic, punk rock, new wave, and rap flash all contained fashion elements asserting individual and group values against the anonymity of urban life. In dress, people can establish personal, idiosyncratic identities of their own or they can conform to group norms. As already indicated, work clothes in particular tend to symbolize bonds of community and commitment to the group and to be influenced by formal dress codes, partly to assert the status of the work group and partly to conform to the expectations of others. Leisurewear, in contrast, tends to provide more opportunities for expressions of individuality. Fashion therefore provides, on the one hand, opportunities for the satisfaction, expression and assertion of uniqueness and, on the other hand, opportunities to satisfy and express a sense of belonging to the group.

The power of fashion norms and conventions is indicated by the fact that as individuals we can begin to change our perceptions of ourselves by changing our dress, that we can come to think of ourselves as modest or immodest, conforming or nonconforming by reference to our dress behaviors rather than by other indicators. Clothing comes to be not simply an expression of character and personality but, rather, a definer of character and personality; we become what we wear; image dictates substance. "If you are not in fashion," wrote Lord Chesterfield in 1750, "you are nobody." As a consequence physical health has been critically linked at times with not only fashion and dress but mental health too. Robert and Jeanette Lauer (1981) write about the "Out-of-Fashion Trauma Syndrome," where anxieties about dress and appearance create mental health problems. In the nineteenth century, they argue, fashion was frequently seen as inhibiting and subverting individual psychological development, whereas in the twentieth century the more positive aspects of fashion in developing self-esteem and self-confidence have been stressed—reflecting the idea, captured in a remark quoted by Herbert Spencer, that the consciousness of being perfectly well-dressed may "bestow a peace such as religion cannot give."

It is particularly in the city or urban environment that dress has become a medium for the display of individuality, a medium for self-advertisement and personal social competitiveness. "One of the chief values of clothing," wrote Elizabeth Hurlock (1971), "is that it enables people to advertise themselves in a way that will win the attention and admiration of others. Many who lack any ability and could not hope to rise above the 'average' on their merits alone, find a satisfactory outlet for this desire for recognition through the medium of dress." As early as the 1920s, Ewen and Ewen report (1982:230), a department store in Los Angeles—Bullock's—was segmenting its female customers into six personality types and promoting fashion sales accordingly. In selecting clothes in terms of these types—Romantic (slender and youthful), Statuesque (tall, remote and blonde), Artistic (enigmatic and "foreign"), Picturesque (soft outlines), Modern, or Conventional (older, stouter and economical)—customers were essentially buying an image or projection of personality, buying a personal and social identity. And the psychologist J. C. Flugel (1966) classified individuals into various types—rebellious, resigned, unemotional, prudish, dutiful, protected, supported, sublimated, self-satisfied—in terms of their attitudes to clothes, clothing choices in this case being seen as an expression of individual personality. In ways such as these, argue Ewen and Ewen, clothing becomes an arena of social dialogue in which individuals express their desires and symbolically seek to satisfy those desires: "Within the expansive parameters of fashion, questions of *class; sexuality* and *gender*; and conflicting vectors of *resistance* and *conformity* have played themselves out visibly and dramatically. In a consumer society, the language and meaning of objects are fused with those of the marketplace" (Ewen and Ewen 1982:233).

It is not surprising to find a close link between the symbolism associated with dress and ideas as to a person's character and personality. The word *personality* is derived from the Latin *persona*, a mask worn by an actor, and has connotations of a presentation of a controlled image for public or private consumption. Character, too, may take on a protean quality, as changeable as clothing fashions. Traditionally character and personality were thought of as relatively fixed and immutable aspects of an individual's identity, suggesting an underlying core of predictability and stability. Such a view has been reinforced by plays, novels and films in which people are expected to act consistently and coherently "in character." But in the twentieth century character and personality have come to be viewed as in part artificial creations, as "the presentation of self in everyday life" in which people project images of themselves that they are often unable to maintain in reality. In the modern urban environment, where individuals find themselves playing a wide variety of roles that may be difficult to reconcile with each other, the adoption of an integrating persona is one way of reducing dissonance and confusion. In the words of Logan Pearsall Smith, "My clothes keep my various selves buttoned up together and enable (them) . . . to pass themselves off as one person."

Personality can become a commodity in itself, a commodity that can be marketed, and this marketing of personality is integrally linked with clothing styles, codes and fashions. Erich Fromm wrote about the development of the "personality market," where success depends largely on the presentation and packaging of the self rather than on ability. People develop a marketing orientation toward themselves, he suggested; they come to experience themselves as commodities that are valued in terms of their *exchange* value, that is, in terms of the price they will fetch in the market, rather than in terms of their *use* value:

The fact that in order to have success it is not sufficient to have the skill and equipment for performing a given task but that one must be able to "put across" one's personality in competition with many others shapes the attitude toward oneself. If it were enough for the purpose of making a living to rely on what one knows and what one can do, one's self-esteem would be in proportion to one's capacities, that is, to one's use value; but since success depends largely on how one sells one's personality, one experiences oneself as a commodity, or rather simultaneously as the seller and the commodity to be sold. A person is not concerned with life and happiness, but with becoming saleable. (Fromm 1947:77–78)

Personality, then, may, in the modern world, be packaged, labelled and branded like a commodity, an integral part of the packaging, labelling and branding being through the medium of clothes. The individual striving for success, suggested Fromm, has to be in fashion on the personality market and has, therefore, both to know what kind of personality is most in demand and how to adapt the presentation of his or her persona to develop those qualities that can best be sold:

Thus, for instance, respectability is sometimes desirable. The salesman in certain branches of business ought to impress the public with those qualities of reliability, soberness and respectability which were genuine in many a businessman of the nineteenth century. Now one looks for a man who instills confidence because he looks as if he had these qualities; what this man sells on the personality market is his ability to look the part; what kind of person is behind that role does not matter and is nobody's concern. (Fromm 1947:84–85)

The end product of this marketing orientation toward one's own personality is, argued Fromm, a high degree of personal insecurity. An individual's self-esteem becomes bound up with fulfilling the desires of others as expressed in the values of the marketplace. Image, not substance, becomes the measure of personal worth. This was a theme developed in Christopher Lasch's book *The Culture of Narcissism* (1980). Lasch argued that an increasingly theatrical approach to life creates "an escalating cycle of self-consciousness—a sense of the self as a performer under the constant scrutiny of friends and strangers." Indicative of this approach were some of the self-help manuals of the 1970s, books such as Robert Ringer's *Winning through Intimidation* (1975), Michael Korda's *Power! How to Get It, How to Use It* (1975), and Robert Shook's *Winning Images* (1977). These books unabashedly insisted that impression management and developing winning images—the appearance and reputation of a winner—were the way to power and success and counted for more than substantive performance or achievement. "Power dressing" is an important element in a winning image; thus Korda, for example, advised his readers on the appropriate briefcase to carry and footwear to buy, Gucci loafers being "power shoes." Like Andy Kagle in Heller's *Something Happened,* if you are unsuccessful, then you should reconsider the way you are dressing and marketing yourself. Other books in a similar vein were John T. Molloy's *Dress for Success* (1975) and *The Woman's Dress for Success Book* (1977) and William Thourlby's *You Are What You Wear: The Key to Business Success* (1978). Molloy argued that his "wardrobe engineering" principles were based on scientific research and opinion polls. His books, suggested Alison Lurie, instruct business men and women "on how to select their clothes so that they will look efficient, authoritative and reliable even when they are incompetent, weak and shifty."

FASHION AND THE BUSINESS MODE

Clothing fashions, then, serve a number of functions in society. In addition to satisfying basic needs for warmth and comfort, clothes provide opportunities for display. Through displays in dress we can establish and assert a personal identity, differentiate ourselves from the group or mass, and "create" or express personality or character. We can declare our membership of leisure and occupational groups and, by conforming to the dress codes of our chosen group, satisfy needs for security and a sense of belonging. Through dress we can indicate our social status, wealth and power, thereby competing economically and socially to enhance our prestige. Norms of modesty and morality may be defined through dress and prevailing attitudes toward gender roles articulated. In addition, the uniqueness of a particular culture, or the spirit of a particular era, may be expressed through clothing fashions.

Fashion businesses have long recognized and capitalized on these social and cultural elements in clothing purchase decisions. They have exploited the economic advantages available in an industry where tastes may change rapidly and where sales may be increased by introducing new styles rather than by improving quality or reducing price. They have exploited the social and status competition implicit in many fashion purchases and used brand names, particularly those associated with European fashion houses and designers like Christian Dior, Jean Patou, Gucci, and Pierre Cardin to sell clothing and accessories at a premium price. They have recognized the willingness of customers to pay for newness and impermanence and to value goods for their symbolic value as much as for their use value. In the United States they have perpetuated the myth of the superiority of French fashions by putting fake French labels in American-made clothes, even though the French fashion trade is dependent commercially on the U.S. market. The fetishism of designer-label clothes has led to a price structure that reflects advertising budgets rather than the quality of materials or of manufacturing methods; in the words of Alison Lurie (1981:133), "Cotton T-shirts that faded or shrank out of shape after a few washings but had the word Dior printed on them were preferred to better-behaved but anonymous T-shirts."

Although there are clearly a variety of commercial opportunities for business entrepreneurs to exploit in the fashion marketplace, opportunities that arise from the very nature of fashion itself, the role of business in *creating* fashion and fashion changes is less clear. Yet the question as to how fashion changes are initiated is critical to understanding the roles of business in the fashion marketplace and, indeed, the role of business in social change generally. The polar positions are that, on the one hand, business institutions *initiate* fashion changes in order to maximize their profit opportunities and, on the other, fashion changes are initiated *outside* the business world and are then picked up, reinforced and diffused by business entrepreneurs. Candidates for initiating fashion changes from *within* the business world are designers and couturiers; manufacturers, especially the manufacturers of cloth; retailers, influenced particularly by their buyers; and independent entrepreneurs. There are three candidates for initiating fashion changes from *outside* the business world. First are the elite fashion leaders who dictate their ideas to designers and couturiers and are sufficiently visible and influential to have those ideas imitated by the mass market. Second are the trend-setters of the streets whose innovative dress ideas are picked up and copied by segments of the population and subsequently exploited by alert entrepreneurs for sale to the mass market (what the black dude is wearing today, suggested Alison Lurie [1981:99], is apt to be in *Esquire* in a year or so. "Urban blacks are the dandies of today, the true heirs of Beau Brummell"). And third are the "sovereign" consumers whose dress "needs" are ferreted out by astute market research methods and then translated into the manufacture of fashions that customers will buy out of instant recognition that their "real" needs can now be satisfied. The claims of technology and technological developments as instigators of fashion changes have already been discussed in the context of the development of ready-to-wear clothes and found wanting. That the whole process of fashion change is irrational and beyond explanation is dismissed, notwithstanding the many apparently unpredictable aspects of the fashion world.

Claims that designers and couturiers are the originators of fashion changes are exemplified in the epithets attached to fashion "dictators" such as Worth, and fashion "dukes" such as Karl Lagerfeld. Adburgham argued for the pre-eminent role of the designer:

The designing of clothes is the most significant of all the decorative arts. A dress designer catches the spirit of the day, the feeling in the air, and interprets it in clothes before other designers have begun to twitch at the nerve ends. . . . Moreover, dress designing is not only the most significant decorative art but also the most important, because it is the most personal. Clothes, unlike furniture and furnishings, china, glass, light fittings, wallpapers, *objets d'art* and *objets domestiques*, are things we must take with us, wherever we go. (Adburgham 1966:39–40)

Others have argued, however, that the designer and couturier can only initiate change as fast as his or her clientele will permit, and that the haute couture clientele has traditionally been a very conservative one.

Many couturiers started as small independent or family businesses: Balenciaga started with a little dress business in Spain, Jeanne Lanvin grew from a slowly increasing demand for her children's clothes, Jean Patou started with a small dress shop, as did Poiret. Schiaparelli, who later captured the custom of many film actresses, started by making clothes in the attic where she lived. It was not until after World War II that international companies began to move increasingly into the ownership of couture houses. Nevertheless, what Lurie called the conspiracy theory of fashion change, "the idea that the adoption of new styles is simply the result of a plot by greedy designers and manufacturers and fashion editors," that fashion changes are the result of "brainwashing by commercial interests," has a lengthy history. In Lurie's view it is an idea that leaves insufficient room for the influence of public taste on fashion changes:

It is not true that the public will wear anything suggested to it, nor has it ever been true. Ever since fashion became big business, designers have proposed a bewildering array of styles every season. A few of these have been selected or adapted by manufacturers for mass production, but only a certain proportion of them have caught on. . . . Garments that reflect what we are or want to be at the moment will be purchased and worn, and those that do not will not, however frantically they may be ballyhooed. (Lurie 1981:11–12)

Mary Quant supported the idea that the key role of the successful ready-to-wear designer was to anticipate shifts in public taste and bring forward fashion ideas appropriate to the spirit of the time: "Good designers—like clever newspapermen—know that to have any influence they must keep in step with public needs . . . public opinion . . . and that intangible 'something in the air.' They must catch the spirit of the day and interpret it in clothes before other designers begin to twitch at the nerve ends" (Quant 1966:74). Inspiration, she argued, could come from many sources: from a Garbo film revival, from Rudolf Nureyev, from a James Bond movie, from television programs, from experimentation, or from visiting places "where you can see the early signs of some new fad or craze beginning to develop amongst the most up and coming trend-setters." But whatever the source of inspiration, it had to be tempered by an appreciation of the possibilities and limitations of mass production methods. Ready-to-wear designers had to work in close cooperation with manufacturers:

The designer has got to learn to drop all sorts of things she wants and sacrifice all kinds of ideas simply because these are ideas which cannot be produced within the price range of a mass market.
    Just as it is pointless to design a Rolls-Royce, then pare it down and down until it is supposed to fit into the mass market of the Mini Minor, so it is pointless in fashion to create a couture design and imagine it can be adequately produced cheaply in quantity.
    You must know your medium from the beginning; from the first moment the designer's pencil goes on paper. Fashion must be created from the start for mass production with full knowledge of mass production methods. (Quant 1966:116)

A sophisticated analysis of the commercialization of fashion is offered by Neil McKendrick. McKendrick demonstrates that consumer behavior was so rampant in late eighteenth-century England and the acceptance of commercial attitudes so pervasive that there can be no doubting that by 1800 the first of the world's consumer societies had emerged. In addition late eighteenth-century England was a society where the desire for novelty and change was so extensive that Dr. Johnson complained that men were even "to be hanged in a new way." McKendrick argues that until this period the history of costume had been remarkably stable and that various forces had been working against frequent fashion changes—poverty, custom and tradition, a stable society with established social strata, and the general scarcity of fashion objects. Thus, for example, in Japan the kimono had remained virtually unchanged for perhaps a thousand years. What, therefore, McKendrick asks, gave rise to the fashion explosion of eighteenth-century England, to a situation in which large numbers of people in society "felt that they *must* be in fashion, whether they liked it or not, even to the point of ridicule. It was no longer forbidden fruit or an atypical social need. It was now . . . socially required of one to be in fashion" (McKendrick 1982:40).

McKendrick's answer is that the fashion explosion was led by commercial interests, that "commerce increasingly took over the manipulation and direction of fashion. Men and women increasingly *had* to wear what commerce dictated, had to raise or lower their hems or their heels at the dictates of the cloth manufacturers and the shoe sellers." Certainly there were favorable social and economic circumstances for this fashion explosion, particularly in better communications between London and provincial England as a result of new canals, turnpike roads and a more efficient coaching system. But it was the role played by businessmen and entrepreneurs that was of vital importance. The eighteenth century was a period when a wide range of commercial techniques were developed in retailing—loss leaders, self-service schemes, inertia-selling campaigns, product differentiation policies, market segmentation, mass advertising campaigns—a portfolio of techniques that the modern marketing manager would be proud to sport. And in the world of fashion merchandising eighteenth-century England saw the burgeoning of new means of spreading fashion news in addition to the traditional hawkers and pedlars; new were the fashion plates, fashion prints, and fashion magazines, as well as the advertisements in newspapers and journals and in ladies' pocketbooks and almanacs. Epitomizing these commercial developments, suggests McKendrick, was the development of the English fashion doll.

Records of the fashion doll date back to 1396. Traditionally the doll, a fully dressed, elaborately coiffured mannequin, often life-size, was brought over from Paris to give the English court an indication of current French modes in dress, hairstyles and accessories. By the beginning of the eighteenth century one doll a year was the norm and, after the Queen and her ladies-in-waiting had assimilated the doll's fashion lessons, it would be passed on to the London fashion shops and then further afield: "One was advertised in *The New England Weekly Journal* in 1733 where it was announced that for two shillings you could look at it, and for seven shillings take it away." The spread of fashion intelligence in this way was slow and was subject to the dictates of the French court and the control of the English one rather than to the interests of business. By the 1790s an English fashion doll had supplanted the French one. It was a flat fashion model about eight inches high cut out of cardboard, was printed by the thousands and eventually came to be sold for a few pence. It was packed in a neat paper envelop together with six sets of costume so that different combinations of dress and coiffure could be fitted to it. A cheap and effective form of advertising, it was also marketed as a children's toy. Different sets of the dolls were available, specifically aimed at different markets, the market being segmented along class and professional lines. The fashion doll was, writes McKendrick, "a vivid symbol of both the extensions of the market and the means by which the market was extended":

By the end of the eighteenth century the competitive, socially emulative aspect of fashion was being consciously manipulated by commerce in pursuit of increased consumption. This new fashion world was one in which entrepreneurs were trying deliberately to induce fashionable change, to make it rapidly available to as many as possible and yet to keep it so firmly under their control that the consuming public could be sufficiently influenced to buy at the dictate of *their* fashion decisions, at the convenience of *their* production lines. (McKendrick 1982:43)

There are, in sum, a variety of theories and part theories setting out to explain fashion change, an indication in itself of the complexity of the issues involved in such an analysis. In the course of this and the previous chapter many of these theories, like the trickle-down versus bottom-up theory, the time spirit theory, the Veblen effect, and the diffusion theory, have been touched upon and the respective roles of technology and of the consumer in fashion changes have been discussed. The role of business, if not always clear in its details, is certainly central to an understanding of fashion change. Business has not merely mirrored fashion changes but, at times, both created such changes and exploited and reinforced changes that have been initiated elsewhere in the community. In the world of fashion, business has been an integral part of the process of social change, creating, controlling, following or reinforcing fashion behavior.

Essentially there have been two modes of business practice in the fashion world, a strategic managerial mode and an opportunistic entrepreneurial one. These two modes are summarized in Figure 2. The first mode, the managerial mode, operates on the assumption that the fashion market can be successfully managed. In this mode the appropriate perspective for a

Figure 2
Business Modes in the World of Fashion

	MANAGERIAL	ENTREPRENEURIAL
(1) Nature of marketplace	Manageable	Exploitable
(2) Business perspective	Strategic	Opportunistic
(3) Model for fashion change and process of diffusion	Fashion leaders and trickle-down; from elite to mass; design and sell.	Trend setters and bottom-up; from streets to mass; copy and sell.
(4) Sovereignty	Designers; elite clientele; manufacturers; retailers; consumers.	Consumers
(5) Dominant images	Dictation; tyranny	Freedom; folly; Irrationality
(6) Role of business	Proactive; agent of social change; creating values.	Reactive; reflector and reinforcer of social change; carrying values.

fashion business is a strategic one in which changes in the market are seen to be largely predictable and controllable by business interests. A relatively stable group of elite fashion leaders are the focal point for the initiation of fashion changes and designers work with this group in mind as a vehicle for establishing new fashion trends that are subsequently to be diffused to the mass market. However, this mode of operation is not always successful, and fashion history shows examples both of business-led innovations that have been rejected by consumers and of new business-led trends that have swept the market regardless of consumer objections. Even fashion writers themselves have been horrified by some of the clothes that consumers have been persuaded to adopt: "The shadow of a sinister silhouette has fallen across Europe," wrote Adburgham in 1957. "A shapeless shape, an amorphous morp, is advancing upon us from Italy and France. The waistless sack-dress with all its ugly implications stalks across fashion's glossy pages."

The entrepreneurial mode, in contrast, recognizes some of the unpredictable aspects of fashion behavior and of consumer tastes in dress. At its most extreme this mode is captured in the suggestion by René König that the fashion world is one of constant uncertainty characterized by "a completely open-minded curious expectation. . . . An element of pure speculation therefore remains with every fashion collection: fashion-orientated behavior is not only unpredictable as regards the moment of change, it is also selective and lets itself be guided by the most varied external influences" (König 1973:78–79). This view of the fashion marketplace stresses the opportunities that rapid shifts in taste, and the faddish, the whimsical and the irrational, provide for exploitation by the alert speculator and entrepreneur. Fashion trends are seen as starting in the streets rather than in the design offices of haute couture houses. There is no stable group of trend-setters, and the initial impetus for change may come from such disparate sources as black teenagers, counter-culture groups and television programs. The entrepreneur quickly picks up and copies street trends and brings them to the mass market. Whereas in the managerial mode a fashion business may be a proactive agent of social change, in the entrepreneurial mode fashion businesses act as reflectors and reinforcers of social change. Whether creating or carrying social values, however, fashion businesses clearly have a key role in the development and transmission of culture.

NOTES

1. Karl Lagerfeld, "The Uncrowned Duke of Drop-dead Swank," *Time*, 23 April 1984.

2. Quoted in Ewen and Ewen 1982:109.

CHAPTER 10

Packaged Authenticity: Tourism and Culture

FROM GRAND TOUR TO COOK'S TOUR

One could say that every year between July and August some millions of people in advanced industrial countries take vacations, carrying cameras and taking photographs which they then show to their friends and family. Or one could say that every year, in rarely explicit, usually implicit, accord with certain travel agencies, the boards of directors of Kodak and the major camera firms decide to produce a certain number of cameras which will travel around the world, while a certain number of other cameras sold in previous years will remain in circulation. These decisions once made, the cameras set out on their travels with a corresponding number of people to operate them. (Goldmann 1981:88)

Lucien Goldmann's alternative explanations of the travels of cameras were made in the context of a discussion of the relative claims of people versus commodities as the driving force of the modern world. The power of commercial objects and commercial images to transform and control our lives, a theme touched upon throughout this book, resurfaces in the literature on the psychology and sociology of mass tourism.

The most cursory observation of modern tourist behavior quickly exposes a triple consumption pattern at play. First, there is "anticipation as consumption," the pleasure derived from poring over travel brochures and planning travel itineraries. Second, there is the consumption of the tourist attraction itself in its particular locale. The photography of ancient monuments, the enjoyment of a particular cuisine or climate or topography, taking part in the experiences and entertainment available in the locality, and the purchasing of artifacts and souvenirs, these may all be part of this aspect of the overall tourist experience. Third is the re-consumption of facets of this experience in the home locale. This may involve the re-enactment of events through traveller's tales, photographs and film, the giving of gifts purchased on one's travels,[1] the incorporation into one's own lifestyle of foreign modes of dress and behavior, or the adoption of words of a foreign language into everyday greetings or conversation. It is the possibility of this re-consumption that primarily drives modern tourism, that defines the nature of tourist attractions and differentiates the structures of tourist markets. The nature of modern tourism, then, can be better understood by reference to the home cultures of tourists than by reference to those foreign cultures that tourists visit.

Travel for pleasure, as opposed to travel on business, or travel for religious reasons such as a pilgrimage to Mecca or to consult the Oracle at Delphi or to visit the shrine of St. Thomas à Becket at Canterbury, is not a modern phenomenon. Festival and carnival travel was a feature of the ancient world. As early as the eighth century B.C. visitors from Europe and the Middle East travelled to Greece for the Olympic Games, and in the fourth century B.C. thousands flocked annually to Ephesus (now in Turkey) to be entertained by acrobats, jugglers, magicians and a variety of animal acts (Mayo and Jarvis 1981:6). The roads built by the Romans for military reasons also opened up opportunities for ordinary citizens to travel over greater distances in some degree of comfort. Spas and coastal resorts became popular places for city dwellers to go in the summer months. There they could relax in mineral baths and enjoy a variety of theatrical and sporting entertainments. The more affluent Roman citizens could travel overseas for holidays in Egypt, Greece or Babylon.

In England from the late seventeenth century on, the "Grand Tour" of Continental Europe was *de rigeur* for the young aristocrat of means in pursuit of taste or the accoutrements of taste. The phrase was introduced by Richard Lassels, who wrote in *The Voyage of Italy* (1670) that "no man understands Livy and Caesar . . . like him who hath made *The Grand Tour* of France and Italy." For the leisured class—a leisurely Grand Tour could last up to three years—overseas travel was seen as a way of rounding out one's education, particularly since that education was so strongly grounded in classical literature. The early form of the Grand Tour was the classical Grand Tour. It focused on galleries, museums, public buildings and historical and religious monuments, largely excluding in the process any significant interest in the contemporary life and culture of the region. With the development of the romantic movement, however, the attention of travellers shifted from the man-made world to the natural world. The romantic Grand Tour incorporated scenic attractions, particularly those of mountain areas such as the Scottish Highlands and the European Alps. It emphasized a renunciation of the artificiality of society and the industrializing, mechanizing "fever of the world" in favor of a redemptive, if temporary, solace in nature, a "private and passionate experience of beauty and the sublime" (Urry 1990:4). "Only mountains, gorges, defiles and torrents," observed Roland Barthes, had access to the romantic travel pantheon, for only they seemed to encourage "a morality of effort and solitude," a "hybrid compound of the cult of nature and of puritanism (regeneration through clean air, moral ideas at the sight of mountain-tops, summit-climbing as civic virtue)" (Barthes 1973:74).

Others, however, were not convinced of the educational advantages of such travel, especially when the growing number of European spas began to feature in Grand Tour itineraries. Originally set up as health resorts, by the late eighteenth century many of the spas, such as that at Baden-Baden, were notable as vacation spots that provided a range of entertainments such as games, social events, public promenading, grand balls, dancing, and gambling—what J. Myerscough describes as "a concentrated urban experience of frenetic socializing for a dispersed rural elite" (quoted by Urry 1990:5). The author of the picaresque novel *Tristram Shandy*, English writer Laurence Sterne, who himself made a seven-month tour of France and Italy in 1765, described travellers as "idle people that leave their native country and go abroad for some reason or reasons which may be derived from one of these general causes—Infirmity of body, Imbecility of mind or inevitable necessity." Adam Smith, who on his return from a visit to France in 1764 devoted himself to his work on *The Wealth of Nations*, had little time for the young sons of the gentry and their Grand Tours. The travelling scion of a noble family, he observed, "commonly returns home, more conceited, more unprincipled, more dissipated, and more incapable of any serious application, either to study or to business, than he could well have become in so short a time had he lived at home." And if a French commentator is to be believed, then neither education nor tolerance were enhanced by the English tourists' experience of overseas travel: "In a hundred there are not two who seek to instruct themselves. To cover leagues of land or water; to take punch or tea at the inns; to speak ill of all nations, and to boast without ceasing of their own; that is what the crowd of the English call travelling" (Swinglehurst 1974:70). It was these travelling young Englishmen of rank and fortune, complained Fraser Rae in 1891, rather than the members of tourist groups, who gave the English in Italy a reputation as eccentric and wealthy lunatics.

In modern times a vestige of the Grand Tour idea is present in the pressures on young Australians and New Zealanders to round off their education with OE—Overseas Experience. This generally incorporates travel to London, alone or with a partner or a few friends. London is then used as a working base from which to mount periodic forays through the British Isles and to explore the countries of the European continent, either hitchhiking or with a hired car or campervan. After one or two dark English winters enduring economic and physical hardships living in the single-room flats of London's bed-sitterland, the young Aussies and Kiwis start their long migration to the sunshine of home. This may involve further travels in Canada and the United States or, for the more adventurous, travel overland to Singapore to catch a flight to Sydney, Melbourne or Auckland. OE and the overseas trip are socially valued acquisitions for young professionals and the middle classes in Australia and New Zealand. They have a similar status as conversational lubricant to that played by the weather in Britain, the state of the roads in Nigeria, the condition of your liver in France, and the Super Bowl in the United States.

Both the classical and romantic Grand Tours and OE trips of Australians and New Zealanders were structured around individual travel and extended periods of time in a foreign country. Whether travelling on foot or by campervan, speed of movement from place to place was not the essence of the experience. In contrast group tours, package tours of limited duration, mass tourism as we now know it, are dependent upon the development of transport technologies that can move large numbers of people between fixed points to fixed timetables and schedules. Initially the railway, and later the motorcoach and the plane, have been crucial in the development of tourism as opposed to travel. This development of tourism—that is, the organization of tours as a business—is particularly associated with the Englishman Thomas Cook and the growth of the business of Thomas Cook and Son.

Born at Melbourne in Derbyshire in 1808, Thomas Cook was an only child whose father died when he was four years old. At the age of ten he left school and went to work to help support his mother, who ran a small shop. After laboring work for a penny a day in the gardens of the Melbourne estate, he was apprenticed to his uncle, a wood-turner. His apprenticeship completed, he left Melbourne and went to work in Loughborough, Leicestershire, in a book-printing and book-publishing house connected with the General Baptist Association. A religious man himself, in 1828 Thomas Cook was appointed a Bible reader and village missionary for the county of Rutland. The following year he travelled 2,692 miles on his missionary work, 2,106 of them on foot (Rae 1891). In 1832 he married the daughter of a Rutland farmer and set himself up in business in Market Harborough as a wood-turner. He became an active member of the temperance movement and in 1840 founded the *Children's Temperance Magazine*. It was while walking 15 miles to a temperance meeting in Leicester the following year that he thought of the advantages of using rail travel to further the cause of the temperance movement. Consequently, with the agreement of his temperance society friends, Thomas Cook approached the Midland Counties Railway to run a special train from Leicester to Loughborough for a large public gathering being organized by the Temperance Society on 5 July 1841. The excursion train carried 570 passengers the 12 miles from Leicester to Loughborough and back for a shilling each, with a musical accompaniment provided by a brass band. Tea and buns were provided at Mrs. Paget's Park for no extra charge. Although the Mechanics' Institutes had run train excursions for their members prior to 1841, the Thomas Cook and Son jubilee history claimed that the 5 July 1841 excursion was "the first *publicly advertised* excursion train which was run in England," adding the cautious rider that "should it turn out that Mr. Thomas Cook was anticipated, he is none the less an originator, because he never heard of anyone doing what he had accomplished" (Rae 1891:23).

The success of the 1841 Loughborough excursion led to Thomas Cook's being approached by other societies for advice on the organization of similar ventures. In the following three summers he was fully occupied in organizing excursions for temperance society members and for Sunday-school children. In September 1843, for example, over 4,500 children and teachers made a day trip by train from Leicester to Derby and back. Abandoning his wood-turning business, Cook moved to Leicester. Although he continued to print and publish books, he was devoting more and more time to his tour business: "The notion of running an excursion train for the convenience of a party who were desirous of making a demonstration in favor of temperance was the exciting cause of Mr. Cook making the simplification of travel a business for himself in order that it might be a pleasure and a boon to his fellow-men" (Rae 1891:25–26). In 1844 Thomas Cook "arrived at an understanding" with the Midland Counties Railway Company's directors to make trains available for his excursions, and the following year advertised his first pleasure trip, an excursion from Leicester to Liverpool. This involved coordinating travel arrangements across four railway networks, advance visits by Thomas Cook to hotels and places where stoppages were to be made en route, and the preparation of a guide for passengers, the *Handbook of the Trip to Liverpool*:

Stoppages were to be made on the way, while arrangements were made for crossing to the Isle of Man or to Dublin, and the steamer *Eclipse* was chartered to convey excursionists to the Welsh Coast. Mr. Thomas Cook compiled, printed, and published a small guide, containing notices of the places of interest on the way, and the sights which were to be visited. (Rae 1891)

When 350 passengers landed from the *Eclipse* at Caernarvon in Wales, "one man only among the natives could speak enough English to act as guide."

If Wales was an exotic destination for Thomas Cook's Midlands excursionists, then Scotland, his next tour destination, was even more so. Since there was no rail link to Scotland at that time, Cook's tour from Leicester to Glasgow went by steamer from Fleetwood in Lancashire to Ardrossan in the Firth of Clyde. The 800-mile return trip, made by 350 tourists, cost one guinea. Along the way the local enthusiasm for tourist visitors was such that crowds gathered for their arrivals and departures, and bands, entertainment, civic welcomes and public speeches were organized on their behalf. By the end of 1850 Thomas Cook could write, "I had become so thoroughly imbued with the tourist spirit that I began to contemplate foreign trips, including the Continent of Europe, the United States, and the Eastern Lands of the

Bible" (Rae 1891:42). In 1851 he founded a travel magazine, *The Excursionist*, and organized a series of excursion trains to the Great Exhibition at the Crystal Palace in Hyde Park, London, where visitors could contemplate not only the wonders of Victorian technology but the dress designs of Frederick Worth. To enable working men and women to make the journey to London, Thomas Cook set up exhibition clubs through which would-be excursionists could accumulate their fares by the payment of weekly installments. Democratic sentiments regarding the educational and social value of such an excursion were still uppermost in Cook's mind:

The Great Exhibition is mainly indebted for its astonishing interest to the skill and industry of mechanics, artisans and other operative classes. And in many instances the honor of invention and execution which properly belongs to those classes is monopolized by the principles of manufacturers (who may be mere noodles) or the wealthy millionaire, whose gold had made him representative of the products of better men's brains and hands. (Swinglehurst 1974:35)

The development of tours of Continental Europe, of Egypt (Cook's established a regular steamer service on the Nile in 1873), the Holy Land, the United States, and New Zealand meant that the clientele for Thomas Cook's business were no longer working-class folk but increasingly drawn from the middle and leisured classes—"the English clergymen, physicians, bankers, civil engineers, and merchants, who honored me by accepting my escort to Italy last year," Cook wrote in defense of his customers in 1865. Nevertheless, travel as a vehicle of liberal education remained a cornerstone of Victorian ideology and was a viewpoint sustained and promoted by Thomas Cook throughout his life. He felt, wrote the official company historian, that "he had a mission in the world. . . . He believed that the more his fellow men saw of each other the better they would understand each other's ways, that the more the world was known by the dwellers in it, the truer would be their knowledge, and that intercourse by travel was one form, and not the least effective, of missionary enterprise" (Rae 1891:132). It was a characteristically optimistic Victorian vision of the benefits to be gained through technological development and the spread of Western, particularly British, civilization.

Not all commentators, however, were so sanguine about the development of mass tourism. Charles Lever, the British vice-consul in La Spezia, writing in *Blackwood's Magazine* under the pseudonym Cornelius O'Dowd, complained of the growing evil of the "Continental Excursionists," droves of whom were deluging the cities of Italy:

They never separate, and you see them forty in number pouring along a street with their director—now in front, now at the rear, circling round them like a sheep-dog— and really the process is as like herding as may be. I have already met three flocks, and anything so uncouth I never saw before, the men, mostly elderly, dreary, sad-

looking; the women, somewhat younger, travel-tossed and crumpled, but intensely lively, wide-awake and facetious. . . .
These Devil's dust tourists have spread over Europe, injuring our credit and damaging our character. Their gross ignorance is the very smallest of their sins. . . . Foreigners may say, "We desire to be able to pray in our churches, to hear in our theaters, to dine in our restaurants, but your people will not permit it. They come over, not in twos and threes, but in scores and hundreds, to stare and laugh at us. They deride our church ceremonies, they ridicule our cookery, they criticize our dress, they barbarize our language. How long are we to be patient under these endurances?" Take my word for it, if these excursionists go on, nothing short of another war, and another Wellington, will ever place us where we once were in the opinion of Europe. (Rae 1891:150–51; 154–55)

Charles Lever, who had in his youth beggared himself gambling in Baden-Baden, was an exemplar of eccentric English behavior in foreign climes. Not content with vilifying Thomas Cook's customers in the pages of *Blackwood's Magazine*, Lever spread the story among his Italian acquaintances that "these tourists were convicts whom the Australian colonies had refused to receive, and that they were sent to Italy by the English Government under arrangement with Mr. Thomas Cook, who was to drop a few in each Italian city, where they were let loose and suffered to go whither they pleased" (Rae 1891:151).

By the time Thomas Cook died in 1892, his firm had come, in the words of Fraser Rae (1891:11), "to be generally recognized as the terrestrial Providence of the travelling public." In that 50 years from 1841 to its 1891 jubilee, Thomas Cook and Son had gone from organizing a 12-mile excursion trip for a temperance meeting to a global travel organization. It published tour information in English, French and German. It published maps and time-tables and guide books, and it produced pamphlets and advertising materials in offices in Europe, India, the United States and Australia. It had its own banking and currency exchange department, issued its own notes and letters of credit payable at its branch offices and agencies throughout the world, and provided shipping and emigration facilities for administrators and colonists of the expanding British Empire. And almost everywhere the railway went, Thomas Cook was sure to follow. "The number of miles of railway in operation throughout the world is 360,495 and Messrs. Thomas Cook and Son supply tickets which are available over 344,739" (Rae 1891:312).

THE CULTURES OF TRAVEL AND TOURISM

During the nineteenth century, in Britain and on the Continent of Europe, travel by train progressively replaced travel by stage coach. Initial resistance to the new technology of the "mechanized horse" stemmed in part from popular fears about the dangers of railway journeys. The large-scale technological accident was a product of industrialization and took some getting

used to for people who associated catastrophes primarily with natural phenomena. In the early days of railway travel it was commonly supposed,
claimed Rae, that "no journey by rail could be undertaken without loss of
life." Whatever the merits of this claim, it was certainly the case that Victorian medical practice recognized a specific form of psychic trauma associated with train travel (Schivelbusch 1986), the forerunner of twentieth-
century fears of flying. One of the effects of tourist excursions by train,
therefore, was not only to familiarize a large number of people with a new
technological environment but to popularize the idea of a trip by train as
something to be undertaken for pleasure.[2]

Just as in the twentieth century there is nostalgia for the age of the steam
locomotive, so in the nineteenth century there was nostalgia for the days of
the stage coach. Coach travel was seen as having more "personality." In
particular, it facilitated social encounters and encouraged communication
between the passengers. Train travel in Europe was divided along class lines
from the outset, adopting the prevailing distinctions between private and
public coach travel and between those who rode inside the coach and those
who rode outside. On trains the working classes travelled in boxcars, which
initially were uncovered. The privileged classes travelled in rail carriages
that were modelled on private horse-drawn coaches. Thus the technology
of train travel was immediately cast in a cultural mold, a mold constructed
of social inequalities.[3] In addition, however, the relative smoothness of train
travel in comparison with coach travel gave literate passengers the option
of reading rather than conversing with each other. Wolfgang Schivelbusch
(1986) argues that the "exclusively bourgeois occupation" of reading while
travelling replaced the intensive conversation and social interaction so celebrated in eighteenth-century novels about coach travel. "Have you got
something to read?" was (and is) a common enquiry of the departing train
(and plane) traveller. The development of the railways stimulated the sale
of books and magazines. In Britain in the late 1840s major booksellers established stalls at railway stations. In 1848, for example, W. H. Smith ob-
tained exclusive rights to sell books and newspapers on the Birmingham
Railway, and he opened his first bookstall at Euston Station in London
(Schivelbusch 1986). Station lending libraries were also established for the
benefit of passengers.

In the United States the structures of train travel were markedly different
from those that developed in Europe. Water travel rather than land travel
influenced the design of American railway compartments. American passenger coaches were modelled on the spaciousness and openness of the
cabins and saloons of river steamboats and canal packets rather than on the
confined space of the horse-drawn carriage. The invention of the double-
axled "bogie" undercarriage in place of the rigid-axled European rolling stock
made possible the construction of a longer passenger car. It was a car more
suited not only to the large distances that were covered by the American

railroads but also to the egalitarianism of white American society: "The classless open car was economically, politically, psychologically and culturally the appropriate travel container for a democratic pioneer society, while the compartment car, on the other hand, expressed the social conditions prevailing in Europe" (Schivelbusch 1986:103).

Although the American Pullman car was safer and more comfortable than the European passenger car, it was never generally adopted by the European railroads. In Europe class consciousness, and the desire of the middle classes in particular for the maximum possible personal privacy when travelling, entrenched the three-class compartment structure as the norm. Where Pullman-style coaches were introduced, they were generally for the exclusive use of first-class passengers and aristocratic patrons. The Belgian Georges Nagelmackers, for example, was a great admirer of George Pullman's sleeping cars. In 1876 he established the Compagnie Internationale des Wagons Lits under the patronage of Leopold II, the King of the Belgians. The company provided luxury sleeping cars and restaurant cars to the national railroad networks of the European continent. It also ran its own luxury trains, the most famous of which was the Orient Express service initiated in 1883. The Orient Express is today an upmarket tourist attraction.

The social distinction between the individual traveller and the mass tourist, evident in the contrast between the snobbery associated with the Grand Tour and the vulgarity ascribed to day trippers and excursionists, was repeated in the development of motor touring in the United States in the twentieth century. The early motor tourists saw themselves as escaping from the confined structures and organized disciplines of railway timetables. For them the packaged holiday structured around train travel and chaperoned by the excursion agent was tourism. They, in contrast, were nomadic gypsies free to roam the countryside in search of excitement and adventure, travellers in the literal sense of the word where travel was work ("travail"):

As evidence of suffering and triumph, early tourists decorated their cars with banners—"Kansas City to Los Angeles," "Ocean to Ocean." Proclaiming distant origins and even more distant destinations, these appropriately worn pennants showed, in effect, what pioneers had been through. . . .

Dusty tonneau, battered fender, travel-stained khakis, weather-beaten canvas, these, too, were evidence of having gotten through. Dust was a particularly welcome symbol, a theme of many motorist signs, like the humble "Just a Little Dusty" scrawled on the rear of a road-weary Model T or the polite but proud "Pardon My Dust." Some autocampers mounted tin cans on radiators as emblems of their ascetic but functional diet, their worldly vagabondage, their defiance of more pretentious standards. In addition to physical documentation, tourists savored impressive stories of hair-raising escapades, near collisions, and ingeniously repaired radiators, to be recounted with relish and embellishment to fellow wayfarers at garages, camp fires, and hotels, or to envious neighbors at home.

For the sake of memory alone, it was good to have trouble. "The peaceful motorist who has no major trouble has a pleasant enough time," Emily Post allowed, "but after all he gets the least out of it in the way of recollections." (Belasco 1979:34)

Early motor tourism was symbolized by freedom from constraint. It was viewed as pioneering work at the frontiers of a new mobility. At the same time it was, wrote Phil Patton (1986:232–33), "a search for the old values," "a way to see America, the real country, populated by 'real Americans,'" and to see America "as if you were the first to see it: regain the sense of discovery of the first explorers and pioneers." The pioneering cultural associations of early motor tourism were picked up by the auto-manufacturing companies. Cars took on the names of explorers—De Soto, Cadillac, and Hudson, for instance.

In England Thomas Cook had seen the development of excursion travel and package holidays as providing the working classes with access to places and experiences hitherto the exclusive reserve of the rich. Similarly in the United States motor transport and car ownership were promoted as part of a general democratization of work and leisure. A 1924 Chevrolet advertisement, suggested that owning a car was like being president of one's own railroad and boosted the cultural, educational and political importance of the car:

What has been the effect of the automobile on our composite national mind?—on our social political and economic outlook?

The once poor laborer and mechanic now drives to the building operation or construction job in his own car. He is now a capitalist—the owner of a taxable asset.
. . .

Evenings and Sundays he takes his family into the country or to the now near town fifty to one hundred miles away. He has become *somebody*, has a broader and more tolerant view of the one-time cartoon hayseed and the fat-cigared plutocrat.

How can Bolshevism flourish in a motorized country having a standard of living, and thinking too high to permit the existence of an ignorant, narrow, peasant majority?

Is not the automobile entitled to the major credit in this evaluation of our standard of citizenship? (Stern and Stern 1978:21)

Using touring literature and trade journals, Warren James Belasco (1979) shows how the inexpensive, communal "squatter-anarchism" of autocamping gradually gave birth to the mass consumption anonymity of the roadside motel and its supporting fast food franchises.[4] He traces the demise of the roadside camp and of travel off the beaten track, and the emergence, first of free municipal campgrounds and then of private camps with tourist cabins and facilities. The word *Mo-tel* was coined by James Vail in 1925. His Motel Inn in San Luis Obispo, California, was primarily a hotel with special provisions for motor travellers. Nevertheless, during the next ten years many private tourist camps upgraded their facilities to cater for the more "respectable" market provided by the "better class" of tourists. With the development of the motel and the motor court the old democratic culture of travel with its "vision of meeting and mixing on the great public space of the road" gave way to "family-oriented privacy and convenience" (Patton 1986:199): "As antimodernist gypsies, these tourists wanted simplicity, self-sufficiency, and comradeship; as modern consumers, however, they valued comfort, service and security. Ultimately, the gypsy gave way to the consumer, not because the urge to stray off the beaten path was insincere or unimportant but because the bourgeois route was safer and easier" (Belasco 1979:5).

As transport technologies changed and journey times shortened, so nostalgia grew for the earlier forms of travel and tourism. Each superseded transportation system—the stage coach, the steam train, the riverboat—has become at one time or another an object of nostalgia, an object for reconstruction in the form of a modern tourist attraction. During the development of the motel industry some people looked back fondly to the democratic camaraderie of the days of auto gypsying and autocamping. With the building of the interstate freeways, old roads like Route 66—"America's Main Street"—were reshaped through songs and stories into valued symbols of a better or simpler age, an age in which gas station operators were roadside sages and waitresses had hearts of gold: "It was the memory of old dangers, perhaps, that sharpened subsequent memories of an ideal roadside past, of the magic diner or cafe with the sun streaming through the windows and the breeze through a screen door with a Rainbo bread sign, where the taste of homemade apple pie blended with the constant rush of the passing traffic" (Patton 1986:234–35).

"WHEREVER YOU GO, THERE YOU ARE":[5] THE SOCIOLOGY AND PSYCHOLOGY OF TOURISM

The authentic travel experience, the authentic tourist experience, is, like all golden ages, always of some other time or place. Dean MacCannell (1976) introduces his analysis of the modern tourist with an apposite quote from Baudelaire to the effect that "life is a hospital where each patient is dying to change beds." The tourist's search for authenticity, and the efforts of the tourist industry to package and sell such authenticity as part of its product, is doomed to failure at the outset. There is a logical absurdity in the notion of authentic experience as a manufactured product, in the notion that an authentic lifestyle can be marketed, or that authentic character or personality can be shaped by the demands of the world of business. Many commentators have observed the paradox of tourists travelling in search of authentic cultural experiences, experiences that are destroyed or changed by the presence of those self-same tourists:

International tourism is like King Midas in reverse; a device for the systematic destruction of everything that is beautiful in the world. (Turner and Ash 1975:15)

It is an irony of modern travel that those who flee off the beaten track often beat a path for those they flee. (Belasco 1979:71)

Nevertheless, the promise of authenticity is still an important aspect of tourism and travel promotion. MacCannell sees the tourist's desire for the acquisition of authenticity in the popularity of access to other people's working lives as a tourist experience. Visits to workplaces—the sewers of Paris, coal mines, factories, slaughterhouses, stock exchanges—have been popular since the end of the nineteenth century. In modern times they have been supplemented by industrial museums and by the reconstruction of working environments—sheep shearing displays, cattle ranches, gold digging and panning, film studios—solely for tourists. These latter tourist attractions have been variously described as "pseudo-events" (Boorstin 1964) and "staged authenticity" (Urry 1990). They derive their appeal from their approximation to some presumed reality, a reality that can be partially entered into in a controlled manner and, perhaps most important of all, escaped from at will.

Other cultural productions for tourists—the artificial presentation and reconstruction of native lifestyles, participation in local customs of feasting and dancing, the stage-managed events of the international tourist calendar— share these qualities of packaged authenticity. For the traveller who seeks a genuine rather than manufactured experience of another culture, authenticity is always just around the corner:

Each new vacation alternative promised personal liberation from business world constraints, and . . . each invited mass participation and commercial elaboration. The success of each innovation thus tended to undermine its original attractions. Private campgrounds grew too luxurious, rock festivals too institutionalized, Greece too mercenary. Backpackers had to make reservations for popular park trails. But such frustrations spawned new ventures: gliders, the Galapagos Islands, jogging, four-wheel drive. The business prospects were as bright as the search was self-defeating. (Belasco 1979:173)

The pursuit of "real" holidays and "real" travel is like the quest for the Holy Grail, only it is a quest now catered for by the travel industry. As part of its Campaign for Real Holidays, the British newspaper The Independent published in 1989 The Independent Guide to Real Holidays Abroad: The Complete Directory for the Independent Traveller. These real holidays have two main characteristics (Urry 1990:95). First, they involve "visiting somewhere well away from where the mass of the population will be visiting; examples include the Maldives, Syria, or Bolivia." Second, real holidaymakers will use "delicatessen" travel agents to reach their destinations; that is, they will use small "specialist agencies that promote particular operators to a discriminating, independent-minded clientele." In practice the big agencies moved quickly to cater for the real holiday market. Thomas Cook's 1990–91 brochure "Escorted Journeys" promoted, "instead of the old Cook's Tour,"

an exciting new concept—the Escorted Journey. This is not a trip for the tourist but a voyage of discovery for the traveller, not just an enjoyable holiday but also an enriching experience. . . . There is no packaging about the Escorted Journey. There's lots of time to relax and explore by yourself. And Thomas Cook treats you not just as an individual but as a VIP. . . . You can relish the thrill of seeing faraway places and savoring new experiences, secure in the knowledge that Thomas Cook provides a service that is both personal and global. . . . This is truly travel à la carte, with an extra slice of variety available in destinations as remote as magic Mauritius and the secret kingdom of Nepal. Choose from our menu or dream up a travel dish of your own. Thomas Cook will do the rest.

Perhaps the ultimate destinations in these quests for real holidays are the places described by P. J. O'Rourke in *Holidays in Hell*: "A ramble through Lebanon," "Weekend getaway: Heritage USA," "Christmas in El Salvador," "Through darkest America: Epcot Center," "Thirty-six hours in Managua— an in-depth report." In the words of the promotional blurb on the back cover of the Picador edition, *Holidays in Hell* is

a package tour of traveller's tales from places as appealing to the average sun 'n sensation seeker as the inner circles of Dante's *Inferno*. . . . Sadly disenchanted with the traditional tourist trail, P. J. O'Rourke has chosen to visit those destinations that feature all too rarely in the travel brochures, largely because they are in a perpetual state of war, revolution or shortage of everything from hot dogs to toilet paper.

But even the desperate war zones are populated by what V. S. Naipaul calls "return-ticket revolutionaries" on their political holidays and by tourists in search of real world experiences:

Also present in Angola, Eritrea and God-knows-Where are the new breed of yuppie "experience travellers." You'll be pinned down by mortar fire in the middle of a genocide atrocity in the Sudan, and right through it come six law partners and their wives, in Banana Republic bush jackets, taking an inflatable raft trip down the White Nile and having an "experience." (O'Rourke 1989:71)

Perhaps, suggests O'Rourke, the only thing left to do is "stay home in a comfy armchair and read about travel as it should be—in Samuel Clemens's *Huckleberry Finn*." It was a perspective shared by a reviewer of Redmond O'Hanlon's *Into the Heart of Borneo*, an account of a trip into the uncharted interior of Borneo in search of the rare Borneo rhinoceros. Preparation for the trip was carried out in the assault course headquarters of the Special Air

Service. Giant leeches, 16-foot pythons, butterflies feeding off your sweat, temperatures of 110 degrees Fahrenheit with 98 percent humidity, and a diet of rice and spiny liver fish periodically offset by the hazards of local hospitality in the form of stewed lizard were among the excitements of the adventure: "How wonderful it is, the reader marvels, never, ever, to have to go to the Borneo jungle! Travel? Our writers will do that for us, thank goodness" (Dinnage 1985).

If the authentic is so elusive and, when tracked down, so potentially terrifying, then tourism can be redirected along two alternative but complementary routes. One is to seek safety in apparently authentic reconstructions of the past. As Umberto Eco (1987:7) observed in the context of the full-scale reconstruction of the Oval Office at the Lyndon B. Johnson Library in Austin, Texas, "The 'completely real' becomes identified with the 'completely fake.' " It is the same pattern of commercialization that saw Bloomingdale's linking up with the Metropolitan Museum of Art to present China in New York and to sell to the American consumer "authentic" imported Chinese handcrafts that had been manufactured exclusively for the Lexington Avenue store (Silverman 1990). And it is the pattern of tourist development that sees Britain being increasingly enmeshed in the reconstruction of its past, to the point where commentators have suggested, not altogether ironically, that the whole country should be declared one great heritage museum.

The other route is to go the whole hog and celebrate in the tourist experience the unreal, the inauthentic, the fake, the escapist fantasy. The inauthentic, like the sham castles, follies and hermitages built by eccentric English aristocrats in the eighteenth century,[6] takes on style and panache. Tourism becomes play. This is the Disney version of tourism, a world where the swamp of Mosquito County is turned into Orlando's "Hollywood East," a top commercial tourist destination that attracts over 13 million visitors a year and can be replicated in Tokyo and Paris. It is a tourism for a postmodern sensibility tuned to the ephemeral nature of distinctions between the real and the unreal. It is the tourism of Umberto Eco's *Travels in Hyperreality*:

Disneyland not only produces illusion, but—in confessing it—stimulates the desire for it: A real crocodile can be found in the zoo, and as a rule it is dozing or hiding, but Disneyland tells us that faked nature corresponds much more to our daydream demands. When, in the space of twenty-four hours, you go (as I did deliberately) from the fake New Orleans of Disneyland to the real one, and from the wild river of Adventureland to a trip on the Mississippi, where the captain of the paddle-wheel steamer says it is possible to see alligators on the banks of the river, and then you don't see any, you risk feeling homesick for Disneyland, where the wild animals don't have to be coaxed. Disneyland tells us that technology can give us more reality than nature can. . . . Here we not only enjoy a perfect imitation, we also enjoy the conviction that imitation has reached its apex and afterwards reality will always be inferior to it. (Eco 1987:44; 46)

Dreams, then, can become reality; indeed, better than reality. There is pleasure both in anticipation of the tourist experience and, however short-lived, in the consumption of the tourist industry product. In this respect modern tourism, like modern fashion, illustrates key aspects of Colin Campbell's thesis that "a dialectic of novelty and insatiability" lies "at the heart of contemporary consumerism."Max Weber's *The Protestant Ethic and the Spirit of Capitalism* focused, inter alia, on the psychology of production. Campbell, in *The Romantic Ethic and the Spirit of Modern Consumerism*, argues for equal attention to be given to the psychology of consumption. The Protestant Ethic, while sanctioning wealth and economic success through hard work, emphasized the moral and spiritual benefits of physical and mental labor. Hedonism, play, and the spontaneous enjoyment of life were frowned upon as forms of idleness; money-making itself was work, not pleasure. The production ethic focused on economic man and woman, economic rationality and a progressive view of history in which technology is tightly linked to material progress through the production and consumption of the products and artifacts of work. In this it was modernist in its conception. The consumption ethic, in contrast, is linked by Campbell to a conception of men and women as basically hedonistic and romantic and to a society in which consumption is a religious or quasi-religious experience. The spirit of modern consumerism is one of play rather than of work, pleasure rather than duty. In the consumer society products are valued because of bizarre, magical, fetishist, irrational, or romantic connotations rather than utilitarian ones: shopping is entertainment, dress is experience, travel is fun. Technology increasingly services this world of imaginative play rather than the world of work. With the acquisition of consumer durables largely taken for granted, the focus shifts to the software associated with leisure and play—to electronic games, virtual reality machines. Technologies are developed that enable the individualized consumption of images rather than the mass consumption of artifacts.

The mystery of consumer behavior, argues Campbell (1987:37), is "its character as an activity which involves an apparently endless pursuit of wants; the most characteristic feature of modern consumption being its insatiability." Such behavior is driven by the twin forces of a "revolution in rising expectations" and a "revolution in rising frustrations," with expectations continually outstripping realization of those expectations. Campbell sees the origins of these consumer wants, not in some instinctive human greed, nor in status competition, nor in the manipulation of images and symbols by advertisers and marketers, but in the widespread adoption of the habit of covert daydreaming:

Individuals do not so much seek satisfaction from products, as pleasure from the self-illusory experience which they construct from their associated meanings. The essential activity of consumption is thus not the actual selection, purchase or use of products, but the imaginative pleasure-seeking to which the product image lends itself, "real" consumption being largely a resultant of this "mentalistic" hedonism. Viewed this way, the emphasis upon novelty as well as that upon insatiability both become comprehensible. (Campbell 1987:89)

From this perspective the basic motivation underlying modern consumerism is not materialistic, since it is not satisfied by the acquisition of material objects. Rather, it is hedonistic in that its primary goal is pleasure rather than satisfaction. Thus the tourists' purchase of a holiday package is driven by a desire to "experience in reality the pleasurable dramas which they have already enjoyed in imagination."

Such a pattern of consumption, argues Campbell, is destined to breed disillusion and an addictive search for the new and novel. It sets up a "dynamic interaction between illusion and reality" in which daydreaming and fantasizing are a permanent mode, but satisfaction is infrequent and short-lived. It also stimulates, as tourism illustrates, the manufacture of experience, the provision of a sense of authenticity that is both more real than reality and more nearly matched to illusions of reality. In this process advertising provides the link between romanticism and consumption. However, "although advertisers make use of the fact that people day-dream, and indeed feed those dreams, the practice of day-dreaming is itself endemic to modern societies and does not require the commercial institution of advertising to ensure its continued existence" (Campbell 1987:91). Nevertheless, the selling of images and the promotion of products, lifestyles and experience in terms of their symbolic associations are integral aspects not only of the tourist industry but of business culture generally.

NOTES

1. Or *before* or *after* travelling. As indicated in Chapter 3, a shop in Tokyo's central station sells souvenirs, artifacts and special delicacies from all the regions of Japan so that travellers can purchase the obligatory gifts for their family members and work colleagues without the inconvenience of carrying them in their luggage.

2. Some early locomotive names emphasized the workhorse character of the new technology (*Puffing Billy*, 1813; *Tom Thumb*, 1830). Others emphasized the exploration of new frontiers (*The Rocket*, 1829; *The Comet*, 1835; *North Star*, 1837). With the rapid growth of passenger rail transport, softer, more feminine names were added; in 1847, for example, a new locomotive was named *Jenny Lind*.

3. In the light of this it is curious to find that some colonial administrators in India in the nineteenth century hoped that the introduction of the railways, by forcing high-caste Brahmins to mix with low-caste farmers and laborers, would accelerate the breakdown of caste barriers (Adas 1989:225).

4. It was the automobile that was instrumental in the initiation and growth of franchising as a form of business development. From the 1890s onward auto dealerships were franchised, and later gas stations. It was a system of business that received a further boost from the construction of the new interstate system in the

1950s and 1960s. A number of major fast-food franchises date from that period; see, for example, Patton 1986:178–85, on the development of Kentucky Fried Chicken.

5. Buckaroo Banzai (O'Rourke 1989).

6. Complete with hired hermits who spent their working hours in the grottoes and caves of the hermitage.

CHAPTER 11

Sport: "It Is Not Like American Business, It Is American Business"[1]

SPORT AS CULTURE

And specially, from every shires ende
Of AMERICA to COOPERSTOWN they wende
The holy BASEBALL HEROES for to seke,
That hem hath holpen whan that they were SIX.[2]

In traditional societies, as we saw in the case of the Trobriand Islands, sport is closely integrated with cultural rituals; not with pilgrimages to the shrines of martyrs perhaps, but certainly with other symbolically significant community events. The Olympic Games of ancient Greece, for example, were the chief feature of a festival held at midsummer every four years in honor of the supreme god, Zeus. While the festival was underway a sacred truce was proclaimed so that athletes, poets, orators, traders and visitors from the various Greek states could travel to Olympia in safety. Other festivals and games of the time had their origins in celebrations held to honor the accomplishments of gods or in funeral rites for those killed in battle. Athletics and horse-racing were accompanied by poetry and music competitions. Such festivals developed both artistic and athletic prowess, encouraged a strong sense of the unity of the Greek people and established a role for athletics in the education of the young.

The modern Olympic Games sought to rekindle the Greek ideal of harmony between physical and intellectual pursuits and to sustain a festival quality. The 1900 games, for example, were connected to the Paris Universal Exhibition, and the 1904 games to the St. Louis World Fair. The inspiration of the modern Olympics, however, was drawn as much from the public school education system of Victorian England as from the festivals of ancient Greece.

Baron Pierre de Coubertin, who organized the first of the modern games in 1896, coupled a "devotion to the Hellenic trinity of body, mind and spirit" with "a compelling faith in the character building qualities of English sports education" (Lucas 1981:23). This English sports education was underpinned by the philosophy of "Muscular Christianity."[3] In leading the reformation of the anarchical,[4] immoral, and vicious British public schools, the Reverend Thomas Arnold, the headmaster of Rugby School from 1828 to 1842, promoted education that was geared to the inculcation of religious and moral principles, the development of intellectual abilities, the assimilation of "gentlemanly" codes of conduct, and the encouragement of athletic proficiency through compulsory organized games. Initially favored more by pupils than by staff, team games so improved the keeping of discipline that they were rapidly assimilated into the formal curriculum. The idea that competitive sports, especially team sports, were an appropriate vehicle for teaching moral behavior became an integral part of the Muscular Christian tradition. First, however, school games had to discard their reputation for encouraging brutality and violence. This was done through rule making and codification of the games and through merging the ethics and codes of games with the ethics and codes of civilized behavior in the wider community. The term "ungentlemanly conduct," for example, was introduced into the laws of Association Football in 1880. To this day, professional footballers in Britain can be fined or suspended by their clubs for ungentlemanly conduct on the field of play.

A further presumption of the philosophy of Muscular Christianity was that the codes of moral behavior acquired and the personal character developed through competitive sport were transferable to the "game of life." As Sir Henry Newbolt's poem "Vitaï Lampada" (1892) illustrates, they were particularly transferable to war:

> There's a breathless hush in the Close tonight—
> Ten to make and the match to win—
> A bumping pitch and a blinding light,
> An hour to play and the last man in.
> And its not for the sake of a ribboned coat,
> Or the selfish hope of a season's fame,
> But his Captain's hand on his shoulder smote:
> "Play up! play up! and play the game!"
>
> The sand of the desert is sodden red,—
> Red with the wreck of a square that broke;—
> The Gatling's jammed and the Colonel dead,
> And the regiment blind with dust and smoke.
> The river of death has brimmed his banks'
> And England's far, and Honor a name,
> But the voice of the schoolboy rallies the ranks:
> "Play up! play up! and play the game!"

This is the word that year by year,
While in her place the school is set,
Every one of her sons must hear,
And none that hears it dare forget.
This they all with a joyful mind
Bear through life like a torch in flame,
And falling fling to the host behind—
"Play up! play up! and play the game!"

The links between sporting prowess and military prowess and the analogies between sport and war have a long pedigree. In Britain the idea that the 1815 Battle of Waterloo was won on the playing fields of Eton continues in educational folklore. Paul Hoch (1972) argued that Baron Pierre de Coubertin, in founding the modern Olympics, was motivated more by military issues than by the high ideals of his Olympic movement. In disgust at the overwhelming defeat of French forces by Germany in the Franco-Prussian War of 1870–71, Coubertin looked upon international sporting contests as a way of "toughening up" French youth and "reinvigorating" the French nation. In the Gulf War of 1991 sporting metaphors were frequently used during military briefings of the press to describe the allies' campaign strategies and performance, not least by the allied commander, General Norman Schwarzkopf, who compared part of his forces' ground attack on the Iraqi army to a Hail Mary play in American football. Military language also seeps back into sport. Nowhere is this more evident than in the aggressive language of bodybuilding, where biceps are known as "guns," shoulders as "cannonballs" and various exercises are carried out to bomb, blitz, shred, rip, burn, blast, destroy, chisel and torture recalcitrant and undisciplined muscles into shape; the body becomes a battlefield, sport becomes war, and Arnold Schwarzenegger becomes The Terminator.

The emphasis on the educational and personal values to be derived from participation in sports had a number of effects in British and American schools and colleges. In British public schools and their imitators in the British colonies and elsewhere, staff appointments were frequently made on the basis of sporting rather than academic attainments. Leadership roles were given to senior students who had demonstrated sporting prowess, such students becoming important role models for younger members of the school. The prestige of the school in the community and vis-à-vis other schools also tended to rest on its sporting accomplishments. In the United States success in intercollegiate competition, particularly in basketball, baseball and football, became a key element in defining the relative prestige and status of educational institutions. As intercollegiate sports grew in popularity, so they were increasingly looked to as a source of revenue to the institution. They provided a focus for the development of alumni associations, for the recruitment of top students and for college public relations. By the 1880s the popularity of college football was such that it presented business opportunities that were gratefully seized by entrepreneurs both inside and outside the colleges: "Undergraduate sports programs were taken out of the hands of the undergraduates, and placed in the hands of a small elite clique of alumni, usually from the wealthiest families . . . [so that] the sports program *became* the college" (Hoch 1972:43). The consequent distortion of educational programs has been documented by Murray Sperber (1990). His research demonstrated that intercollegiate sports programs, far from being major revenue generators for the colleges, survive only because of the diversion of funds from academic programs.

Character building through sport, sport as training in moral behavior, and sport as preparation for life were concepts infused in nineteenth-century British public school education with the ethos of the amateur. Sports and games were played by the leisured classes in a climate that stressed the importance of the game itself rather than a win-at-all-costs mentality. Indeed, the term "amateur" was synonymous with membership of the gentlemanly or upper classes. Artisans and laborers who played sports without any financial rewards were not accorded amateur status. In some instances they were banned from amateur contests on the grounds that the better physical shape they enjoyed as a consequence of their manual labors gave them an unfair advantage! Similarly, practice and training were frowned upon as being likely to undermine natural grace and talent (Holt 1989:100). The amateur gentlemanly ideal was fundamental to Coubertin's Olympic Games though it had nothing to do with the original games of ancient Greece. In the games of 1896 many of the participants were tourists who happened to be in Athens at the time. All of them were gentlemen from the leisured classes (Pitt 1979). No prize money was to be associated with the new Olympic Games. Participants were to be exclusively amateur in status and in their commitment to their sport. This Olympic ideal was enshrined in the baron's speech at the opening of the 1908 games in London (Arnold 1983:7): "The most important thing in the Olympic Games is not to win but to take part, just as the most important thing in life is not the triumph but the struggle. The essential thing is not to have conquered, but to have fought well." The values were "an odd amalgam of Christian gentility, masculinity and Social Darwinism." Great emphasis was placed on the aggression and ruthlessness necessary for successful leadership but tempered with "an altruistic courtesy in triumph, compassion to the defeated and stress upon fair play" (Whannel 1983:41). The ideals of English amateur sportsmanship, of motivation through love of the game rather than through an overwhelming desire to win, permeated American college sport around the turn of the century. Walter Camp, "The Father of American Football," was fond of regaling students with lines from William Makepeace Thackeray's ballad "The End of the Play" (1848):

Come wealth or want, come good or ill,
Let young and old accept their part,
And bow before the Awful Will,
And bear it with an honest heart,
Who misses or who wins the prize.
Go, lose or conquer as you can;
But if you fail or, if you rise,
Be each, pray God, a gentleman.

Maintaining the amateur and gentlemanly status of the Olympic Games against encroaching professionalism was a long, drawn out and ultimately futile struggle. The state subsidies for athletes from Eastern Europe and the commercial sponsorship of Western sportsmen and women—the growth of "shamateurism"—forced the International Olympic Committee (IOC) to revise the rules governing Olympic Games participation. In 1974 they permitted "broken time" payments for athletes (thereby allowing reimbursements for loss of income while in training), legitimized sponsorship and lifted the restrictions on the time that athletes could spend away from home in training and competition. Although the IOC was prepared to abandon its defense of the amateur code, not all national associations were so flexible:

A ten-year-old boy has been expelled from an athletics club for breaching his amateur status by winning a 10p bag of sweets.
Montrose Athletic Club in Scotland told Andrew Williamson to leave because he took part in a local highland games race last Sunday and won the sweets by coming second in the race for boys and girls aged 10 and under. He has now been deprived of his amateur status.
The club has told the boy's angry mother that it is only upholding the rules of the Scottish Amateur Athletics Association. Its secretary, Mr John Ward, said yesterday that it was "most unfortunate. The boy was advised before the games that taking part in any of the games activities would be against the rules of the SAAA. He competed and we had to take this action." (Guardian, 9 August 1985)

THE IDEOLOGIES OF SPORT

The amateur code and ethos was a product of the British class structure. Indeed, the emphasis on sports education applied primarily to those who were expected to fill leadership roles in the society. For working-class children physical and moral education was encouraged not through the playing of games but through the discipline of quasi-military drills (Goldlust 1987:19). The role of sports and games in the socialization of children and in the transmission of cultural values has been of major interest to social scientists. Studies have focused on the ways in which sports and games reflect and reinforce social structures and their underlying ideologies:

Games of "skill," for example, have been found more commonly in societies in which success and achievement were highly esteemed; games of "strategy" more commonly in communities where children were encouraged to be clean, obedient and independent; while games of "chance" seem to occur in poorer societies, those which need children to work early, which reward adult behavior among the young, and in which the dream of the "lucky win" transforming rags to riches is common. (Hutchinson 1983:3)

In the United States the Horatio Alger doctrine of success through the character virtues of hard work, perseverance, frugality, sobriety, ambition, and respect for authority have been transferred to the sporting arena. Eldon Snyder (1974:362) has commented on how sports coaches inculcate in their players "such value orientations as hard work, achievement orientation, competitiveness, aggressiveness, and discipline." Tales of rags-to-riches through sports accomplishments are the modern version of the mythology of log-cabin presidents. Major league baseball in particular, "America's oldest and most venerable professional sport" (Scully 1974:221), with its ethos of fair play and its meritocratic symbolism, was presented as an avenue for upward mobility for the educationally disadvantaged and an escape route from the ghetto for immigrants and blacks.

More radical commentators on the links between modern sports and contemporary culture have described the ideology of sport as the mirror image of the ideology of capitalism. Marxist analysis views sport as essentially a conservative force, propping up the status quo, conditioning the masses into spectator roles, a twentieth-century opiate of the people:

We can . . . see how different sports, the sports industry, and the ideology of sports, arose as a consequence of the developing material conditions of capitalist society, and how the sports industry functioned to facilitate the smoothness of authoritarian capitalist class relations generally; how it helped to socialize workers for their coglike roles on the assembly lines; how it built up a symbiotic relationship with the developing mass media industry; how sports and the media helped socialize workers to think of themselves mainly as passive consumers; how sports spread the poisons of competitiveness, elitism, sexism, nationalism, militarism and racism—all of which have kept the international working class divided against itself; and, finally, how there has developed within the sports world itself a movement of athletes to build a more human society. (Hoch 1972:12)

Other writers have traced parallels between changes in prevailing American ideologies and changes in sporting values. Thus the values of the early era of American capitalism are seen to be reflected in the "Lockean game" of baseball: "Baseball is a Lockean game, a kind of contract theory in ritual form, a set of atomic individuals who assent to patterns of limited cooperation in their mutual interest" (Novak 1976:59). Steven Riess used professional baseball's myths, symbols and rituals to explore American mores, values and beliefs during the period from 1890 to 1920. He found in baseball of the progressive era an ideology expressive of a small-town agrarian society. The myth of baseball is the myth of an indigenous, classless and egalitarian American game, originating in the countryside and typifying all that was best in American democracy. Owners are projected as benevolent and philanthropic citizens operating their franchises out of concern for the local community's welfare. Local clubs are seen as a focal point for developing a sense of community spirit and for promoting hometown pride. Through participation in the game and its rituals, American-born children will learn traditional American values and immigrants will be quickly assimilated into the dominant WASP culture.

"Although," comments Steven Riess (1980:7), "most of the ideology's basic elements were false, fans accepted its veracity, and that perception helped shape their attitudes and behavior. The public saw baseball as a true reflection of contemporary society." The reality was somewhat different to the myth. Gerald Scully records that as early as 1867 negro players and clubs were banned from playing against white teams. The ban was not totally effective at first. Negroes were advertised as Cubans or Indians or Spaniards; the first Negro professional team—the Cuban Giants—spoke in fake Spanish when they took the field. Nevertheless, from 1885 to 1947 there were no black major league players, and from 1898 to 1946 black Americans were confined to their own leagues. Those who dominated the administration and management of major league baseball had other concerns than community welfare. They were entrepreneurs deeply involved in the politics of urban development and often closely tied to the political machines of the big cities. Although fans of the game, their chief interest was in using their franchises, their contract players and their ball park real estate to make a profit. And the players themselves, as the 1919 Black Sox scandal illustrated, were not all paragons of moral virtue. The events of 1919, however, demonstrated the pervasiveness of the public's expectation that the morality of sports should be better than the morality of politics: "The world of baseball began to be seen as a moral world above the corruption of the urban political landscape. This *moral* sports / *immoral* politics dichotomy was dramatized in the 1919 Black Sox scandal, where the tampering with the World Series produced a sense of moral outrage that far transcended the tempest over the Teapot Dome" (Lipsky 1981:61). (The continuing power of this traditional baseball ideology, of the values enshrined in it, and of the threat to those values that the Black Sox case encapsulated, can be seen in the 1989 Phil Aldon Robinson film *Field of Dreams*.)

As sport became big business, its ideology shifted. The specialization, rationalization and bureaucratization characteristic of Taylorism and Fordism spread to the world of professional sport. The team became more important than the individual, and the psychology of the team an important factor in achieving sporting, and business, success. "Being a good team player" was synonymous with being "a good corporate man." Richard Lipsky (1981:60) argues that it was "no accident that as American society became more complex and bureaucratic, the more corporate games of football and basketball rose to popularity." Others argued that the role of the player in these corporate-modelled sports teams was analogous to that of the alienated worker on the industrial assembly line. Largely unseen owners stand at the top of a hierarchy of command that works its way down to the ordinary player through middle layers of managers and coaches, captains and quarterbacks:

In football, like business but unlike almost any other game, every pattern of movement on the field is increasingly being brought under the control of a group of non-playing managerial technocrats who sit up in the stands (literally *above* the players) with their headphones and dictate offenses, defenses, special plays, substitutions and so forth to the players below. It is no longer a game. It's a business. And there is too much at stake to leave this business to the players. If the trend continues, it will be a rare pro quarterback who will be allowed to decide on his own plays. (Hoch 1972:9)

Specialization, meticulous preparation, and rigorous training in technique, rather than creativity, flair, and the ability to do the unexpected, were seen as the keys to success in the competitive jungle of professional football. Former offensive lineman Jerry Kramer described in *Instant Replay* (1969) how his team trained under legendary coach Vince "Winning-is-the-only-thing" Lombardi:

He makes us execute the same plays over and over, a hundred times, two hundred times, until we do every little thing automatically. He wants to make the kick-off team perfect, the punt-return team perfect, the field-goal team perfect. He ignores nothing. Technique, technique, technique, over and over and over, until we feel like we're going crazy. But we win. (quoted in Blair 1988:86)

Kramer presents a number of images of the Lombardi-trained team. Alongside the associations of the team with a machine are associations with war, with a patriarchal family, and with the business corporation: "Lombardi chewed on us again tonight. . . . First he compared the Packers to a large corporation, like General Motors or IBM or Chrysler, and he said that a large business cannot tolerate mistakes. 'We've got seventy people here in camp,' he said. 'If the ones we have can't do the job, we'll get some more' " (quoted in Jones and Smith 1978:157). It is a long way from the original idea of play in human culture. This was a conception of play as a non-obligatory activity, circumscribed by agreed rules yet allowing individual players latitude for innovation and initiative. Play involved make-believe and a conscious awareness that although it was intensely absorbing, it nevertheless was an escape from the realities of life. It was an unproductive activity. It did not generate wealth or the production of goods or the acquisition of social status. It was an activity "connected with no material interest, and no profit can be gained by it" (Huizinga 1949:13).

It would be wrong to suggest, however, that modern sports, dominated as they are by business interests, business considerations and business methods, have completely lost touch with their cultural origins in games, in ritual, in dance and in theater. Cricket and football pitches are referred to as "sacred ground" or "hallowed turf." Matches are preceded by prayers, devotions, hymn singing and other religious or quasi-religious observances. The players themselves go through their own rituals of superstition, psyching themselves up for the coming contest. Fans (literally "fanatics") dress or make up in the colors of their teams and perform ritual celebrations of victory and consolations for defeat. Big sporting occasions are accompanied by ever more elaborate musical and visual spectacles: skydivers, cheerleaders, fireworks, national pageantry, marching bands, patriotic and team songs, gymnastic displays. Major events and festivals—the SuperBowl, the soccer World Cup, the summer and winter Olympics, the Wimbledon tennis championships, the Kentucky Derby, the Melbourne Cup, the Grand National Steeplechase—mark the ritual passage of the seasons and the years. The folklore of epic contests and heroic players lives on in quiz shows, in record books and in a vast array of sporting publications.

David Voigt has argued that modern sports are as full of fetishes and fetishism as any primitive cult. As evidence he cites sports and fitness crazes—the jogging and running fetishists who "zealously follow punishing regimens which they believe will result in magical payoffs like improved mental or physical abilities" and "an ability to piss white water once a day" (Voigt 1983). He illustrates the anthropomorphizing of sports equipment with the story of the professional golfer who, after a disappointing performance on the greens, held his putter under the water and screamed, "Drown you SOB," later lashing the recalcitrant club to the rear of his car and dragging it sparking down the highway. And he cites the modern mania, born of the nineteenth-century scientific and industrial revolutions, for calibration, quantification and measurement that stimulates an obsession with setting, monitoring and breaking performance records. It is this obsession, and the deification of record-holders that accompanies it, that is the basis of the remarkable sales success of the *Guinness Book of Records* and of *Soap* character Bert Campbell's determination, on learning that he has only a few months to live, to do something, anything, that will qualify him for entry to that Guinness pantheon.

The moral codes and educational values of the sports world are caught in a variety of aphorisms. These aphorisms or maxims suggest that such codes and values are appropriate guides for everyday behavior. Some stress aggression and competitiveness: "Just win, baby";[5] "Winners never quit and quitters never win"; "When the going gets tough, the tough get going"; "Winning isn't everything, it's the *only* thing"; "The bigger they are, the harder they fall." Others place greater stress on concepts of fairness, respect for the rules and the acceptance of defeat with a good grace: giving an opponent "a sporting chance," not "hitting below the belt," being a "good loser," or "It's not cricket." These may in turn evoke nostalgia for the perceived values of a bygone age, an age that predated commercialism and professionalism in sport, an age when games were about "old-fashioned virtues," about "standards: of play, of behavior, of spectatorship"; and when administrators were more concerned with preserving the "mysticism" and "protecting the heritage" of their sport than with making a profit from it (Blofeld 1978:64). Such an age was more imaginary than real. The gentility and behavioral codes of tennis were breached long before the advent of Ilie Nastase's self-promotional antics and John McEnroe's sulphurous rages and theatrical violence. In the 1920s the Wimbledon Ladies' Champion was the Frenchwoman Suzanne Lenglen, a "*prima donna* of the courts, all temperament and tantrums," whose "unsporting" behavior shocked the English. Prior to the Wimbledon championship of 1925, the weekly magazine *Punch* wished "success to the Lawn Tennis Association in its attempts to put an end to the exhibitions of bad manners, bad temper, and bad language which were too much in evidence at last year's tournament":

> The players of the present glare
> Argue, expostulate and swear,
> Lift hands in anguish to the skies
> And blank the umpire's blinking eyes.
>
> *Punch* 13 May 1925:511

Nevertheless, sporting heroes, like all cultural heroes, are expected to offer pithy and moralistic comments about the secrets of their success, secrets that might provide suitable guidance for success in life itself. It is a tradition that was nicely parodied by the baseball pitcher Satchel Paige. He ascribed his 20-year dominance of the black leagues to the observance of six golden rules, rules that he claimed could make anyone great (Pitt 1979):

1. Avoid fried meats which angry up the blood.
2. If your stomach disputes you, lie down and pacify it with cool thoughts.
3. Keep the juices flowing by jangling around gently as you move.
4. Go very light on the vices, such as carrying on in society. The social ramble ain't restful.
5. Avoid running at all times.
6. Don't look back. Something might be gaining on you.

SPORT AND THE MARKET

The origins of modern professional sport lie in the second half of the nineteenth century. The English Football Association (FA) was formed in

1863 and immediately took steps to clean up a game that for centuries had been a byword for violence. Having watched an English football (soccer) match in 1829, a Frenchman had asked, "If this is what they call football, what do they call fighting?" (Walvin, 1975:179). Initially the FA was dominated by the amateur gentlemen who played for clubs in the south of the country. Many of these clubs had emerged from churches, schools and universities and were the product of the public school ethos of Muscular Christianity and the cult of team games. But soccer was also popular among working people, and a number of clubs were established in workplaces. In London, for example, West Ham United was originally a team from the Thames Ironworks, and Arsenal a team from the Woolwich munitions factory. The Midlands Club Coventry City emerged from the Singer sewing machine factory. Other clubs, notably Stoke City, Crewe Alexandra, and Manchester United, were founded by groups of railway workers, the growth of the railways after 1840 having transformed the possibilities for competition among workplace and other teams.

The popularity of soccer among working men, particularly in the industrialized Midlands and the north of England, and the ever-increasing crowds of spectators the matches attracted, led to the introduction of admission charges to games. James Walvin (1975) records that at first the income received from gate takings was an embarrassment to the FA, who gave the money to charity. The northern clubs, however, increasingly pumped the money back into the game, building stadiums, purchasing equipment and, illegally at first, paying their players wages and attracting new players by the payment of transfer fees. By the mid–1880s professionalism was common in the clubs of northern England and they were regularly advertising in the Scottish newspapers to attract new players. Many members of the FA considered professional sport to be unacceptable, breaching the amateur and gentlemanly codes of ethics held dear by the leisured classes. Nevertheless, the FA gradually came to terms with professionalism in soccer. In 1883 the players in FA Cup semi-finals and finals were permitted reimbursement of their railway fares, and in 1885 professional soccer was legalized. Amateur soccer and professional soccer separated along class and regional lines. It was a pattern that was to be followed in Britain by the split in the Rugby Football Union formed in 1871. In 1895 the northern clubs, anxious to compensate their predominantly working-class players for lost earnings, formed their own professional Northern Union. In 1922 this became the Rugby League, leaving the Rugby Football Union as the guardians of the amateur game. To this day in Britain players who join league clubs, or who infringe their amateur status in other ways, are banned for life from participation as players, coaches or administrators in union clubs.

The growing professionalism of British soccer toward the end of the nineteenth century—the payment and contracting of players on a full-time basis and the spiralling transfer fees, for example—created pressure on the clubs to turn themselves into profit-seeking business organizations. It would be misleading to suggest, however, that professionalization brought the total commercialization of the game. Businessmen, politicians and professionals invested time, energy and money in their local soccer clubs for prestige as well as for profit:

For politicians . . . what better way was there of establishing a reputation, of ensuring that one's name was before the eye of the male electorate and for posing as a man of the people, than by belonging to the people's game; to the local football club? Similar motivations drew local businessmen. Booming clubs attracted businessmen's spare cash (for shares) and enhanced in numerous and indefinable ways their commercial status in the town. Manufacturers and entrepreneurs, newspaper proprietors and merchants, established themselves as patrons, benefactors (and, less obviously, as beneficiaries) of local teams, giving employment in their businesses and providing enjoyment for the crowds, many of whom were their workmen, voters and clients. (Walvin 1975:83)

This patronage of football clubs by wealthy individuals has continued for over a hundred years, though in the modern era the wealthy patron is as likely to be a rock star as a wealthy industrialist.[6] In the view of Garry Whannel, even though British soccer clubs have operated since the 1890s as limited liability companies, it is too simplistic to argue that they have been run purely along business lines: "Clubs have been controlled mainly by local businessmen, not for gain so much as for power and influence in the community and as a hobby. Some would suggest that many of football's problems stem precisely from the fact that it is *not* run as a business" (Whannel 1983:25). It is his view that the pressures toward commercialization of sport in the twentieth century have come not so much from professionalization and the motivations of club owners as from the entertainment and advertising industries. This is an issue to which we will return shortly.

Patterns of development in American sports have some similarities with those in England. American football, initially a hybrid of soccer and rugby, developed through intercollegiate sport with the formal codification of rules by the Intercollegiate Football Association in 1876. It was seen as "a training ground for the competitiveness that American elites regarded highly and rewarded handsomely" (Blair 1988:84). By 1906, when the forward pass was approved, American football had adopted its own distinctive patterns. Among the most significant of these was the structural segmentation of the game into discrete plays. This breaking up of the natural flow of the game put a premium on organization and skill rather than creativity, flair and luck as the key to victory. It allowed for "scientific planning" in the direction of the course of play and for a highly specialized division of labor among the players. As such it was a reflection of what John Blair has described as the modularity in American culture, a systems view in which things are conceived of in terms of subsystems of replaceable component parts. It was a pattern reinforced in 1950 when the rules of football were changed to permit unlimited substitution, further entrenching the intense specialization that had become so characteristic of the game. That the goal kicker in American football only kicks (and consequently may be on the field of play for less than a minute in an entire match) is a constant source of amazement to Europeans brought up on a diet of rugby or soccer:

The latter two games use players in ways made consonant with a preindustrial conception of labor, the European craftsman who made one entire musket at a time, as opposed to the world sponsored by the American System of Manufactures, wherein each participant performs a limited range of actions with theoretically greater efficacy. In the industrial circumstance, of course, the machine embodies the specialization rather than the individual worker, but the characteristics of the systems as such are congruent. (Blair 1988:87)

A similar modularity is evident in the Americanization of the English game of rounders. Blair quotes the observation of an Englishman in 1904 on the transmutation of rounders into baseball: "The Americans have a genius for taking a thing, examining its every part, and developing each part to the utmost. This they have done with our game of rounders and, from a clumsy primitive pastime, have so tightened its joints, and put such a fine finish on its points that it stands forth a machine of infinite exactitude" (Blair 1988:92).

By 1904 professional baseball was firmly established in the United States. Admission charges for spectators had been introduced in 1868, and as early as 1869 the Cincinnati Reds were prepared to announce that they were an all-salaried team. Two years later the National Association of Professional Base Ball Players was formed and the first championship for professional teams was organized. The control of the sport by the players was, however, short-lived. In 1876 a group of team owners set up the National League of Professional Base Ball Clubs. Entry to the league was restricted to teams from cities with a minimum population of 75,000. Money was invested in sports fields, in press promotion and in salaries for players. Secretly in 1879 and openly in 1880, the National League owners introduced a reserve clause into the contracts of five players per team. This gave the owners the right to reserve the services of those players and to prevent them from playing for other teams in the league. Appalled by what they described as a "slave system" of employment, the players established their own league—the Players' League—but, though popular with fans, it could not acquire the financial resources and press coverage of the National League competition and survived only one season.

SPORT AS ENTERTAINMENT

Sport has a long-standing relationship with the media. Sports reporting in newspapers goes back to the early eighteenth century. In the middle of the nineteenth century the development of the wire telegraph made possible the daily publication of the results of sports contests. It also led to the creation of centralized news agencies and meant that newspapers were no longer confined to printing only local news. There quickly developed in the newspaper industry a popular belief that it was the sports pages that most boosted sales and circulation. It was a belief later supported by readership surveys demonstrating that a third of the newspaper-reading public read *only* the sports pages. The development of the wire telegraph facilitated the growth of the mass circulation popular newspaper. The development of professional sports leagues in the same period meant that the promotion of sports and the promotion of newspapers went hand in hand. Sports events were used to help sell popular newspapers, and the newspapers were used to promote sports events. It was a relationship of reciprocal free publicity. Journals and newspapers made no payments to the sports that were effectively helping to promote their circulation. And sports bodies made no payments to the journals and newspapers whose coverage was effectively advertising and promoting their matches. By the end of the nineteenth century a large proportion of the popular daily press coverage was devoted to reports of sporting events and to announcements of, and commentary on, forthcoming contests.

The symbiotic relationship between sports and the media continued with the advent of radio and, later, television. However, the commercial relationship between sports and broadcasting was significantly different to that between sports and the press. This is particularly clear in the case of television, an ideal medium for exploiting the live action and universal appeal of sporting contests. In its infancy the technology of television was most suitable for covering one-on-one sports contests that took place in a restricted area, that is, in sports like boxing and wrestling. The development of more sophisticated outside broadcast facilities, of multi-camera coverage of games and, later, of instant replay meant not only that team games could be covered by television but that they could be covered in ways that gave the home spectator a view of the total spectacle of an event that might not be available to the gate-paying spectator. Clearly television coverage threatened the viability of the live event, both in the potential loss of gate receipts and in the consequent loss of the gladiatorial atmosphere created by the physical presence of fans at the venue, the atmosphere that in part prompted the television coverage of the event in the first place.

A number of accommodations between the television networks and the sports organizations were entered into in attempts to offset the potentially damaging commercial impacts of television on sport. These included payments from the networks for the rights to cover particular events or sports, blackouts on television coverage in the particular vicinity of a match, and delayed telecasts. In part these were all mechanisms either to compensate clubs for loss of gate receipts or to protect them from such a loss. Generally

National League organizations control national broadcasting rights and local clubs control the broadcasting of games that are not part of the nationally negotiated package. Under legislation passed by Congress in 1961, the combination of clubs in a league to sell national broadcasting rights was exempted from the antitrust laws. Rights payments, however, soon became more than a form of compensation. In the early days of commercial television, sport was necessary to attract viewers and, in so doing, to promote the sales of television sets. Then as now, the attraction of viewers through sport was also a major avenue to the attraction of advertising revenues. Networks were soon encouraged, both by their dependence upon advertisers and by the pressures from increasingly entrepreneurial and profit-seeking sports organizations, to bid competitively with each other for exclusive television rights to major sporting attractions.

These commercial arrangements tying together advertisers, television networks and sports bodies had a number of major impacts on the nature of the sports themselves and on their popularity. Although baseball is still described as America's national game, it is football that is more compatible with television and has consequently grown in popularity since the advent of televised sport. The segmentation of football fits well with the need for advertising breaks, and the predictability of the game's playing time facilitates its scheduling for television. In football, as elsewhere, administrators have willingly cooperated in developing the entertainment values of their sport and in the scheduling of their contests to fit in with the imperatives of network programming. The start of the 1988 Seoul Olympics, for example, was brought forward a week to fit in with the contractual commitments of ABC and NBC to televise baseball's playoffs and World Series respectively. The structures of a number of games were significantly altered to make them more amenable to television coverage. The tie-breaker set was introduced into tennis both to develop the pace and excitement of matches and to make their length more predictable—and hence easier to schedule for television coverage. In sumo wrestling the three-minute "maturing" rule was introduced for similar reasons. Originally a highly formal religious ritual, the short-lived physical clash of sumo wrestlers had traditionally been preceded by elaborate protocols of psychological, physical and spiritual preparation, or maturing, lasting for up to ten minutes or more. Similar time constraints to sumo's three-minute maturing rule have been progressively introduced in a number of other sports events, for example, weightlifting; high, long and triple jumps; pole vaulting; discus, hammer and javelin throwing; springboard diving; and chess. In all cases they are designed to force athletes to get on with the real action, the visual entertainment. In golf, television has favored coverage of 72-hole stroke-play tournaments rather than match-play tournaments primarily because stroke-play rounds of golf have a predictable length and are guaranteed to cover the last five or six holes of the course, the holes where fixed television camera positions have been set up.

A number of other sports have been transformed or revitalized by television. The television version of wrestling is pure theater. In Britain in the 1960s the game of snooker was dying of neglect (the game's nearest equivalent in the United States is pool). Its image was that of a game for ne'er-do-wells and the unemployed, an image fostered by its popularity in the depression of the 1930s when smoke-filled snooker halls were one of the few available places for meeting with one's friends and for cheap entertainment. By the 1960s there were only a handful of manufacturers of snooker and billiard tables and equipment left in Britain, and they were desperately trying to diversify into other, more popular and respectable fields such as lawn bowls. All that changed, however, with the advent of the BBC's televised snooker tournament Pot Black in the late 1960s.[7] Now tuxedoed professional players—the best of them millionaires—play the game with intense concentration in a reverential atmosphere more akin to church than beer-hall, the silence occasionally broken by the respectful applause of the audience and the hushed calling of the break score by a graveyard-voiced commentator.

Other changes in sports practices have also been ascribed to the influence of television. "Time outs" are allegedly called to coincide with commercial breaks, and allegations have been made that in professional basketball the referees readjust the penalty count to prevent one team from falling too far behind in the game, a good close match being more likely to keep the television audience in contact with the game and its accompanying advertisements. While sports entrepreneurs and administrators have always been keen to introduce more drama and fast-moving action into their games, the tendency has been accentuated by the presence of television and the recognition that professional sport is part of the entertainment industry. As part of that industry sport has developed its own star system, its own lives of the rich and infamous, its own media-created public personas, its own news fillers of gossip and trivia about its heroes and villains. Professional sportsmen and women are increasingly presented, and present themselves, first and foremost as entertainers in competition not so much with each other as with other claimants on the consumer's discretionary entertainment dollar. Personal competitiveness is merely a useful marketing ploy to be exploited in the promotion of ticket sales and the attraction of a large television audience. Thus, for example, the 1989 WBC title match between Sugar Ray Leonard and Tommy Hearns was advertised as "The War" in the expectation that the viewing audience would take more interest if they perceived the contest as a grudge match, no matter how blatantly manufactured. Sports commentary too is sucked into the entertainment and advertising mode. Its language is the language of hyperbole, of exaggeration and sensationalism and superlatives. And in international contests it is chauvinistic to the point of absurdity.

SPORTS SPONSORSHIP

We feel the Games are the ultimate in amateur sports. We would be embarrassed not to be involved.
—Brian Porter, Manager of Olympic Marketing for Anheuser-Busch, an $11 million sponsor of the 1984 Los Angeles Games
(*Time*, 18 June 1984).

Sports organizations have a number of sources of income in addition to membership fees, gate receipts and the sale of television rights. These include the sale of food, beverage and souvenir concessions for the venues of the club or league, the sale of advertising space at those venues, the sale of programs and, in some sports where there is a transfer system, the sale of players. The profitability of many major professional sports is now partially dependent, however, on a further source of income—corporate sponsorship. Corporate sponsorship of sports is not a new phenomenon. Whannel records that at the 1908 London Olympics Oxo had the marathon catering franchise and gave all the runners an Oxo Athlete's Pack containing samples of the company's products. In 1928 Coca-Cola shipped a thousand cases of its "official soft drink" to accompany the U.S. team to the Amsterdam Olympics. However, in the late 1960s and through the 1970s and 1980s sponsorship grew to massive proportions. This growth was partly triggered by growing restrictions on the direct advertising of tobacco and tobacco products following the publication in 1964 of the surgeon general's report *Smoking and Health*. Tobacco companies developed a number of strategies to circumvent the intentions of government directives on advertising. These included such marketing ploys as "piggyback" advertising, where tobacco brand names are displayed in advertisements for other products; parallel marketing, where cigarette brand names are attached to non-tobacco products; and the embedding of tobacco advertisements in major movies—Philip Morris, for example, paid $350,000 to have its brand name shown in the appropriately titled James Bond movie *Licensed to Kill*. The largest part of the industry's effort, however, went into the sponsorship of sport (Deeks 1992).

From the sponsoring company's point of view, sports sponsorship can offer a number of benefits. It can glamorize the company's products or services by association with well-known sports stars and with youthful and healthy activities. It can stimulate general public goodwill toward the company, demonstrably raise public awareness of the corporation and increase morale among the organization's own employees. Since the demographic makeup of sports fans varies from sport to sport, sponsorship can provide a form of advertising that is tightly focused on a desired target market. With the development of sponsorship has come a growth in sports marketing and of sports promotion agencies. Sports marketing is designed to provide the research, information and cost-benefit data needed by a company considering investing in sports promotion as part of its business development strategy. Sports promotion agencies specialize in designing sponsorship and advertising packages that match a product or a company to a specific target market. Their role involves liaison among commercial sponsors, sporting organizations, the advertising industry and the media. Since a crucial element in the sports sponsorship package is television coverage of the proposed event or events, liaison with the television networks is particularly important. Former professional sportsmen and women frequently find employment in sports marketing and promotion as well as in corporate sales and public relations departments.

From the point of view of the professional clubs and their players, sponsorship can make a major contribution to the costs of promoting and administering tournaments, of improving facilities, and of providing prize money and other incentives to attract top performers to the club. It also provides direct material benefits to the players in the form of free sports clothing and equipment, though this may not always be to their liking. In the 1982 European athletics championships, for example, the management of the Polish team banned their world-ranking high jumper from the competition because he refused to wear the officially approved brand of shoe. In many other sports, individual athletes have taken exception to the official sponsors' products, either on the grounds of quality or personal preference or for political reasons.

The 1984 Los Angeles Olympics has been marked out as representing the high noon of corporate sports sponsorship. Because of the financially disastrous experience of its North American predecessor, Montreal, in hosting the 1976 Olympic Games, the citizens of Los Angeles and of southern California had voted not to give any public money to the Olympics. However, under the skillful and forthright direction of Peter Ueberroth, who had been a successful entrepreneur in the travel industry and went on, after the Olympic Games, to become baseball commissioner, the LA Olympic Games showed a profit of $125 million. ABC paid $225 million for the television rights to the games (45 percent of the games' entire operating budget) and over $180 million was raised in corporate sponsorship by the U.S. Olympic Committee and the Los Angeles Olympic Organizing Committee, presided over by Ueberroth. Major sponsorships were limited to 32 companies who paid from $4 million to $13 million in a mixture of cash, goods and services. For example, $5 million plus 500,000 Snickers bars and 500,000 bags of M&M candies were donated by confectionery company M&M/Mars. Levi

Strauss clothed the 700 members of the U.S. team and the 40,000 Olympic Games staff. IBM lent 200 personal computers and other computer technology. Other companies outside the elite group of official sponsors were granted designations as official suppliers. In addition estimates were that sponsoring companies spent a further $500 million plus in advertising and promotion of their involvement in the Olympic Games.

There were critics of the commercialization of the Los Angeles Olympics. In the European press the games were dubbed the McLympics, and one American weekly complained that they were "beginning to look like a TV docudrama about the last days of capitalism." Nevertheless, the Los Angeles model of games management has subsequently become the norm for major international sporting festivals, copied with varying degrees of success. The highly profitable 1988 Seoul Olympic Games met over half of its operating costs from the worldwide sale of television rights for $407 million and corporate receipts of $128 million from 23 corporate sponsors, 57 suppliers and 62 licensees (Official Report: Games of the XXIVth Olympiad, Seoul, 1988, v.1:221). After the heavily boycotted and financially disastrous Edinburgh Commonwealth Games of 1986, the 1990 Auckland Commonwealth Games were described by the organizing committee chairman, businessman David Johnson, as the "commercial games." They were designed to run largely along business lines, funded by sponsorship, the sale of television rights, gate receipts and voluntary labor. As in Seoul, companies were sold rights as official sponsors, official suppliers or official licensees. Unysis designed, supplied and ran the games' computer network at its own cost, and Kodak developed a new photographic identification card system for athletes and officials, a system it subsequently offered to the organizers of the 1992 Barcelona Olympics. In the event the Auckland Commonwealth Games could not be sustained solely by business and commercial involvement, and both local and central government picked up a substantial bill for the shortfall in games funding.

The growing linkages and dependencies between business and sport, and the development of business management approaches to sports administration, are readily observable in the running of major sports festivals. For a number of reasons these events are now generally impossible to fund without the sale of television rights, commercial sponsorship, major government funding or a mixture of all three.[8] One reason is their size—the sheer number of participating sports men and women and their accompanying coaches and team managers and officials place major burdens on the host communities in terms of accommodation, food and travel. A second reason is the highly expensive electronic communications infrastructure that has to be established to make events an attractive proposition for the all-important purchase of television rights—the setting up of media centers with video feed facilities, computerized work stations, and communication satellite access. And a third reason is the continual raising of expectations among the television viewing public in terms of the entertainment values of sporting events, expectations that lead to a constant demand for bigger, better, more spectacular—and more expensive—events than last time.

However, the links between business and sport are not confined to professional sport or to major international tournaments. They also pervade the everyday practice of business management. Sporting metaphors and the language of sports are ubiquitous in business and permeate business ideology. What is known as the unitary management ideology, for example, places great stress on the idea of the business organization as a team in which all must pull together to support the goals of management. The ability to engender team spirit is deemed to be an important quality in any would-be business manager, and being a good team player a necessary personal attribute. Management development workshops and role plays focus, among other things, on team-building exercises. At a more macro level corporate strategy is frequently described in terms of having a corporate game plan and a set of organizational goals. Products are described as winners and losers, and their managerial sponsors as product champions. New projects may be kicked off, and their initial stages described in terms of reaching first base. Managers will be encouraged to "go for it," a term that has its origins in American football. Individual managers whose performance is below par or not up to scratch may be transferred to another position or sidelined. As can be seen, a variety of terms from a number of sports are jumbled together, sometimes distorting their original meanings.

There are further ways in which sports values and business values are intertwined. Empirical studies suggest that there is a general perception among business managers that the personality traits associated with sports achievement are also associated with managerial success (Warn 1989). The self-motivation, need for achievement, discipline, competitiveness, persistence, goal setting, and responsiveness to rewards for effort that lead to individual sporting success are thought to be important traits of successful managers. There is an even greater belief in the transferability of skills from team sports to the business arena, that participation in team sports develops the communication skills, the commitment to the group, the mutual support systems, and the acceptance of common goals needed by successful managers. Another common analogy is that between the role of the business manager and that of the sports coach. Successful performance in these roles are seen to require an ability to motivate others, to communicate effectively, to provide appropriate reinforcement and encouragement, to delegate and to organize, to analyze performance, to adjudicate disputes, and to reward and sanction behavior. It is not surprising, therefore, that many managers believe that recruitment to managerial positions is influenced by the sporting achievements of the candidates.

NOTES

1. M. R. Real (1975) on the organization of professional football.
2. Philip Roth, *The Great American Novel.*
3. During the reign of Queen Victoria 295 out of a total of 695 cricketing "blues" from the Universities of Oxford and Cambridge became Anglican clergymen (Whannel 1983:41).
4. In 1797 at Rugby School and in 1818 at Winchester School, for example, the authorities had found it necessary to call in the armed militia to quell riots and regain control of the schools (Goldlust 1987:17).
5. Motto of the Los Angeles Raiders Football Team.
6. Similarly in the United States in the 1980s owning a minor-league baseball club became trendy among celebrities like actors Bill Murray and Robert Wagner, athletes Don Drysdale and Roman Gabriel, and singers Jimmy Buffett and Conway Twitty (Lamb 1991:56).
7. The first snooker match on BBC-TV was broadcast in black and white on 8 September 1950. It was only the advent of color broadcasts of the game in 1967, however, that attracted a worldwide audience (London, Museum of the Moving Image).
8. NBC paid $401 million for the U.S. rights to the Barcelona Olympics; the asking price for Atlanta is $600 million. The European Broadcasting Union, a consortium of European television networks, paid $90 million for Barcelona and $275 million for Atlanta.

CHAPTER 12

Schemes for Dreams: Commerce and Culture

CULTURE AND COUNTERCULTURE

A number of reservations have been expressed and a variety of questions raised about the growing impact of business on culture. Is the morality of business and the market economy, for example, a sufficient code of conduct for human behavior in the modern world? Should the engineering principles and management ideologies developed in complex technological systems be used in the design of educational programs? Does the concentration of ownership and control in the media foreshadow a new Orwellian manipulation of mass consciousness? Are there viable alternatives to the dominance of business practices, business values, business symbols, and business languages in the shaping of modern culture and society?

This search for alternatives to business culture is explored in the present chapter. The proposition is that business culture is now the standard culture of the Western world. Within the framework of that standard culture, however, a number of alternative cultures and subcultures exist. Some of these act to modify the behaviors that are conditioned and sanctioned by the dominant business culture. In addition, countercultures periodically seek to establish themselves outside the orbit of business culture, rejecting that culture in toto and seeking to replace it with something else. Whereas coexistence with the dominant culture is accepted by members of alternative cultures and subcultures, counterculture groups seek to replace the dominant culture or to protect themselves as totally as possible from its impacts.

Some examples from within the world of business may clarify these distinctions. Many small businesses, and some large ones too, are family firms. In such businesses it is not uncommon for interpersonal and familial considerations to impinge on business decisions in significant ways, ways that may not be wholly compatible with the maximization of profit (Deeks 1976). Similarly in societies where kinship networks are still central to the social structure, business behaviors may be shaped as much by the ethics of kinship as by the ethics of the market (Reddy 1991). In other enterprises business organization and business practices may be significantly shaped by the owners' ideological commitments and beliefs—whether religious, political or ecological. Even in large-scale business enterprises such matters may be determined in part by the professional codes and occupational subcultures of members of the firm. In all these instances some alternative non-business value system, drawn from a subculture or an alternative culture, is introduced into the business arena to modify the prevailing economic rationality of decision making within the enterprise.

Countercultures, in contrast, reject such accommodations with the dominant culture. Some of these are cultures of preservation. The Amish, for example, in their community of Lancaster County, Pennsylvania, have sought to sustain the values and practices of a seventeenth-century Swiss religious sect, the Mennonites. They farm and produce primarily for their own communal use. Wherever possible they reject modern technology, retaining horse-drawn transport, using wind and water power to preserve a pre–Industrial Revolution lifestyle, and producing handmade toys for their children. They keep alive their own language, manage their own schooling system and have their own publishing house and printed literature. The emphasis in schooling is on the acquisition of practical skills and simple crafts, and children are engaged in work from an early age. Work is a shared activity linked to the seasonal rituals of farm life or to the communal efforts of building and maintenance, a feature of Amish life illustrated by the barn-building sequence in the 1985 film *Witness*. The Amish ideology gives priority to communal needs, emphasizes personal humility and discipline, discourages competitiveness and condemns laziness and luxuries. The simplicity of manner and tastes prized by the culture is reinforced through dress codes.

Amish culture is a form of counterculture that Milton Yinger described as "value-oriented." It seeks to protect and preserve a set of values that are threatened by economic, social and political developments in the broader society. The focus of such a counterculture is activity within the community. Two other prominent varieties of counterculture in Yinger's schema, are those that are "power-oriented" and those that are "participation-oriented." The power-oriented countercultures seek to subvert and replace the dominant culture, or some critical aspect of it, generally through a process of political action. In their attack on business culture they emphasize the concentrations of wealth and power, the inequitable income distribution, and the commercialization of human relationships that flow from the free play of the market economy. From this perspective, socialist and communist ideologies with their goals of social transformation through fundamental rearrangement of economic relationships are power-oriented countercultural movements. They provide a focus for political action in societies with low per capita income.

In participation-oriented countercultures, suggests Yinger, the attack on the dominant business culture has a different emphasis. It is an attack on the prestige accorded to material possessions and to technology, and on the consequent development of societies that are seen to be spiritually impoverished. The goal of participation-oriented countercultural movements is one of self-realization, personal growth and the development of new insights and experiences. The focus is on transformation through psychic and interpersonal activity rather than through political or community activity. Feeling may be given priority over rational thought, and an anti-work or no-work ethic may be developed. Generally such counterculture movements arise in rich rather than poor societies. The 1970s ideology of dropping out, "doing your own thing" and "finding yourself" reflected such a participation-oriented countercultural mode.

Truth... is attained not by arid research but by mystical insight. It is found in populist, homespun wisdom, in direct experience with the cosmos, in meditation, in chants, in drugs, in sensory deprivation, in sensitivity to the messages of the intuitive right hemisphere of the brain—all this set over against science, technology, the knowledge of the expert, and cold rationality. (Yinger 1982:97)

It is a mode that stimulates exactly that modularity of personality that John Blair argues is so characteristic of American culture, a culture that encourages individuals to think of themselves as free to change at will their jobs, their personalities, their partners. In its positive guise it manifests an openness to innovation, an acceptance of change and a toleration of alternative lifestyles. On the negative side is an increasing fragmentation of experience and an acute sense of alienation:

The consequence of a willingness to encounter everything is that you experience nothing. A life that careens wildly from one posture to the next is not enriched by any of them; the self does not grow as a result, but sinks into a deepening promiscuity of being. There is no authentic gratification in this mode of being, but only a combination of listlessness, triviality, identity confusion, and an unappeasable need for sensation. (Selzer 1979:194)

The narcissistic New Consciousness movement of the 1970s represented a retreat from political action as a means of bringing about social and cultural change. In Christopher Lasch's view the "culture of narcissism" was the final outcome of the culture of competitive individualism; it "carried the logic of individualism to the extreme of a war of all against all, the pursuit of happiness to the dead end of a narcissistic preoccupation with the self" (Lasch 1980:xv).

Utopian literature shares common points of departure with countercultural movements. The stimulus for much utopian writing is dismay at the nature of the dominant culture and the prevailing social system. Utopian models alert us to question the basic principles and ideologies that manage and control contemporary society. In presenting models of some future world, writers have sought to detail the characteristics of an alternative "better" society (utopia) or to extend imaginatively to some future time the negative consequences of continuing along some current cultural paths (dystopias). Whereas utopias hold up an image of a society that we might collectively wish to work toward, dystopias like Aldous Huxley's *Brave New World* (1932) and George Orwell's *Nineteen Eighty-Four* (1949) present pictures of societies we might create if we do not change our collective course.

Both utopian and dystopian writing contain a mixture of extrapolative and normative models of the future. In the extrapolative models, current technological, economic and business developments are projected forward and their consequences for social and organizational life explored. In the normative models an ideal future society is constructed around a set of values and ideologies that guide the design of new forms of social and organizational life. In addition to describing some future ideal society, many utopian writers suggest the political, social, economic or technological mechanisms necessary to achieve it. Utopian thinkers, suggested Paul Goodman, rather than being impractical, unrealistic and naive, are people who "still think that machines are meant to be useful, that work is a productive activity, that politics aims at the common weal, and in general that something can be done" (Goodman 1962:12). That such ideals should be characterized as utopian is a measure of the general cynicism about the possibilities of significant change in the prevailing social system.

TECHNOCRATIC AND CRAFT UTOPIAS AND THE ENGINEERED SOCIETY

The Utopian Socialist writers of the early years of the Industrial Revolution sought to come to terms with the social, political and cultural consequences of the economic and technological changes taking place around them, particularly those changes that divided capital from labor and increased the gap between rich and poor. In their utopian designs some of these writers embraced the new technologies and the opportunities those technologies made available. Henri Saint-Simon (1760–1825), for example, saw society as being composed of two great classes. One class was the producers (*les industriels*) and included workers, capitalists, scientists, technicians, artisans, artists, and educators—all those who made some direct contribution, through their work, to the common welfare. The other class was the idlers (*les oisifs*). In this class were the privileged, the landed aristocracy, the nobility, the church hierarchy, officers of the crown, magistrates, and the army—those who did not work or who made no productive contribution to society. Saint-Simon's utopian society was one in which everyone worked (the idlers disappeared through peaceful means) for the good of the whole community. Men of arts and letters (*les savants*), acting in the general public interest, set the economic and spiritual goals of the society. The day-to-day management of economic affairs was to be placed in the hands of those who understood industry and commerce—the bankers, businessmen and technocrats—but without individualistic capitalist competition. Saint-Simon's utopian views were popular and influential, and he has been described as "the precursor of socialism, the precursor of the technocrats, and the precursor of totalitarianism" (Carr 1964:2).

Whether to accept or reject the costs and benefits of science and technology is a key theme in utopian novels. Francis Bacon's fragmentary utopian sketch *The New Atlantis* (1626), for example, was

> an explicit attempt to replace the philosopher with the research scientist as the ruler of the utopian future. New Atlantis was a pure technocratic society. Replete with research institutions aimed at advancing technological progress, scientific rationality was located at the very core of the community. Its research institutes were described as "the very eye of the kingdom." (Fischer 1990:67)

In contrast, Samuel Butler's satirical romance *Erewhon* (1872), while not presenting Erewhonian society in utopian terms, nevertheless portrayed it as one that is uncontaminated by sophisticated technology. Indeed, in Erewhon all machines were destroyed after a philosopher had prophesied that they would eventually supersede the human race.

The advent of industrialization, the love-hate relationship over technology and "progress" and the culture divide between the world of science and technology and the world of literature and the arts, have markedly influenced the utopian novels of the nineteenth and twentieth centuries. Of the technocratic utopias, Edward Bellamy's *Looking Backward 2000—1887*, published in 1888, was one of the most influential and widely read. Within ten years of its publication, 400,000 copies had been sold in the United States, over 250,000 in Britain and the book had been translated "into the language of every civilized country" (Taylor 1964:205). Like most of the technocratic literature, Bellamy's vision is of a world organized in accord with scientific and technical principles. He sees such a world having an order and form that cannot be achieved through the messy and conflictual apparatus of politics. His utopian technocratic society is formed by a process of industrial evolution rather than through the mechanisms of democratic party politics.

The organization of business in Bellamy's utopia is highly centralized and authoritarian. A central state bureaucracy directs the industries of the nation through a system of industrial guilds. The organization of industry into large-scale enterprises within the framework of a corporate state creates, in Bellamy's vision, a highly productive society. It also facilitates the elimination of the four wasteful aspects of a competitive capitalist market economy: "first, the waste by mistaken undertakings; second, the waste from the competition and mutual hostility of those engaged in industry; third, the waste by periodical gluts and crises, with the consequent interruptions of industry; fourth, the waste from idle capital and labor, at all times" (Bellamy 1967:245). Bellamy's is an organizational utopia as much as a technological one, reflecting the "prodigiously multiplied efficiency which perfect organization can give to labor."

A spate of utopian writing followed the 1888 publication of Bellamy's book: "Between 1888 and 1900 there appeared altogether over sixty Utopias—an average of five a year—which deal specifically with the abuses and possible reform of society" (Taylor 1964:206). These included works with such titles as *Looking Further Backward*, *Looking Forward*, and *Looking Beyond*, many of them using Bellamy's own utopian framework. It was a tradition that lived on. In 1973 Bellamy's future society was updated by Mack Reynolds in *Looking Backward from the Year 2000*. Reynolds adopted Bellamy's industrial guild system for the central planning and coordination of production and distribution but revised Bellamy's vision of the year 2000 to take account of the technological capabilities of the 1970s. Reynolds's novel is an extrapolative and optimistic technological utopia. Everyone in his future society has a guaranteed annual income and there are no differentials of wealth. There is almost no employment. Junior positions in business have been largely automated out of existence and the service sector has been revolutionized by computerization and automation, all items being electronically purchased from home and electronically delivered. An individual has a 1 in 50 chance of landing a job, and all the available jobs require high levels of education and aptitude. Those who are employed work at home for six hours a day, four days a week and retire at age 45 if they have not been bumped from their jobs before that by the computers. Farmer Edie, for example, works in her Pennsylvania home managing, by remote control, 20 automatic tractors on a farm the size of the state of Kansas. For those with no employment, work is continued on an amateur basis as hobby and as play. In this utopian leisure society higher-education facilities are greatly expanded in accord with the principle of lifelong education. Studies are carried out at home through access to communications satellites and computer data banks.

Not all the utopian socialists shared Saint-Simon's vision of a technocratic meritocracy in which technical experts had a predominant role in the running of society and social problems were resolved by scientific and technological means. Charles Fourier (1772–1837), for example, saw the ideal society as being structured in terms of small communities rather than in a science of large-scale organization and administration. Fourier's utopian communities were agriculturally based. He rejected large-scale industry and its work disciplines in favor of willingly given and productive labor in self-sufficient communities that were in harmony with the natural world. Robert Owen

(1771–1858), a wealthy manufacturer, keen social reformer, and active trade unionist, was the founder of the cooperative movement in Britain. His utopian vision sought to bring together the benefits of industrialism and advanced technology with the ideals of a communal society. His experimental communities—New Lanark in Scotland and New Harmony in the United States—were designed to combine industrial and agricultural work in independent and self-sufficient villages of "unity and cooperation."

Just as not all the utopian socialists accepted Saint-Simon's view of the desirable future, so too not all the utopian novelists accepted the technocratic utopia of Bellamy and his imitators. William Morris's *News from Nowhere* (1890) was a direct reaction to Bellamy's work. Bellamy accepted the machine and the advance of technology. For him science and technology were instruments for progress toward the elimination of poverty by the exploitation and mastery of nature:

In *Looking Backward*, he accepts the advance of technology, welcomes it, and attempts to build it into a complete system of human values. Bellamy's Utopian society owns, therefore, devices which are the equivalent of the radio and television; it tills its farms with power-drawn plows; and it manufactures its goods in gigantic mills which, unlike the factories of the nineteenth century, are as thoroughly habitable as they are powerful—airy, cheerful, and all but noiseless. (Taylor 1964:192)

Morris, in contrast, rejects some of the machines and much of the machinery of the industrial age and rejects too the whole organizational paraphernalia supporting Bellamy's technocratic society. In *News from Nowhere* Morris constructs a society of small and static rural communities, a pastoral society in harmony with nature. Community activities revolve around the land and the festivals of the agricultural season, such as harvesting, and around cooperative work to meet the needs of the community. There are no factories and no large-scale enterprises. Workshops are provided as informal meeting places for those who wish to work together.

In Morris's arts and crafts utopia the ethic of craftsmanship is paramount. Morris was happy to see work that was irksome to do by hand—work that was "revolting and destructive of self-respect"—being done by machines. But for work that was a pleasure to do by hand, power tools and power-driven machines were a threat rather than a promise and should not be used. In his utopian community, handicrafts are revived and craftsmanship relearned. There is no money economy, no one is paid for his or her work and there are no artificial incentives or other forms of coercion to work. Consequently the only reward for good work is the reward of creation. All work in *News from Nowhere* is a form of pleasure, either individual or communal, and necessary for a sense of well-being: "Happiness without happy daily work is impossible."

Morris's model society is built on a romantic and nostalgic view of medieval

England as a golden age of craftsmanship and a time of simplicity and austerity in which possessions and luxuries were regarded as sources of spiritual corruption. In his various lectures on art, socialism, democracy, and capitalism, Morris repeatedly praised the roughness of the work of medieval sculptors and craftsmen, seeing in that roughness a sign of "the life and liberty of every workman who struck the stone." By comparison he found the fine craftsmanship of the eighteenth century to be the "rigid, cold, inhuman" product of a slavish copying of pattern books. And the machine products of his own time, while they had "a certain high finish, and what I should call shop-counter look," were dull and lifeless and had a mechanical quality that could be produced only by turning the worker into a tool. Under a system of handiwork, in contrast,

no great pressure of speed was put on a man's work, but he was allowed to carry it through leisurely and thoughtfully; it used the whole of a man for the production of a piece of goods, and not small portions of many men; it developed the workman's whole intelligence according to his capacity, instead of concentrating his energy on one-sided dealing with a trifling piece of work. . . . It was this system, which had not learned the lesson that man was made for commerce, but supposed in its simplicity that commerce was made for men, which produced the art of the Middle Ages, wherein the harmonious co-operation of free intelligence was carried to the furthest point which has yet been attained, and which alone of all art can claim to be Free. (William Morris lecture on "Art and Democracy," Henderson 1967:303)

Modern futurology literature, on the basis of forecasts of the negative impacts of computerization on opportunities for paid employment, suggests a variety of developments along the road to a leisure society. These include the breakdown of the Protestant work ethic, the growth of service-sector employment and of leisure industries, guaranteed income schemes, artificially enforced consumption, bi-occupationalism (in which an individual has both a job in a high-demand skill and one in a chosen field of endeavor), multi-staged careers, retirement at age 38, expanding lifelong educational opportunities, the substitution of ecological thinking for economic thinking, the revival of small decentralized communities and so on (Brigard and Helmar 1970). Among these glowing brave new worlds is the development of arts and craft–based activities and enterprises with primarily recreational goals. In their desire to provide people with purposeful, if unpaid, employment and an opportunity for creative work, these schemes share common ground with William Morris's utopian visions. In their bourgeois consumption patterns, however, some of them may be more fanciful than the socialist Morris would have anticipated or approved of: "Every home will have its trampoline, sauna, swimming pool and piano. . . . Hobbies, leisure and work will all be the same thing. . . . Everyone will have the time and the opportunity to develop latent interests in opera, ballet, writing, painting and all arts and entertainment" (Marshall 1983).

The craft utopians adopt what I have described elsewhere as a "literary medieval" stereotype about business (Deeks 1976:187). It is a perspective that treats "small" as "beautiful," extolling the virtues of the small business enterprise and, by implication, warning of the "badness" of "big" business. The literary medieval business world is one of family firms, tightly knit into their local communities, operating businesses that are largely in harmony with nature. It is a world in which the business owner is typically conservative, a craftsperson rather than an entrepreneur, the upholder of traditional values and beliefs, skeptical of progress, proud of the personal loyalties within the enterprise and of the firm's reputation for a quality product. It is a Horatio Alger world beloved of Senate small business committees; they see the small enterprise as being "a great motive force among our people. It stimulates expression of the fundamental virtues of thrift, industry, intelligence, schooling, home ties, and family pride—in short, those fireside virtues which have counted for so much in developing our strength and character" (quoted by Bunzel 1962).

As a focal point of stability and order in a rapidly changing environment, the literary medieval entrepreneur is the antithesis of the archetypal capitalist of classical economic theory, the risk-taking, profit-maximizing, economically motivated individualist who is competitive, materialistic and single-minded in the pursuit of personal wealth. The utopian craft business is the antithesis too of the centralized large-scale industries of the technocratic utopias. In the modern world, however, the entrepreneurial ethos of competitive individualism and the management ideology of the technocratic large-scale corporation are more potent shapers of society and culture than the traditional craft or communal enterprise or family firm. One result has been the rapid exploitation of the natural environment by business rather than the development of a business system that is in harmony with the natural world. Some writers have stressed the dilemma posed by the decline of the dualistic world view that separates humankind from nature: "Man has tended to become so dominant on earth that he is now approaching a position where he constitutes one of the principal aspects of his own environment and in which environmental mastery would require the subjugation even of human nature by man" (quoted by Leiss 1970:578–79).

The need to use science to control human behavior and to recreate a society where humankind and nature are in harmony was the major theme of B. F. Skinner's utopian novel, Walden Two (1948). Skinner creates his utopian society by behavioral engineering. In Walden Two, the principles and techniques of behaviorist psychology are used to ensure that although members of the community are practically always doing what they "want" to do, what they "choose" to do, "we see to it that they will want to do precisely the things that are best for themselves and the community. Their behavior is determined, yet they're free." In Walden Two's participation-oriented culture, the prescription for the good life constitutes a minimum of unpleasant labor, a chance to exercise one's talents and abilities, intimate and satisfying personal relationships, the preservation of good health, and opportunities for rest and relaxation. Work is kept to a minimum in order to avoid or minimize the psychological problems that arise from uncreative and uninteresting employment. The average working day is one of four hours, and there is a regulatory system of labor credits that give positive reinforcement to the principles of no failure, no boredom and no duplication of effort. The technological advantages of the modern world are exploited within a framework of cooperative living, a framework that makes the benefits of mass production and labor-saving devices available to everyone.

In *Walden Two* the individual is subordinated to the group. This is achieved through cradle-to-grave behavior modification. Behavioral engineering is used in community education, in the psychological management of the community, in solving the psychological problems arising from group living, and in the training out of individual emotions that are seen to have no beneficial function in a cooperative society. *Walden Two*'s scientists and planners are moving toward an even more desirable situation, one in which they can design individual personality and control individual motivation and temperament. Although this foreshadows some of the possibilities of genetic engineering, it is a position that had already been satirized in literature. Aldous Huxley's novel *Brave New World* (1932), for example, opens with a description of the Central London Hatchery and Conditioning Center where test-tube babies are decanted "as socialized human beings, as Alphas or Epsilons," predestined and conditioned to accept and to like "their unescapable social destiny":

On Rack 10, rows of next generation's chemical workers were being trained in the toleration of lead, caustic soda, tar, chlorine. The first of a batch of two hundred and fifty embryonic rocket-plane engineers was just passing the eleven hundredth meter mark on Rack 3. A special mechanism kept their containers in constant rotation. . . . "They learn to associate topsy-turvydom with well-being; in fact, they're only happy when they're standing on their heads."

One man's utopia is another man's dystopia. *Walden Two* had a generally hostile reception; *Life* magazine described it as "a travesty of the good life." Skinner's vision, of human nature engineered for the social good, exchanges the competitive jungle of individualism for the claustrophobic tyranny of totalitarianism. For behind the apparently benign manufacture of happiness and contentment in *Walden Two* lies a hierarchical structure of authoritarian control, a class structure of planners, managers, scientists and workers. Skinner's defense of his utopia and its controls was that it simply made explicit what was a fact of life: "All men control and are controlled. The question of government in the broadest possible sense is not how freedom is to be preserved but what kinds of control are to be used and to what ends" (Douglas 1971:131). In Skinner's view his utopia was being castigated as an undesirable dictatorship primarily because it was a planned community. If the same community had developed through a process of cultural evolution, it would, Skinner believed, have been warmly welcomed.

In *Walden Two* there are no mechanisms of consent by the controlled in the methods and purposes of their subordination, no controls over the controllers, no guards on Frazier, Walden Two's main planner-creator and self-appointed guardian of the communal good. It is the problem of all blueprints for utopia. How do you get from here to there? Bellamy's technocratic utopia is the consequence of an evolutionary process. His corporate state evolves from large-scale business enterprise and is founded on faith in human rationality and cooperativeness. In contrast, Morris's craft utopia is brought into existence by revolutionary political action. The transition to a decentralized form of communism is brought about by using the class action of a general strike to precipitate civil war and the breakdown of the world market economy.

BUSINESS AND POSTMODERNISM[1]

For some writers, the desire to reshape communities, reshape human behavior, reshape life itself—a desire so fundamental to utopian literature—is anathema:

Reshaping life! People who can say that have never understood a thing about life—they have never felt its breath, its heart—however much they have seen or done. They look on it as a lump of raw material which needs to be processed by them, to be ennobled by their touch. But life is never a material, a substance to be molded. If you want to know, life is the principle of self-renewal, it is constantly renewing and changing and transfiguring itself, it is infinitely beyond your or my theories about it. (Boris Pasternak, *Dr. Zhivago*)

Indeed, in the twentieth-century, grand designs to reshape whole societies have had murderous consequences. Dystopian rather than utopian visions have seemed a more appropriate reflection of a Western world increasingly skeptical of the benefits both of institutionalized technological systems and of religious and secular templates for creating new economic and social orders. Disillusionment with human progress through scientific and technological advances affected not only utopian literature but science fiction. During the 1960s science fiction, "a genre which had hitherto been a home for social optimism, coupled with a far-seeing faith in science and technology, became devoted instead to social discontent and cosmic despair" (Mellor 1984:20). The growing distrust of political statements, of communalistic political philosophies, and of utopian social agendas, and a decline in political activism and rational political debate, leave a vacuum at the core of modern politics that cannot be filled by the marketing of political images. Political pluralism, far from being an expression of vibrant debate about routes to a better future, becomes merely an aimless kind of tolerance underwriting the social and economic status quo.

Modernism expressed a "positive, technocratic, and rationalistic" vision of the world appropriate to utopian writing, an un-self-conscious confidence in technology and scientific rationality as the key to a better life. Postmodernism, in its rejection of "meta-narratives" and its "intense distrust of all universal or 'totalizing' discourses" (Harvey 1989:9), provides the appropriate intellectual climate for dystopian literature. Implicit within aspects of postmodernist thinking is a new freedom for business activity and for the dissemination of the values of a business culture. The modernist tradition, like the utopian one, constrains business within the framework of some broader social order and social values. It sanctifies the intervention of the state as an agency for the rational planning of a new economic order or a more just and humane society, precipitating a whole range of conflicts between business and government, business and the community—conflicts over capital accumulation, resource utilization, labor exploitation, control of the media, equal employment opportunity, the protection of personal privacy, and so on. Postmodernist thinking expresses freedom from constraints, the constraints of rationality, of history, of time and place, of social structure, of custom and practice, of organization and technology, and of government and the state. Whereas from a modernist perspective the separation of business from society and from culture made some analytical sense, indicating some underlying assumptions about the subordination of business to the interests of the broader community,[2] in a postmodernist framework this is no longer the case. In the postmodern world there is a more symbiotic relationship between business and culture, business and society, a symbiosis caught in terms such as "business culture," "the enterprise culture," "the enterprise society." This symbiosis has been facilitated by the dominance of the Hayekian or Friedmanite meta-narrative about the over-riding superiority of the free market (the ideology of market capitalism described in Chapter 3), a meta-narrative to which business is generally sympathetic, and the decline of alternative meta-narratives about ways of reconciling public benefits with private vices or of establishing the nature of the "community interest" or the "public good."[3] When Irving Kristol (1978) proposed two cheers for capitalism, his analysis was grounded in recognition that in practice the alternatives ranged "from the hideous to the merely squalid." The third cheer was absent because of Kristol's perception of the spiritual limitations of capitalism. The "bourgeois mode of existence" lacked a "transcendental" dimension. Capitalism, with its emphasis on individual economic self-improvement, generated "an unromantic, prosaic way of life" and failed "to satisfy the spiritual hunger for something larger, more heroic, more exalted than 'bettering one's condition' " (Podhoretz 1981:102).[4] Others have seen precisely this absence of a transcendental dimension as sufficient reason to accord capitalism a third cheer, since for all its limitations it was not a system that demanded the unquestioning loyalty and adoration of those who worked within it. From this perspective of the "innocence of commerce" the reification of the ideology of market capitalism as the dominant ideology of the Western world in the latter half of the twentieth century could be seen as counter-productive.

In the transition from modernism to postmodernism, however, more has changed than the rejection of state plans and grand social designs. The focus of business activity has shifted to encompass not only the traditional expropriation and exploitation of resources—land, labor, and capital—but also the expropriation and exploitation of language, symbols, and images, the very currency of knowledge and consciousness. It is not only an ideology compatible with business interests that has emerged as the dominant ideology in recent years. As we saw in Chapter 5, business languages and symbols have come to permeate the cultural mainstream, embedding themselves in the collective consciousness and increasingly conditioning private and public thinking about a variety of non-business issues. These languages and images, promoting as they do the ethics of consumption and the morality of market behavior, are business ideology in disguise. As they spread, so culture is progressively reconstructed in a manner compatible with business practices and values. In this process of reconstruction commerce and culture are fused. John Urry (1990:85), for example, writes of the

dissolving of the boundaries between what is artistic production and what is commercial. Developments here include the growth of "free" artistic pop videos to sell records, of pop songs appearing first within advertisements, of major artistic talents employed within the production of adverts, and the use of "art" to sell products via sponsorship. Commerce and culture are indissolubly intertwined in the postmodern.

There are many other examples of this fusion process and of the blurring of the boundaries between business and culture, boundaries fundamental to the systems models so favored by modernism. Commercial sponsorship of the modern museum, the sale of reproductions of works of art in museum shops—turning museum artifacts into assets that can be marketed and merchandised—and the joint promotions run by museums and department stores illustrate the phenomenon.[5]

Shops and museums have a great deal in common. Urban, predominantly middle class, dedicated to exhibition, committed to consumption, either of images, ideas or goods. Once separated only by the availability of their content (for sale in the stores, only for display in the museums), new attitudes and new technologies tend to erode this distinction between merchandise and collections. (Bayley 1989:5)

London's Science Museum has been criticized for its reconstructions of a Sainsbury supermarket and a McDonald's burger bar. In 1991 it mounted an exhibition, "Running on Air," devised by Nike to link up with the television advertising campaign for the company's new Air 180 running shoe. Nike was not charged for the display space, a situation that an official of the Association for Business Sponsorship of the Arts described as "utterly astonishing. Nike must be laughing all the way to the ringing cash tills. Museums can't live in the markets part of the time and in cloud-cuckoo-land the rest, imagining they are totally pure because they haven't accepted any money. Nike is getting a great deal of commercial benefit out of the association: the museum should be selling its own excellence rather than giving it away free" (*The Independent*, 7 May 1991:14).

In the mass media it is often difficult to distinguish editorials and news from advertisements. In professional sport, play and games are restructured to fit the demands of commerce and the entertainment industry. Popular culture in particular is replete with pastiche and bricolage, indiscriminately merging cultural icons and commercial images. Madonna recreates herself as Marilyn Monroe. Reality Nirvana Tuttle puts on new personalities every day:

I can be vamp, tramp, flapper, sleaze, mod, postmod, Pop Art, disco, retro, rococo, go-go, gypsy, new wave, new romantic, New Look, Carnaby Street, Cossack, Bonnie and Clyde, directoire, debutante, existentialist, belle époque, buffalo girl, baby doll, Barbarella, punk, postpunk, Pre-Raphaelite, even *preppy* if I want to, which is almost never.

I can be any one of these things, and I never know which one I'm going to be when I wake up in the morning. It's *exciting*. (Tulloch 1990:41–42)

Lennon and McCartney tunes are reprocessed as advertising jingles, and Elton John and Louis Armstrong play side by side in a Diet Coke ad. Following the successful creation of the cyborg T–1000 in *Terminator 2*, the possibility of using "morphing" techniques to make a film with a computer-generated Marilyn Monroe is under discussion. Digital sampling technology allows pop songs to produce rhythm tracks drawn from such diverse origins as Gregorian chants, church bells, bites of hits from earlier times and the whispered verses of the Marquis de Sade. Such arbitrary appropriation and imitation of the past is, argues Norman Cantor (1988:380), a principle characteristic of postmodernist culture in the arts and literature.[6] The "youthcult fiction of the 1980s," writes Josephine Hendin (1990:219),

is a fiction not of insurgency but of cultural collaboration. What stands out is an assimilation, to the point of wholesale adoption, of advertising culture. Labels, name brands, surface signs have become the sole social referents and methods of character definition. In this literature, character is entirely the product of acts of appropriation indistinguishable from buying.

By 1987 there were reportedly more shopping centers in America than post offices or secondary schools (Schiller 1989:99). Shopping becomes entertainment; shopping centers, "Galleria."[7] Shopping malls, "decorated sheds which are part museum, part church," are the spiritual home of post-modern life, "places where the solemn rituals of high consumption capitalism are carried out" (Bayley 1989:77), seeking to provide through speculative as well as actual consumption the transcendental experiences supposedly missing in the heart of the bourgeois lifestyle. The malls are illustrative of the increasing corporate destruction and control of public space and are designed to standards in which community space is subservient to commercial needs (Schiller 1989:99). Department stores become tourist attractions; in the food halls of Harrods in London's Knightsbridge district, Japanese tourists queue to have their photographs taken. Major buildings are constructed to add glitz to corporate images: "Post Modern architecture and design is a *bricolage* of styles and allusions, an art of surface effects made possible by the deregulation of history. . . . In the Post Modern era culture is truly the handmaiden of commerce. Architecture *is* a form of advertising" (Bayley 1989:22).

The fusion of commerce and culture so characteristic of postmodernism has been a major theme of this book. It underpins the idea of business culture set out in Chapter 2 and the subsequent exploration of the percolation of business languages, symbols, images and values into the broader community. It is clearly evident in the specific industries described in the latter part of the book. Chapter 7 commented upon the way in which the entertainment-oriented values of commercial television distorted the presentation of news, and Chapter 11 highlighted the interconnections between television and sport. Both the fashion industry and the tourist industry have some quintessential postmodern aspects. In fashion, image triumphs over substance, and fickleness, stylistic derivativeness, eclecticism and irrationality co-exist with socially controlling dress codes. In modern tourism, technologically created "realities" and commercially constructed tourist "experiences" mirror the facades of postmodernism and provide a commentary on postmodernist debates about the nature of authenticity. Across the industries themselves there is a series of interconnections. A television program, *Miami Vice*, stimulates fashion and tourism.[8] Thomas Cook's railway excursionists travel to the 1851 Great Exhibition in London and the 1855 Paris Exhibition to view, among other things, the dresses of Frederick Worth.

Such fusions and connections do not represent the interlockings of a tight cultural system with precise boundaries but are random surprises sprung from commercial history and practice. They should alert us to the fact that a close relationship between commerce and culture is not something new or exclusive to the world of postmodernism. Art Nouveau was a decorative style that originated in a shop of that name set up in Paris in 1895 (Bayley 1989:47). The 1851 and 1855 exhibitions were commercial and cultural showcases whose design influenced the great museums and department stores developed simultaneously in the second half of the nineteenth century. The first of the great department stores, the Bon Marché, opened in Paris in

1869, included an art gallery. In 1902 the French architect Julien Guadet described such stores as "museums of merchandise" (Bayley 1989:44). Emile Zola, in his 1883 novel *Au Bonheur des Dames*, describes such a store as a "cathedrale de commerce moderne"; in the center of the store *Au Bonheur des Dames*,

> on a straight line from the main entrance, a broad gallery ran from one end of the shop to the other, flanked on the right and left by two narrower galleries, the Monsigny Gallery and the Michodière Gallery. The courtyards had been glazed in and transformed into halls; and iron staircases rose from the ground floor, iron bridges had been thrown across from one end to the other on both floors. It so happened that the architect was intelligent, a young man in love with modernity. . . . Everywhere space and light had been gained, air was freely let in, the public had plenty of room to move about beneath the audacious curves of the wide-spaced trusses. It was the cathedral of modern business, strong and yet light, built for a multitude of customers. . . . A whole world was opening up there amidst the life echoing beneath the high metal naves.

In the pre-industrial world, too, commerce and culture were inextricably meshed in the organization of public space. The precincts of the cathedrals and churches of medieval Europe frequently provided the location for markets and fairs (see Moore 1985). Describing the nature of public space at that time, Nicholas Adams (1991) writes of "a startling interpretation of religious and civic business, one that continued well into the modern era. Cathedrals in the Middle Ages, one might say, were more like what we would think of as civic centers than the civic centers themselves." Much the same might be said of those modern cathedrals of commerce, the shopping malls—more like civic and religious centers than the civic and religious centers themselves, but privately rather than publicly owned.

What has changed, however, as Chapter 3 indicated, is that in the post-modern world the economy is no longer "a branch of religious morality, based on Biblical texts and classical teaching and indoctrinated into the public through standard sermons, morality plays, and econo-religious tracts warning of the spiritual consequences of the abuse and misuse of money" (Fischer 1985:14). In the contemporary world the economy is an extension of business ideology, based on classical laissez-faire texts and teaching, and indoctrinated into the public through advertisements, commercial sponsorships, and educational programs extolling the spiritual satisfactions to be derived from the accumulation, use and misuse of money. By default rather than design, business is the only religion of postmodernism.

BUSINESS CULTURE: REPRISE

The idea of a business culture—the theory of a business culture sketched out in Chapter 2—seems particularly appropriate in the context of the debate about postmodernism and the post-Soviet world order. It posits the dominant role of business in the construction of contemporary society and culture, placing business at the center of the material, intellectual and spiritual life of the Western world. It postulates a general acceptance of business values—the values of free enterprise and profit maximization, of individual property ownership, and of private and corporate capital accumulation—as the shared values underpinning the idea of community. In a business culture the market is seen as the most valued mode for the provision and exchange of material goods and services. As such a culture spreads its tentacles wider, so the market comes to be seen as the ideal mode for the provision and exchange of all facets of the non-material culture. Love, sex, personality, religion, health, education, leisure, all become commodities in the marketplace, and the mechanism of material exchange becomes the dominant mechanism for social, psychological and political exchange.

If culture is viewed as "the collective programming of the mind" (Hofstede 1980:25), then a business culture is one in which this collective mental programming is dominated by the ideologies, values and practices of business. The premise and conclusion of the present work is that business institutions and ideas play the leading role in the social construction of modern life. They provide the "shared designs for living," "the shared models people carry in their minds for perceiving, relating to, and interpreting the world about them," that Louise Spindler (1977:4) argues are the very essence of culture. Such an integrating perspective sees culture as providing a coherent, unifying context for living. In a business culture that context is defined and designed by business ideas and practices and by business languages and symbols.

Debates about culture, however, have not only emphasized culture's integrating aspects. At the other end of the spectrum is a view that emphasizes the "dissonant, conflictual, self-contradictory," "multilayered, fragmented character" of culture (Marx 1988:x–xi). Rather than the melting-pot metaphor implicit in the idea of a business culture is a metaphor of culture as a rich tapestry or mosaic of divergent elements lending color and variety to contemporary society. From this perspective business stands, as it always has, at the point of cultural interchange and transaction. Like some ancient port of trade, business is conveniently placed to ameliorate or accommodate cultural clashes and to facilitate the transmission and diffusion of the products and values of different cultures. But business culture itself is merely one of many cultures in a world defined by a greater awareness and appreciation of cultural difference, a world of cultural pluralism. From such a perspective the impact of business on culture is essentially neutral, or it can potentially be neutralized by nurturing and sustaining cultural divergence within the society or the state.

Certainly the idea of a cultural mosaic is an apt metaphor for many aspects of contemporary Western life. It is not incompatible, however, with the theory of a business culture. The globalization of economic activity, the growth of multinational enterprises, and the expansion of McLuhans's global village made possible by communications technology create the conditions for the development of a business culture that is broader-based than the nation-state. The precise boundaries between culture, society and nation-state become not only more difficult to identify but also highly permeable. A perspective of a cultural superstructure dominated by the melting-pot ethos of the world of business, and a mosaic of cultural substrata from which new business opportunities are periodically generated and exploited, seems an appropriate way of accommodating the idea of a unifying business culture with more traditional notions of cultural fragmentation and diversity. A similar pattern of melting pot and mosaic can be seen, particularly in Europe, in the contemporaneous breaking down of economic boundaries between nation-states and a resurgence in nationalism and ethnic conflict. Thus many of the new European states see the need for sustaining some common economic framework, or for entering into an expanded European Community, while at the same time trying to evolve national and local political structures that recognize ethnic and cultural diversity.

We have, then, something of a paradox. The general argument advanced is that through its growing dominance of technology, language, images and values, business has captured the cultural highground. Business increasingly shapes the perception and experience of life in the Western world and creates the primary culture, the context for living. Ironically, however, alongside the inevitable decline of cultural pluralism that this growing hegemony of the business culture represents, we find an increasing awareness and appreciation of cultural difference, a greater textual variety within a growing contextual conformity.

In the tension of such a paradox lies both hope and fascination. The membrane between text and context is highly permeable and the broader framework of the business culture will continue to be influenced by the values of a diversity of local communities and constituencies. Thus there develops a sense in which in a business culture it is, at one level, all the same, yet, at another level, everywhere different, that, as G. K. Chesterton grumbled, the world was "nearly reasonable, but not quite." Certainly in this book it is the "not quite" that I have focused upon—the irrational aspects of business behavior, the bizarre bazaar, the strangeness of our taken-for-granted world. Marginal as they may be to the mainstream of business activity, it is the elements of the "not quite" that displace, disorient and surprise us, and make us look at business culture both critically and imaginatively. Perhaps the celebration of the "not quite" is justification for these explorations of the ambiguities of the contemporary world.

NOTES

1. Definitions of modernism and postmodernism, like definitions of culture, are matters of controversy and debate.

2. For example, Alvar Elbing (1970) developed a "social value theory of business" and Robert Heilbroner (1969) wrote of "economic means—social ends."

3. It is interesting to speculate as to what impact the demise of the command economies will have on the general debate about alternative economic systems. One view is that the Western-style liberal democratic market economy has won and the debate is closed. Francis Fukuyama's claim of "the End of History" illustrates this perspective. Another is that the end of the Soviet system in Eastern Europe will allow the West to focus attention on the defects of the market economy without the fear that in doing so it is losing some points in an ideological cold war. This would lead to renewed interest in alternative models of market-based economic systems— the "participatory market economy" or the "socialist market economy" or the "green economy," or to use Bloch and Parry's phrase, a "long-term transactional order" (see Chapter 3). In 1992, for example, MITI, the Japanese Ministry of Trade and Industry, announced its intention of developing a hundred-year program to put Japanese business at the leading edge of technological developments designed to alleviate, if not solve, environmental problems.

4. Even the emptiness of consumer materialism, as Bernice Martin (1981) observed, can be processed and packaged into a strong sales message: Thus the marketability of "lifestyles" and of "authenticity" and "expressive experience," and the commercialization of countercultural motifs and images.

5. The relationship between Bloomingdale's and New York's Metropolitan Museum was referred to in Chapter 10. In London the Victoria and Albert Museum subsidiary, V&A Enterprises, collaborated with the Habitat home furnishings store to promote a new range of textiles, the "Habitat/V&A Collection." Herbert Schiller (1989) has argued that corporate involvement in public galleries has led to the exclusion of the works of artists not "approved of" by commercial sponsors; the museum has been "enlisted as a corporate instrument" and "made an adjunct to the consciousness industry" (Schiller 1989:92).

6. Art and literature, like fashion, have a long tradition of borrowing, adapting, reiterating themes and motifs from the past and working them into a contemporary idiom; they are full of the resonances and allusions ascribed by Cantor to postmodernist culture.

7. "Gallery became a synonym for museum after antique sculptures were first displayed in the Galleria of the Vatican" (Bayley 1989:74 n).

8. "The Civic Virtues of 'Miami Vice,' " *The Economist*, 21 September 1985:41.

Bibliography

Adams, Nicholas. 1991. In *The New York Review*, April 25:49.

Adas, Michael. 1989. *Machines as the Measure of Men: Science, Technology, and Ideologies of Western Dominance*. Ithaca, N.Y.: Cornell University Press.

Adburgham, Alison. 1961. *A Punch History of Manners and Modes, 1841–1940*. London: Hutchinson.

————. 1966. *View of Fashion*. London: George Allen and Unwin.

Agnew, Jean-Christophe. 1986. *Worlds Apart: The Market and the Theater in Anglo-American Thought, 1550–1750*. Cambridge: Cambridge University Press.

Alston, J. P., and L. A. Platt. 1969. "Religious Humor: A Longitudinal Content Analysis of Cartoons." *Social Analysis*, 30:217–22.

Anderson, R. E., and M. Friemuth. 1975. "Cartoons Confront Computers." *Creative Computing*, March 1975:50–52.

Anderson, Ronald E., and Elaine Jolly. 1977. "Stereotyped Traits and Sex Roles in Humorous Drawings." *Communication Research*, 4(4):453–84.

Arnold, Peter. 1983. *The Olympic Games: Athens 1896 to Los Angeles 1984*. Sydney: Golden Press.

Bagdikian, Ben H. 1983. *The Media Monopoly*. Boston: Beacon Press.

Baker, Samm Sinclair. 1969. *The Permissible Lie: The Inside Truth about Advertising*. London: Peter Owen.

Baritz, Loren. 1965. *The Servants of Power: A History of the Use of Social Science in American Industry*. New York: Wiley.

Barshay, Robert. 1974. "The Cartoon of Modern Sensibility." *Journal of Popular Culture*, 8(3):523–33.

Barthes, Roland. 1973. *Mythologies*. St. Albans, Hertfordshire: Paladin (originally published in French in 1957).

Barton, Bruce. 1924. *The Man Nobody Knows: A Discovery of the Real Jesus*. Indianapolis: Bobbs-Merrill.

Barwise, Patrick. 1971. "Behavioural scientist." *Financial Times*, December.

Bayley, Stephen (ed.). 1989. *Commerce and Culture: From Pre-Industrial Art to*

Post-Industrial Value. Tunbridge Wells, Kent: Penshurst Press for the Design Museum, London.

Beard, Miriam. 1938. *A History of Business*. 2 vols., Ann Arbor: University of Michigan Press.

Belasco, Warren James. 1979. *Americans on the Road: From Autocamp to Motel, 1910–1945*. Cambridge, Mass.: MIT Press.

Bellamy, Edward. 1967. *Looking Backward 2000–1887*. Cambridge, Mass.: The Belknap Press of Harvard University Press.

Belshaw, Cyril S. 1965. *Traditional Exchange and Modern Markets*. Englewood Cliffs, N.J.: Prentice-Hall.

Berger, Arthur Asa. 1984. *Signs in Contemporary Culture: An Introduction to Semiotics*. New York: Longman.

Bergson, Henri. 1911. *Laughter: An Essay on the Meaning of the Comic*. London: Macmillan.

Billington, Sandra. 1984. *A Social History of the Fool*. New York: St. Martin's Press.

Birmingham, Stephan. 1984. *"The Rest of Us": The Rise of America's Eastern European Jews*. Boston: Little, Brown.

Bjerke, Bjorn. 1986. "What We Say to Students Makes a Difference." Paper presented to Inter-University Conference of Teachers of Management and Business, University of Waikato, New Zealand.

Blair, John G. 1988. *Modular America: Cross-Cultural Perspectives on the Emergence of an American Way*. Westport, Conn.: Greenwood Press.

Bloch, Maurice, and Jonathan Parry. 1989. "Introduction: Money and the Morality of Exchange." In *Money and the Morality of Exchange*, ed. Jonathan Parry and Maurice Bloch. Cambridge: Cambridge University Press.

Blofeld, Henry. 1978. *The Packer Affair*. London: Collins.

Bogardus, Emory S. 1945. "Sociology of the Cartoon." *Sociology and Social Research*, 30(11):139–47.

Boorstin, Daniel. 1964. *The Image: A Guide to Pseudo-Events in America*. New York: Harper.

Borgmann, Albert. 1984. *Technology and the Character of Contemporary Life: A Philosophical Inquiry*. Chicago: University of Chicago Press.

Bowie, Norman. 1982. *Business Ethics*. Englewood Cliffs, N.J.: Prentice-Hall.

Bradney, Pamela. 1957. "The Joking Relationship in Industry." *Human Relations*, 10(2):179–87.

Brenton, Howard, and David Hare. 1985. *Pravda: A Fleet Street Comedy*. London: Methuen.

Brigard, Raul de, and Olaf Helmar. 1970. *Some Potential Societal Developments, 1970–2000*. Middletown, Conn.: Institute for the Future.

Bunzel, J. H. 1962. *The American Small Businessman*. New York: Knopf.

Campbell, C. 1987. *The Romantic Ethic and the Spirit of Modern Consumerism*. Oxford: Basil Blackwell.

Cantor, Norman F. 1988. *Twentieth-Century Culture: Modernism to Deconstruction*. New York: Peter Lang.

Carnegie, Andrew. 1962. *The Gospel of Wealth*. Cambridge, Mass.: Harvard University Press.

Carr, E. H. 1964. *Studies in Revolution*. New York: Grossett and Dunlap.

Cawelti, J. G. 1965. *Apostles of the Self-Made Man*. Chicago: University of Chicago Press.

Chamberlain, J. 1948. "The Businessman in Fiction," *Fortune*, 38(5):134–48.

Cochran, T. C. 1959. *Basic History of American Business*. Princeton, N.J.: Van Nostrand.

Cooper, M. H., and A. J. Culyer. 1968. *The Price of Blood*. London: Institute of Economic Affairs.

Corwin, Norman. 1986. *Trivializing America*. Secaucus, N.J.: Lyle Stuart.

Coser, Rose Laub. 1959. "Some Social Functions of Laughter: A Study of Humor in a Hospital Setting." *Human Relations*, 12(2):171–82.

Crews, Frederick. 1989. "The Parting of the Twains." *The New York Review*, July 20.

Cribb, Joe (ed.). 1986. *Money: From Cowrie Shells to Credit Cards*. London: British Museum Publications.

Curwen, Peter J. 1981. *The U.K. Publishing Industry*. Oxford: Pergamon Press.

Darnton, Robert. 1985. *The Great Cat Massacre and Other Episodes in French Cultural History*. Harmondsworth, Middlesex: Penguin Books.

De Mente, Boye. 1975. *Japanese Manners and Ethics in Business*. Phoenix: Simpson-Doyle.

Deeks, John. 1976. *The Small Firm Owner-Manager: Entrepreneurial Behavior and Management Practice*. New York: Praeger.

———. 1992. "Who's Choking Smoking? Advertising, Sponsorship and Government Regulation of the Tobacco Industry." In *Controlling Interests*, ed. John Deeks and Nick Perry. Auckland: Auckland University Press.

Della Casa, Giovanni. 1958. *Galateo or The Book of Manners*. Harmondsworth, Middlesex: Penguin Books (first published in 1558).

Dettelbach, Cynthia G. 1976. *In the Driver's Seat: The Automobile in American Literature and Popular Culture*. Westport, Conn.: Greenwood Press.

Diamond, Edwin. 1982. *Sign Off: The Last Days of Television*. Cambridge, Mass.: MIT Press.

Dinnage, Rosemary. 1985. "Travelling Light." *The New York Review*, June 13, 29–30.

Douglas, Mary. 1975. *Implicit Messages*. London: Routledge and Kegan Paul, 1975.

———. 1990. "No Free Gifts." Foreword to W. D. Hall's translation of Marcel Mauss, *The Gift*. London: Routledge.

Douglas, Jack D. 1971. *The Technological Threat*. Englewood-Cliffs, N.J.: Prentice-Hall.

Duby, Georges. 1974. *The Early Growth of the European Economy: Warriors and Peasants from the Seventh to the Twelfth Century*. London: Weidenfeld and Nicolson.

Eco, Umberto. 1987. *Travels in Hyperreality*. Picador edition. London: Pan Books.

Edmunds, Lowell. 1981. *The Silver Bullet: The Martini in American Civilization*. Westport, Conn.: Greenwood Press.

Elbing, Alvar O. 1970. *Behavioral Decisions in Organizations*. Glenview, Ill.: Scott Foresman.

Ellul, Jacques. 1965. *The Technological Society*. London: Cape.

———. 1980. *The Technological System*. New York: Continuum.

Elton, Ben. 1989. *Stark*. London: Sphere Books.

Enzensberger, Hans Magnus. 1981. "The Industrialization of the Mind." In *Culture and Society in Contemporary Europe: A Casebook*, ed. Stanley Hoffmann and Paschalis Kitromilides. London: George Allen and Unwin (the essay was first published in 1962.)

Evans, Christopher. 1979. *The Mighty Micro*. London: Gollancz.

Ewen, Stuart, and Elizabeth Ewen. 1982. *Channels of Desire: Mass Images and the Shaping of American Consciousness*. New York: McGraw-Hill.

Eysenck, H. J. 1944. "National Differences in 'Sense of Humor': Three Experimental and Statistical Studies." *Character and Personality*, 13:37–54.

Fischer, Frank. 1990. *Technocracy and the Politics of Expertise*. Newbury Park, Calif.: Sage.

Fischer, Sandra. 1985. *Econolingua: A Glossary of Coins and Economic Language in Renaissance Drama*. Newark: University of Delaware Press.

Fisher, S., and Fisher, R. L. 1983. "Personality and Psychotherapy in the Comic." Chapter 4 in McGhee and Goldstein (1983).

Flugel, J. C. 1954. "Humor and Laughter." In Lindzey, Gardner, *Handbook of Social Psychology*, ed. Gardner Lindzey 709–34, Cambridge, Mass.: Addison-Wesley.

———. 1966. *The Psychology of Clothes*. London: Hogarth Press, Fourth Impression (first published in 1930).

Fowles, Jib. 1982. *Television Viewers vs Media Snobs*. New York: Stein and Day.

Fromm, Erich. 1947. *Man for Himself: An Inquiry into the Psychology of Ethics*. Greenwich, Conn.: Fawcett.

Fukuyama, Francis. 1992. *The End of History and the Last Man*. New York: Free Press.

"Going for the Green: Olympic Sponsors Look for Big Payoffs from Their Million-Dollar Promotions." *Time*, 18 June 1984:54–55.

Goldlust, John. 1987. *Playing for Keeps: Sport, the Media and Society*. Melbourne: Longman Cheshire.

Goldmann, Lucien. 1981. "The Revolt of Arts and Letters in Advanced Civilizations." In *Culture and Society in Contemporary Europe: A Casebook*, ed. Stanley Hoffmann and Paschalis Kitromilides. London: George Allen and Unwin (Goldmann's essay was written in 1968).

Goldstein, Jeffrey H., and Paul E. McGhee. 1972. *The Psychology of Humor*. New York: Academic Press.

Goodman, Paul. 1962. *Utopian Essays and Practical Proposals*. New York: Vintage Books.

Greenberg, B. S., and S. Kahn. 1970. "Blacks in *Playboy* Cartoons." *Journalism Quarterly*, 47:550–60.

Hackett, Earle. 1973. *Blood, the Paramount Humor*. London: Jonathan Cape.

Harris, Marvin. 1987. *Why Nothing Works: The Anthropology of Daily Life*. New York: Simon & Schuster (Touchstone edition).

Harrison, Randall P. 1981. *The Cartoon: Communication to the Quick*. Beverly Hills, Calif.: Sage.

Harvey, David. 1989. *The Condition of Postmodernity: An Enquiry into the Origins of Cultural Change*. Oxford: Basil Blackwell.

Hawthorn, Jeremy. 1983. *Multiple Personality and the Disintegration of Literary Character: From Oliver Goldsmith to Sylvia Plath*. London: Edward Arnold.

Heilbroner, Robert (ed.). 1969. *Economic Means and Social Ends*. Englewood Cliffs, N.J.: Prentice-Hall.

Heller, Joseph. 1974. *Something Happened*. New York: Knopf.

Henderson, Philip. 1967. *William Morris: His Life, Work and Friends*. Harmondsworth, Middlesex: Penguin Books.

Hendin, Josephine. 1990. "Fictions of Acquisition." In Nicolaus Mills (ed.), *Culture in an Age of Money: The Legacy of the 1980s in America*. Chicago: Ivan R. Dee.

Hendrickson, Robert. 1974. *Lewd Food: The Complete Guide to Aphrodisiac Edibles*. Radnor, Penn.: Chilton Book Company.

Hertzberg, Hendrik. 1990. "The Short Happy Life of the American Yuppie." In *Culture in an Age of Money: The Legacy of the 1980s in America*, ed. Nicolaus Mills. Chicago: Ivan R. Dee.

Hewison, William. 1977. *The Cartoon Connection: The Art of Pictorial Humor*. London: Elm Tree Books.

Hibbert, Christopher. 1982. *Edward VII: A Portrait*. Harmondsworth, Middlesex: Penguin Books.

Hoch, Paul. 1972. *Rip Off the Big Game: The Exploitation of Sports by the Power Elite*. New York: Doubleday.

Hofstede, G. 1980. *Culture's Consequences: International Differences in Work-Related Values*. Beverly Hills, Calif.: Sage.

Hollander, Anne. 1975. *Seeing through Clothes*. New York: Avon Books.

Holt, Richard. 1989. *Sport and the British*. Oxford: Clarendon Press.

Horowitz, Ira. 1974. "Sports Broadcasting." In *Government and the Sports Business*, ed. Roger Noll. Washington, D.C.: Brookings Institution.

"How Nike Got a Run for No Money at the Science Museum." *The Independent*, 7 May 1991:14.

Hughes, Thomas P. 1989. *American Genesis: A Century of Invention and Technological Enthusiasm, 1870–1970*. New York: Viking.

Huizinga, Johan. 1949. *Homo Ludens. A Study of the Play-Element in Culture*. London: Routledge and Kegan Paul.

Hurlock, Elizabeth. 1971. *The Psychology of Dress: An Analysis of Fashion and Its Motive*. New York: B. Blom (reprint of 1929 edition).

Hutchinson, Peter. 1983. *Games Authors Play*. London: Methuen.

International Journal of Research in Marketing. 1988. Special Issue on Semiotics and Marketing Communications Research, 4(3):165–256.

James, C.L.R. 1963. *Beyond a Boundary*. London: Hutchinson.

James, Henry. 1978. *The American*. New York: W. W. Norton (originally published in 1877).

Johnson, Nicholas. 1970. *How to Talk Back to Your Television Set*. Boston: Little, Brown.

Jones, David A., and Leverett T. Smith. 1978. "Jerry Kramer's *Instant Replay* and Dan Jenkins' *Semi-Tough*: A Cultural Dialogue." *Journal of Popular Culture*, 12(1):156–67.

Kadis, A. L., and C. Winick. 1973. "The Cartoon as Therapeutic Catalyst." In *Alfred Adler: His Influence on Psychology Today*, ed. Harold H. Mosak, pp. 106–23. Park Ridge, N.J.: Noyes Press.

Klapp, Orrin E. 1949. "The Fool as a Social Type." *The American Journal of Sociology*, 55(2):157–162.

Kenner, Hugh. 1987. *The Mechanic Muse*. New York: Oxford University Press.

Kernan, Alvin B. 1982. "The Taking of the Moon: The Struggle of the Poetic and Scientific Myths in Norman Mailer's *Of a Fire on the Moon*." In *The Imaginary Library: An Essay on Literature and Society*. Princeton, N.J.: Princeton University Press.

Kidder, Tracy. 1982. *The Soul of a New Machine*. Harmondsworth, Middlesex: Penguin Books.

Kolaja, J. 1953. "American Magazine Cartoons and Social Control." *Journalism Quarterly*, 30:71–74.

König, René. 1973. *The Restless Image: A Sociology of Fashion*. London: George Allen and Unwin.

Kristol, Irving. 1978. *Two Cheers for Capitalism*. New York: Basic Books.

Kroeber, A. L., and Clyde Kluckhohn. 1952. *Culture: A Critical Review of Concepts and Definitions*. Cambridge, Mass.: Peabody Museum.

Lamb, David. 1991. "A Season in the Minors." *National Geographic*, 179(4):41–73.

Larsen, Judith K., and Everett M. Rogers. 1984. *Silicon Valley Fever: Growth of High-Technology Culture*. New York: Basic Books.

Lasch, Christopher. 1980. *The Culture of Narcissism*. Abacus edition. London: Sphere Books.

Lauer, Robert H., and Jeanette C. Lauer. 1981. *Fashion Power: The Meaning of Fashion in American Society*. Englewood Cliffs, N.J.: Prentice-Hall.

Laver, James. 1937. *Taste and Fashion*. London: Harrap.

Le Goff, Jacques. 1988. *Your Money or Your Life: Economy and Religion in the Middle Ages*. New York: Zone Books.

Leach, Jerry W. (director). 1975. *Trobriand Cricket: An Ingenious Response to Colonialism*. Film produced by the Office of Information of the Government of Papua and New Guinea, Port Moresby.

Leiss, William. 1970. "Utopia and Technology: Reflections on the Conquest of Nature." *International Social Science Journal*, 22(4):576–88.

Leiss, William, Stephen Kline, and Sut Jhally. 1986. *Social Communication in Advertising: Persons, Products and Images of Well-Being*. New York: Methuen.

Lerner, Daniel. 1964. *The Passing of Traditional Society*. New York: Free Press.

Lewis, Roy, and Rosemary Stewart. 1958. *The Boss: The Life and Times of the British Business Man*. London: Phoenix House.

Lindblom, Charles E. 1977. *Politics and Markets: The World's Political-Economic Systems*. New York: Basic Books.

Lipsky, Richard. 1981. *How We Play the Game: Why Sports Dominate American Life*. Boston: Beacon Press.

Lowe, Donald M. 1982. *History of Bourgeois Perception*. Chicago: University of Chicago Press.

Lucas, J. A. 1981. "The Genesis of the Modern Olympic Games." In *Olympism*, ed. J. Segrave and D. Chu. Champaign, Ill.: Human Kinetics.

Lurie, Alison. 1981. *The Language of Clothes*. New York: Random House.

MacCannell, Dean. 1976. *The Tourist: A New Theory of the Leisure Class*. New York: Schocken Books.

Mailer, Norman. 1970. *A Fire on the Moon*. London: Weidenfeld and Nicolson.

Mangan, J. A. 1981. *Athleticism in the Victorian and Edwardian Public School.* Cambridge: Cambridge University Press.

Marchand, Roland. 1985. *Advertising the American Dream.* Berkeley: University of California Press.

Marly, Diana de. 1980. *The History of Haute Couture, 1850–1950.* London: Batsford.

Marsh, Peter. 1985. *The Space Business: A Manual on the Commercial Uses of Space.* Harmondsworth, Middlesex: Penguin Books.

Marshall, Heather. 1983. "Leisure—The Base of Future Employment." *National Business Review* (New Zealand), November 21:43.

Martin, Bernice. 1981. *A Sociology of Contemporary Cultural Change.* New York: St. Martin's Press.

Martin, Captain Henry Byam. 1981. *The Polynesian Journal of Captain Henry Byam Martin, R. N.* Salem, Mass.: Peabody Museum of Salem.

Marx, Leo. 1964. *The Machine in the Garden: Technology and the Pastoral Ideal in America.* New York: Oxford University Press.

——. 1988. *The Pilot and the Passenger: Essays on Literature, Technology and Culture in the United States.* New York: Oxford University Press.

Mason, Roger S. 1981. *Conspicuous Consumption: A Study of Exceptional Consumer Behavior.* New York: St. Martin's Press.

Mauss, M. 1970. *The Gift.* London: Routledge and Kegan Paul.

Mayo, Edward J., and Lance P. Jarvis. 1981. *The Psychology of Leisure Travel: Effective Marketing and Selling of Travel Services.* Boston: Mass.: CBI Publishing.

McDougall, Walter A. 1985. *The Heavens and the Earth: A Political History of the Space Age.* New York: Basic Books.

McGhee, Paul E., and Jeffrey H. Goldstein (eds.). 1983. *Handbook of Humor Research.* Vol. I, Basic Issues; Vol. II, Applied Studies; New York: Springer-Verlag.

McKendrick, Neil. 1978. "Literary Luddism and the Businessman." General introduction to *Sir Alfred Jones: Shipping Entrepreneur Par Excellence,* by P. N. Davies. London: Europa.

McKendrick, Neil, John Brewer, and J. H. Plumb. 1982. *The Birth of a Consumer Society: The Commercialization of Eighteenth-Century England.* Bloomington: Indiana University Press.

McLean, Iain. 1986. "Should Blood Be for Sale?" *New Society,* 6 June: 10–12.

Melada, Ivan. 1970. *The Captain of Industry in English Fiction, 1821–1871.* Albuquerque: University of New Mexico Press.

Mellor, Adrian. 1984. "Science Fiction and the Crisis of the Educated Middle Class." In *Popular Fiction and Social Change,* ed. Christopher Pawling. New York: St. Martin's Press.

Merritt, G. 1982. *World Out of Work.* London: Collins.

Meyer, Katherine, John Seidler, Timothy Curry, and Adrian Aveni. 1980. "Women in July Fourth Cartoons: A 100-year Look." *Journal of Communication,* 30(1):21–30.

Miller, Roger, and Marcel Cote. 1985. "Growing the Next Silicon Valley." *Harvard Business Review,* July-August: 114–23.

Mills, Nicolaus. 1990. "The Culture of Triumph and the Spirit of the Times." In

Culture in an Age of Money: The Legacy of the 1980s in America, ed. Nicolaus Mills. Chicago: Ivan R. Dee.

Mintz, L. E. 1983. "Humor and Popular Culture." Chapter 8 in McGhee and Goldstein (1983).

Moore, Ellen W. 1985. *The Fairs of Medieval England*. Toronto: Pontifical Institute of Mediaeval Studies.

Mulkay, M. J. 1988. *On Humor: Its Nature and Its Place in Modern Society*. New York: Blackwell.

Novak, Michael. 1976. *The Joy of Sports*. New York: Basic Books.

O'Rourke, P. J. 1989. *Holidays in Hell*. London: Pan Books, Picador edition.

Odendahl, Teresa. 1990. *Charity Begins at Home: Generosity and Self-Interest among the Philanthropic Elite*. New York: Basic Books.

Official Report: Games of the XXIVth Olympiad, Seoul, 1988. 2 vols. Seoul, Seoul Olympic Organizing Committee, 1989.

Pacey, Arnold. 1983. *The Culture of Technology*. Cambridge, Mass.: MIT Press.

Palmore, E. 1971. "Attitudes toward Aging as Shown by Humor." *The Gerontologist*, 181–86.

Park-Curry, Pamela, and Robert M. Jiobu. 1983. "The Computer as Fetish: Electronic Pop God." In *Objects of Special Devotion: Fetishes and Fetishism in Popular Culture*, ed. Ray B. Browne, pp. 328–35. Ohio, Bowling Green University.

Parry, Jonathan. 1989. "On the Moral Perils of Exchange." In *Money and the Morality of Exchange*, ed. Jonathan Parry and Maurice Bloch. Cambridge: Cambridge University Press.

Patton, Phil. 1986. *Open Road: A Celebration of the American Highway*. New York: Simon & Schuster.

Pelling, Henry. 1963. *A History of British Trade Unionism*. Harmondsworth, Middlesex: Penguin Books.

Pilger, John. 1984. *Burp: Pepsi v. Coke in the Ice Cold War*. A report by John Pilger, Central Independent Television (U.K.).

Pilger, John. 1990. *A Secret Country*. London: Vintage.

Pitt, Nick. 1979. *Big Red Diary 1980: Politics in Sport*. London: Pluto Press.

Podhoretz, Norman. 1981. "The New Defenders of Capitalism." *Harvard Business Review*, March-April: 96–106.

Polanyi, Karl, Conrad M. Arensberg, and Harry W. Pearson (eds.). 1957. *Trade and Market in the Early Empires: Economics in History and Theory*. Glencoe, Ill.: The Free Press.

Poliakov, Leon. 1977. *Jewish Bankers and The Holy See: From the 13th to the 17th century*. London: Routledge and Kegan Paul.

Quant, Mary. 1966. *Quant by Quant*. London: Cassell.

Radcliffe-Brown, A. R. 1952. *Structure and Function in Primitive Society*. London: Cohen and West.

Rae, W. Fraser. 1891. *The Business of Travel: A Fifty Years' Record of Progress*. London: Thomas Cook and Son.

Real, M. R. 1975. "Super Bowl: Mythic Spectacle." *Journal of Communication*, 25 (Winter): 20–26.

Reddy, Narendra. 1991. "Managerial Decision-Making in the Island Nations of the

South Pacific." Ph.D. thesis, Department of Management Studies and Labour Relations, University of Auckland, New Zealand.

Redfield, James M. 1986. "The Development of the Market in Archaic Greece." In *The Market in History*, ed. B. L. Anderson and A.J.H. Latham. London: Croom Helm.

Riess, Steven A. 1980. *Touching Base: Professional Baseball and American Culture in the Progressive Era*. Westport, Conn.: Greenwood Press.

Robinson, Dwight E. 1976. "Fashions in Shaving and Trimming of the Beard." *American Journal of Sociology*, 81:1133–39.

Rodgers, William. 1971. *Think: A Biography of the Watsons and IBM*. London: Panther Books.

Rosen, R. D. 1978. *Psychobabble*. New York: Atheneum.

Roth, Philip. 1985. *The Great American Novel*. New York: Viking Penguin.

Runcie, John F. 1980. "By Days I Make the Cars," *Harvard Business Review*, May–June: 106–115.

Saenger, G. 1955. "Male and Female Relations in the American Comic Strip." *Public Opinion Quarterly*, 19(3):195–205.

Schiller, Herbert. 1989. *Culture Inc: The Corporate Takeover of Public Expression*. New York: Oxford University Press.

Schivelbusch, Wolfgang. 1986. *The Railway Journey: The Industrialisation of Time and Space in the Nineteenth Century*. Berkeley: University of California Press (originally published in German in 1977).

Schudson, Michael. 1984. *Advertising, the Uneasy Persuasion*. New York: Basic Books.

Schumacher, E. F. 1973. *Small Is Beautiful*. London: Blond and Briggs.

Schuyler, George S. 1969. *Black No More*. New York: Negro Universities Press (originally published in 1931).

Scully, Gerald W. 1974. "Discrimination: The Case of Baseball." In *Government and the Sports Business*, ed. Roger G. Noll. Washington, D.C.: Brookings Institution.

Seaman, William R. 1992. "Active Audience Theory: Pointless Populism." *Media, Culture and Society*, 14:301–11.

Selzer, Michael. 1979. *Terrorist Chic*. New York: Hawthorn Books.

Shepard, Leslie. 1973. *The History of Street Literature*. Newton Abbot, U.K.: David and Charles.

Silverman, Debora. 1990. "China, Bloomie's and the Met." In *Culture in an Age of Money: The Legacy of the 1980s in America*, ed. Nicolaus Mills. Chicago: Ivan R. Dee.

Sloane, Peter J. 1980. *Sport in the Market? The Economic Causes and Consequences of the "Packer Revolution."* London: Institute of Economic Affairs.

Smith, Henry Nash. 1964. "The Search for a Capitalist Hero: Businessmen in American Fiction." In *The Business Establishment*, ed. Earl F. Cheit. New York: Wiley.

Smither, Robert D. 1984. *Competitors and Comrades: Culture, Economics, and Personality*. New York: Praeger.

Snow, C. P. 1964. *Two Cultures: And a Second Look*. Cambridge: Cambridge University Press.

Snyder, Eldon E. 1974. "Sociology of Sports: Concepts and Theories." *Journal of Popular Culture*, 8(2):361–69.

Sperber, Murray. 1990. *College Sports Inc.: The Athletic Department vs The University*. New York: Henry Holt.

Spindler, Louise S. 1977. *Culture Change and Modernization*. New York: Holt, Rinehart and Winston.

Steele, Valerie. 1985. *Fashion and Erotism*. New York: Oxford University Press.

Stein, Ben. 1979. *The View from Sunset Boulevard: America as Brought to You by the People Who Make Television*. New York: Basic Books.

Stephenson, Richard M. 1951. "Conflict and Control Functions of Humor." *The American Journal of Sociology*, 56(6):569–74.

Stern, Jane and Michael Stern. 1978. *Auto Ads*. New York: Random House.

Streicher, Lawrence H. 1967. "On a Theory of Political Caricature." *Comparative Studies in Society and History*, 9 (1966–67):427–45.

"Striking It Rich: A New Breed of Risk Takers is Betting on the High-Technology Future." *Time*, 15 February 1982:36–43.

Swinglehurst, Edmund. 1974. *The Romantic Journey: The Story of Thomas Cook and Victorian Travel*. London: Pica Editions.

Taylor, Walter Fuller. 1964. *The Economic Novel in America*. New York: Octagon Books.

Tebbel, John. 1987. *Between Covers: The Rise and Transformation of American Book Publishing*. New York: Oxford University Press.

Theberge, L. J. 1981. *Crooks, Conmen and Clowns: Businessmen in TV Entertainment*. Washington, D.C.: Media Institute.

Titmuss, Richard M. 1970. *The Gift Relationship: From Human Blood to Social Policy*. London: Allen and Unwin.

Tulloch, Lee. 1990. *Fabulous Nobodies*. Sydney: Picador (Pan Books).

Tunstall, Jeremy. 1977. *The Media Are American: Anglo-American Media in the World*. New York: Columbia University Press.

Turkle, Sherry. 1984. *The Second Self: Computers and the Human Spirit*. London: Granada.

Turner, E. S. 1965. *The Shocking History of Advertising*. Revised edition. Harmondsworth, Middlesex: Penguin Books.

Turner, Louis, and John Ash. 1975. *The Golden Horde*. London: Constable.

UNESCO. 1982. *Cultural Industries: A Challenge for the Future of Culture*. Paris: UNESCO.

Urry, John. 1990. *The Tourist Gaze: Leisure and Travel in Contemporary Societies*. London: Sage.

Van Nostrand, Albert. 1960. *The Denatured Novel*. New York: Bobbs-Merrill.

Veblen, Thorsten. 1953. *The Theory of the Leisure Class*. New York: New American Library Mentor Edition (originally published in 1899).

Voigt, David. 1983. "No Sex till Monday: The Fetish Phenomenon in American Sport." In *Objects of Special Devotion: Fetishes and Fetishism in Popular Culture*, ed. Ray B. Browne. Ohio: Bowling Green University Popular Press.

Walvin, James. 1975. *The People's Game: The Social History of British Football*. London: Allen Lane.

Warburg, Fredric. 1959. *An Occupation for Gentlemen*. London: Hutchinson.

Warn, Rachel. 1989. "Sporting Professionals: An Inquiry Into the Relationship between Business and Sport." Unpublished M.Phil. thesis. University of Auckland.

Watts, Emily Stipes. 1982. *The Businessman in American Literature.* Athens: University of Georgia Press.

Weber, Max. 1958. *The Protestant Ethic and the Spirit of Capitalism.* New York: Scribner's.

Welsford, Enid. 1966. *The Fool: His Social and Literary History.* Gloucester, Mass.: Peter Smith, Reprinted 1966 (first published, London: Faber and Faber, 1935).

Whannel, Garry. 1983. *Blowing the Whistle: The Politics of Sport.* London: Pluto Press.

Whiteside, Thomas. 1981. *The Blockbuster Complex: Conglomerates, Show Business and Book Publishing.* Middleton, Conn.: Wesleyan University Press.

Wilentz, Sean. 1990. "The Trials of Televangelism." In *Culture in an Age of Money: The Legacy of the 1980s in America,* ed. Nicolaus Mills. Chicago: Ivan R. Dee.

Willeford, William. 1969. *The Fool and His Sceptre: A Study in Clowns and Jesters and Their Audience.* London: Edward Arnold.

Williams, Raymond. 1961. *Culture and Society, 1780–1950.* Harmondsworth, Middlesex: Penguin Books.

————. 1983. *Keywords.* London: Flamingo.

Williams-Mitchell, Christobel. 1982. *Dressed for the Job: The Story of Occupational Costume.* Poole, Dorset: Blandford Press.

Williamson, Judith. 1978. *Decoding Advertisements: Ideology and Meaning in Advertising.* London: Marion Boyars.

Wills, Garry. 1990. "Shylock without Usury." *The New York Review,* 18 January: 22–25.

Winick, C. 1961. "Space Jokes as Indication of Attitudes toward Space." *Journal of Social Issues,* 17:43–49.

Winner, Langdon. 1977. *Autonomous Technology: Technics-out-of-control as a Theme in Political Thought.* Cambridge, Mass.: MIT Press.

Wolfe, Tom. 1965. *The Kandy-Kolored Tangerine Flake Streamline Baby.* New York: Farrar, Straus and Giroux.

————. 1979. *The Right Stuff.* New York: Farrar, Straus and Giroux.

————. 1980. *In Our Time.* New York: Farrar, Straus and Giroux.

Wood, James Playsted. 1958. *The Story of Advertising.* New York: Ronald Press.

Wright, Lawrence. 1968. *Clockwork Man.* London: Elek.

Wuthnow, Robert. 1982. "The Moral Crisis in American Capitalism." *Harvard Business Review,* March-April: pp. 76–84.

Wyllie, I. G. 1954. *The Self-Made Man in America.* New Brunswick, N.J.: Rutgers University Press.

Yates, Norris W. 1964. *The American Humorist: Conscience of the Twentieth Century.* Ames: Iowa State University Press.

Yinger, J. Milton. 1982. *Countercultures.* New York: Free Press.

Index

Acculturation, 14–15, 21
Adas, Michael, 46
Active audience theory, 135 n.10
Adburgham, Alison, 167, 172
Addams, Jane, 159
Advertisements, 1, 59, 68–82, 115, 121, 132, 169, 182, 206, 225–28
Advertising, 3, 67–82, 126, 166, 169, 187–88, 201, 226–27; codes of practice, 78; and computers, 59; culture, 226; ethics, 78–79; and fashion, 150–51, 159, 170; and image of business, 4; language of, 3, 14, 67–68, 71–74, 78; and occupational costumes, 144; and politics, 115; semiology of, 3, 68–71; signs, images, 68, 187; and sport, 204–9; symbolism in, 51; and television, 17–19, 115, 123, 132–34, 226; and tourism, 177
Advertising agencies, advertising industry, 74–80, 116, 134, 202, 208
Affirmative action, 90
Age of arrogance, 26–27
Alger, Horatio, 196, 221
Alienation, 130, 198, 215
Altruism, 40
Amateurs, Amateurism, 4, 14, 120, 194–95, 201

American football, 193–94, 198–99, 202–3, 205, 210, 211 n.5; plays in, 193, 202; rules of, 203
Amish, Amish culture, 214
Anderson, Ronald E., 88, 91, 128
Anthropomorphism: and computers, 58, 60; and sports equipment, 199. *See also* Morphing
Anti-business sentiment, 33, 129
Anticipation as consumption, 173
Argonauts of the Western Pacific (Malinowski), 23
Appropriate technology, 51
Armstrong, Neil, 56
Arnold, Rev. Thomas, 192
'Art Nouveau,' 227
Artificial intelligence, 64
Authoritarianism, 107
Autocamping, 182–83
Automation, 218
Autonomous technology, 49. *See also* Machine-out-of-control

Babbitt (Sinclair Lewis), 82
Bacon, Francis, 217
Bagdikian, Ben, 118
Baker, Samm Sinclair, 80
Banking, 32

Barnum, P. T., 75
Barshay, Robert, 104–5
Barter, 23–25
Barthes, Roland, 69
Barton, Bruce, 6, 80–83
Baseball, 191, 193, 196–97, 203, 205, 208, 211 n.6
Basketball, 193, 198, 206
Baudelaire, 183
Beard, Miriam, 26
Behavioral engineering, 221
Behaviorist psychology, 221
Bellamy, Edward, 217–19, 223
Belshaw, Cyril, 24
Berger, Arthur Asa, 69
Bergson, Henri, 102
Best sellers, best seller lists, 123–25, 135 n.8
Bicycle, 148
Bierce, Ambrose, 140
Big business, 55, 58, 102, 130–31, 197, 221, 223
Biotechnology, 61
Birmingham, Stephen, 158
Bizarre bazaar, 67–71, 230
Blair, John G., 202–3, 215
Bloch, Maurice, 33, 231 n.3
Blofeld, Henry, 17
Blood, blood business, 40–42
Bloomer, Mrs. Amelia Jenks, 146–47, 159
Bloomingdale's, 186
Body language, 69
Bodybuilding, language of, 193
Boesky, Ivan, 43 n.3
Books, book publishing, book selling, 1, 72, 117–25, 180. See also Publishers, publishing industry
Books of etiquette, 143
Borgman, Albert, 50
Bradney, Pamela, 103
Brandon, Barbara, 109 n.1
Brenton, Howard, 117
Broadcasting, 205. See also Television
Brother Jonathan, 103
Bureaucracy, 55, 96, 197
Business: in cartoons, 49, 87–109; case studies, 85; and consciousness, 132

(see also Consciousness industry); and cultural change, 12–15; and culture, 12–15; definition of, 9; dress, 3, 145–46, 165; ethics, ethical issues, 19, 98, 105; gift-giving, 25–26; and government, 19, 21, 224; history, 5–6, 82; ideology, values, 2–3, 20–21, 33, 68–69, 79–80, 83, 89, 98, 105, 210, 213, 224–30; language, 4, 20–21, 83–85, 111, 213, 225–30; in literature, 33, 89, 129; mode, 165–72; and politics, 21; and postmodernism, 223–28; schools, 85, 130; and social change, 9–12, 166; and society, 9–12, 19–20, 224; in society, 11, 33, 151; and sport, 197–98, 209–10; success books, 130 (see also Self-help books, manuals); the third culture, 1–7
Business culture, 1–6, 19–21, 68, 213–15, 224–30; alternatives to, 213; definition of, 19; extended business culture, 2, 20–21
Business executives, 30, 75, 80, 114, 128–30, 165, 169, 202, 217; as anti-hero, 126–30; in cartoons, 87–101, 105, 127; in films and television, 128–30; image of, 75, 129; in literature, 33, 89, 126–30; as role models, 129; stereotyping of, 99, 128–29. See also Managers
Business Power through Psychology (Swift), 82
Butler, Samuel, 137, 217
Byron, Lord, 119

Camp, Walter, 194
Campbell, Colin, 187–88
Cantor, Norman F., 61, 226, 231 n.6
Capital accumulation, 229
Capitalism, capitalist, 19, 31, 35, 39, 196, 209, 217–21, 224–25, 227
Capitalist personality, 37
Car ownership, 182
Caricature, 100–101, 106, 127; of business, 101; theory of, 100, 105
Carnegie, Andrew, 28
Cartoons, cartoonists, 3–4, 87–109, 128

Chaplin, Charlie, 59
Chesterton, G. K., 230
Chirographic culture, 112
Chivalry, 31
Christian theology, tradition,
    Christianity, 31–32, 38, 80, 192
Chronographic imperialism, 62
Civilization, civilized behavior, 46–47,
    65 n.3, 70, 178, 192
Class: consciousness, 181; distinction,
    141; relations, 196; stratification,
    structure, 89, 195, 222
Classical economic theory, 221
Clothes reform movement, 147
Coach travel, 180
Cold War, 52
Collective consciousness, 225
Colonialism, 47
Comic personality, 101
Command economy, 35, 231 n.3
Commerce: and culture, 4, 213–31;
    innocence of, 33, 225
Commercial: culture, 133; games, 209;
    speech, freedom of, 79; values, 107
Commercialism, 2–4, 19, 75, 120, 127,
    200
Commercialization, 83, 114, 186; of
    fashion, 169; of images, 231 n.4; of
    relationships, 214; of the self, 35, 83,
    113, 162–65; of sport, 18–19, 83,
    200, 202, 209
Communal society, 219
Communication: art of, 57; medium of,
    111–12
Communications: media, 12, 112–13;
    skills, 210; technology, 46, 62, 209,
    218, 230
Communism, 223
Community interest, 224
Company dress codes, 145
Competition, competitiveness,
    competitive individualism, 29, 163,
    206, 214–18, 221
Competitive sports, 192
Computational culture, 65
Computer(s), 1, 49, 57, 60, 64, 113,
    226; advertising, 59; age, 11; culture,
    13; and children, 64; data banks, 218;

fetishism, 2, 58–60; firms, names of,
    58–59; gender of, 60; language, 2,
    56–59; as "Man of the Year," 60;
    personality of, 58; science, 5, 61;
    technology, systems, 3, 47, 55, 59,
    209
Computerese, 2, 56–59
Computerization, 218, 220
The Confidence Man (Melville), 75
Conglomerates, 121, 124–25
Consciousness, 2, 12, 39, 60–65, 84,
    111–13, 132–34, 213, 215, 225
Consciousness industry/industries, 3,
    21, 111–14, 131, 231 n.5
Conspicuous consumption, conspicuous
    waste, 23–26, 142
Conspicuous generosity, philanthropy,
    24–28
Consumer: behavior, 187; culture, 13,
    79; materialism, 231 n.4; society, 76,
    150, 161–64, 169, 187; sovereignty,
    159–62, 167
Consumerism, 187–88
Consumption, 187–88; of artifacts, 187;
    ethics of, 68, 187, 225; of images,
    187; psychology of, 67, 187
Cook, Thomas, 176–79, 182, 185, 227
Cook's Tour, 173
Cooperative: movement, 219; society,
    222; work, 219
Corporate: culture, 97 (see also
    Organizational culture);
    entrepreneurs, 122; hierarchy, 97;
    image, 227; man, 198; state, 217, 223
Coser, Rose Laub, 106
Coubertin, Baron Pierre de, 192–94
Countercultures, 213–16; participation-
    oriented, 214–15, 221; power-
    oriented, 214; value-oriented, 214
Couturiers, 153–55, 167
Coxe, Tench, 47
Craft utopia, 218–21, 223
Craftsmanship, 219–20
Cribb, Joe, 29
Cricket, 15–19, 23, 120, 199–200, 211
    n.3
Crinoline, crinolinomania, 138, 156
Crotchet Castle (Peacock), 48

Cult objects, 30. *See also* Fetishes
Cultural: analysis, 68; change, 2, 12–
15, 34, 46, 50, 215, 223; diffusion,
14–16, 21, 51; history, 6;
imperialism, 14, 134; industries, 113;
integration, 19; melting-pot, 229–30;
mosaic, 229–30; pluralism, 21, 229–
30; propaganda, 70; resilience, 17;
stereotypes, 88; superstructure, 230;
symbols, 57 (*see also* Symbols;
Symbolling; Symbolism); system, 13,
50, 227; values, 20, 34, 36, 46, 51,
55–56, 85, 132, 195, 229
Culture, 12–15, 34, 132, 229; of
change, 140; commerce and, 213–31;
and counterculture, 213–16;
definition of, 9, 12–13; key elements
of, 13–14; of the market, 34; of
narcissism, 215; of philanthropy, 28,
39; of travel, 179–83; varieties of, 13.
See also Business culture
Customary society, 150

Darnton, Robert, 6
Day-dreaming, 187–88
Della Casa, Giovanni, 143
Democracy, 35, 161, 197, 220
Demonizing of technology, 50
Denaturing of the novel, 124–25
Denim, denim jeans, denim
democracy, 156–59, 161
Department stores, 159, 162–63, 225,
227–28. *See also* Shops, shopping
Designer-label clothes, 166
Diamond, Edwin, 83, 115–16
Dickens, Charles, 75, 128–29, 155
"Disco News," 116
Disney, Disneyland, 186
Douglas, Mary, 43 n.6, 107–8
Dreams, 187–88, 213
Dress codes, 3, 97, 143–46, 151, 163,
166, 214, 227
Dress laws, 140
Dressing for power, 69
Duby, Georges, 31
Dystopia, dystopian literature, 216,
222–24

Eco, Umberto, 125, 186
Economic: change, 157; freedom, 35;
individualism, 38; man, 187; self-
interest, 37, 42; systems, 231 n.3
Economics of charity, 40
Edmunds, Lowell, 13
Education, 83, 85, 113, 133, 192, 195,
218, 229
Egalitarianism, 181, 197
Electric wire telegraph, 62, 204
Electronic: book, 124; communications,
209; culture, 112–13, 130; games,
187; revolution, 124
Elite fashion, 161
Ellis, Havelock, 148
Ellul, Jacques, 50–51
Elton, Ben, 128
Emerson, Ralph Waldo, 27, 55
Emotional machines, 64
Emulative spending, 142
Enculturation, 20
Engineered society, the, 221–23
English football (soccer), 199, 201–3
English sports education, 192
Enlightenment, the, 64, 112
Enterprise culture, 224
Enterprise society, 224
Entertainment, entertainment industry,
187, 202, 206, 226–27
Entertainment values, 123, 203–7, 210
Entrepreneurial: activity, 12, 205;
ethos, 221; mode in fashion industry,
3, 170–72; motivation, 118;
organizations, 124; publishing
houses, 124
Entrepreneurs, 4, 114, 208, 221; in
cartoons, 89–90; corporate, 122; in
fashion industry, 140, 151, 154, 158,
166–72; in literature, 5, 55, 117,
128–30; Russian-Jewish, 158;
salesmen, 80–81; self-made, 126; in
social and political structure, 30–33;
and sport, 18, 194, 197, 202, 206;
technological, 45
Environment, 221, 231 n.3
Environmental Protection Agency, 49
Enzensburger, Hans Magnus, 111–12
Ethics: of advertising, 78–79; of

consumption, 68, 187, 225; of
craftsmanship, 219; of exchange, 35;
of kinship, 214; of the market, 11,
35, 214; of work, 215 (*see also*
Protestant Ethic). *See also* Business
ethics
Equal employment opportunity, 90,
224
Erotism, 146–49, 151
Evolution, 14, 223
Ewen, Stuart, and Ewen, Elizabeth,
141, 146, 149–50, 157–58, 161–64
Exchange, medium of, 29–30, 34. *See
also* Money
Exchange systems, exchange-based
economy, 2, 17, 19, 24, 36, 39. *See
also* Gift-exchange, gift-exchange
economy
Exchange value, 34–35, 38, 164
Executive desks, 94–95

The Fable of the Bees (Mandeville), 36
Fair play, 194, 196, 200
Falwell, Jerry, 83
Family, family firm, 83, 213, 221
Fashion, 3, 67, 137–72, 187, 231 n.6;
advertisements, 151; and business
modes, 165–72; change, 159, 166–71;
commercialization of, 169; conspiracy
theory of fashion change, 168; doll,
169–70; follies of, 138; images of,
137–40, 162–63; language, metaphors
of, 137–40; leaders, 167, 171;
magazines, 151; merchandising, 151,
162, 169; shifting erogenous zone
theory of, 149; and social control,
139–43; 'Time Spirit Theory' of, 149,
170; 'top down' and 'bottom up'
modes of change, 159, 170; trickle-
down theory of, 141, 153, 159, 170
Fashion industry, 147, 150–53, 158,
227
Fast food franchises, 182, 189 n.4
Federal Communications Commission,
21
Federal Trade Commission, 74, 78
Feiffer, Jules, 101
Fetish, fetishism, 2, 58, 166, 199

Fiction as commerce, as merchandise,
124–25
Film, films, 1, 38, 46, 123, 164, 168,
184, 214, 226
Fischer, Sandra, 34–35
Fisher, S. and Fisher, R. L., 101
Flugel, J. C., 140, 148
Food and Drug Act, 78
Food and Drug Administration, 78
Fordism, 197
Foreign Corrupt Practices Act 1977, 26
Formula writing, 125
Fourier, Charles, 218
Fowles, Jib, 133–34
Franchising, 182, 188 n.4
*Frankenstein, or The Modern
Prometheus* (Mary Shelley), 49
Franklin, Benjamin, 76, 129, 145
Free cities, 33
Free enterprise system, 131, 229
Freedom of commercial speech, 37, 79
Free market, 35–36, 224
Fromm, Erich, 37–38, 164–65
Fukuyama, Francis, 231 n.3
Futurology literature, 220

Game of life, 192
Games, 1, 192, 194–95, 226; ethics and
codes of, 192
Garment industry, New York, 158
Gekko, Gordon, 38, 43 n.3
Genetic engineering, 222
Gentlemanly conduct, 15, 155, 192–95,
201
Gentlemanly profession, 119–21
Gift-exchange, gift-exchange economy,
2, 16, 23–35, 40. *See also* Exchange
systems, exchange-based economy
Gift-giving, 19, 23–26; in business, 25–
26
Gift relationship, 42–43
Gilmour, Rev. M. K., 15
Glenn, John, 55
Global village, 11, 230
Globalization, 230
Goodman, Paul, 216
Government, 39, 131, 209, 224

Grand Tour, the, 173–76, 181; classical, 174–76; romantic, 174–76
The Great Cat Massacre (Darnton), 6
Great Exhibition 1851, 178, 227
Greed, 38
Green economy, 231 n.3
Greenwich Mean Time (GMT), 61–62
Grub Street, 118, 135 n.5
Guinness Book of Records, 199

Hackett, Earle, 41
Hare, David, 117
Harrison, Randall, 87, 89
Haute couture, 3, 150–51, 153–56, 159–62, 167, 172
Hawkins, Stephen, 125
Hawthorn, Jeremy, 5
Hazlitt, William, 141
Headlong Hall (Peacock), 48
Health, health care, 40–43
Heller, Joseph, 128, 145, 165
Hemingway, Ernest, 119
Hewison, William, 87–88, 101, 106
High-tech, high-tech imagery, 45, 58
Hollander, Anne, 152 n.4
Humor, psychology of, 100
Hughes, Thomas, 50, 60
Huxley, Aldous, 216, 222

Ideology, 2, 14–15, 31–35, 39, 68–70, 178, 195–97, 210, 213–16, 225, 231 n.3. *See also* Business ideology, values
Images, 163–65, 187–88, 225–27, 230. *See also* Symbols; Symbolling; Symbolism
Impression management, 165
Individualism, 35, 151, 161, 215, 217, 222
Industrial age, 219
Industrial espionage, 45, 47
Industrial revolution, 11–12, 46–47, 199, 216
Industrial society, 126
Industrialization, 4, 46, 179, 217; of the mind, 3, 112–13; of time and space, 61, 63

Information age, information society, 11, 46
Information systems, 61
Information technology, 46
Innocence of commerce, 33, 225
Intercollegiate sports, 193–94, 202
Institutionalized technology, 2, 52, 58, 65, 223
The International (Christian) Lightning Trust (Twain), 80
Irrationality, images of, 137
Invisible Hand, 36

James, Henry, 127
Jesus, 80–83
Johnson, Dr. Samuel, 71
Jokes, 107–8
Jolly, Elaine, 88, 91, 128
Journalism, 3, 117, 126; models of, 116

Kadis, A. L., 104
Kernan, Alvin, 55–57
Kidder, Tracy, 58
Klapp, Orrin, 103
Kluckhohn, Clyde, 12
Knopf, Alfred, 119, 121
König, René, 172
Kramer, Jack, 18
Kramer, Jerry, 198
Kroeber, A. L., 12
Kristol, Irving, 224

Language: of advertising, 67–74, 78, 82; and blood, 40–41; of business, 3–4, 111, 213, 225, 227, 229–30; and consciousness, 84–86; and cultural imperialism, 133; of fashion, 137–40; as key element of culture, 13–15, 214; and market economy, 34–35, 39; of sport, 4, 210; of sports commentary, 206; of the technological culture, 56–57
Lasch, Christopher, 162, 215
Laver, James, 149
Lauer, Robert and Jeanette, 141, 149, 163
Leach, Jerry, 15–16
Leacock, Stephen, 100

Le Goff, Jacques, 31–32
Leisure society, leisure industries, 220
Lever, Charles, 178–79
Lewis, Sinclair, 82–83
Lifelong education, 218
Lind, Jenny, 75, 188 n.2
Lipsky, Richard, 198
Literary culture, 1, 124
Literary Luddites, 130
Literary romanticism, 55–56, 58
Literature, 1, 2, 5, 33, 49, 56–57, 68, 111, 214, 217, 220, 222, 226, 231 n.6; of business, business executives, 111–35
Litterateurs, in publishing, 122–25
Lombardi, Vince, 198
The Lord's Work (Wolfe), 83
Low, David, 109 n.4
Lowe, Donald M., 112
Lucile, 142, 148
Lurie, Alison, 165–68
Luddites, 47, 157

MacCannell, Dean, 183–84
Machine age, 11
Machine-out-of-control, 95
Machine-regulated time, 62
Machine(s), 216–17, 219–20; as measure of mankind, 47; mind of, 64; personality of, 58; spiritual qualities of, 58
Magazines, magazine publishing, 78, 121, 125
Mailer, Norman, 2, 54–58
Malinowski, Bronislaw, 23
The Man Nobody Knows (Barton), 80–81
Man-machine systems, 95
Management, 4–5, 20, 93–94, 97, 107, 209–10, 217; authority, 108; ideologies, 213, 221; systems, 122
Managerial: alienation, 130; behavior, 107; class, 12, 19; mode in fashion industry, 3, 170–72; success and sports achievement, 210; technocrats in sport, 198
Managers, 5, 90, 94, 97, 128, 140, 210. *See also* Business executives

Mandeville, Bernard de, 36
Manufacturing system, 48
Market: capitalism, ideology of, 35, 224–25; culture of, 34–40; economy, 2, 11, 25–39, 70, 111, 213–14, 218, 223, 231 n.3; ethic, 35, 214; exchange, 25, 29–30, 33; freedoms, 37; ideology of, 35, 39, 70; and moral crusades, 36; morality of, 34–40, 41, 225; segmentation, 163, 170; sport and, 200–203; system, 20, 36; values of, 35, 48, 229
Marketing, merchandising, 68, 71, 79, 122–23, 151, 158, 162, 169, 187, 206–8, 223, 225
Marketing of personality, 164
Marketing orientation, 37–38, 164–65
Marly, Diana de, 153–56
Martini, symbolism of, 13
Mason, Roger S., 26
Martin Chuzzlewit (Dickens), 75
Marx, Karl, 111
Marx, Leo, 60
Mass communications, 70, 100
Mass consumption, 159
Mass fashion, mass-produced clothing, 151, 157–59, 161–62
Mass market, marketing, 162, 167–68
Mass production, 158–59, 162, 168, 222
Mass tourism, 173, 176, 178, 181
Maxwell, Robert, 121
Mayhew, Henry, 156
McKendrick, Neil, 129–30, 169–70
"Me Decade," 65
Mechanical society, 48
Mechanization, 157
Media, 4, 19–20, 113–15, 196, 226; impact on culture, 134; imperialism, 135; industries, 114; organizations, 17; studies, 113, 135 n.10. *See also* Sport and the media; Television
Medical science, practice, 52, 83
Mercantilism, 35
Merchandising. *See* Marketing
Mergers, megamergers, 121–22
Metaphor, 34–35, 210
Metropolitan Museum of Art, 186
Mind-making industry, 113–14

Military uniforms, 158
Mintz, L. E., 106
Miti (Ministry of Trade and Industry, Japan), 231 n.3
Modern Times (Chaplin), 59
Modernism, modernist, 61, 187, 224–25, 230 n.1
Modularity in American culture, 202–3
Monetary exchange, 30
Money: cowries, 30; economy, 31, 33, 219; lenders, lending, 31–33 (*see also* Usury); making, 27, 31; properties of, 34
Monopoly, 37
Morphing, 226

Naipaul, V. S., 185
Narcissism, 151
Neo-Luddites, 47
Newbolt, Sir Henry, 192
New Consciousness, 65, 215
New Book, the, 160, 226
New Thought Movement, 82
New Yorker, The, 87, 89, 100–101, 106
News, 226; models of, 116; organizations, 119; and television, 116
Newspapers, newspaper publishing, 117–19, 131, 135 n.2, 159, 169, 201, 203–4; acquisition, 118; ownership, 118–19, 202
Nightingale, Florence, 139
"Noblesse oblige," 27, 39
"Nouveau riche," 27, 126, 155
Novelization, 123
Novels, 164. *See also* Literature
Nuclear age, 11, 46

O'Rourke, P. J., 185
Occupational costumes, 144
Occupational subcultures, 214
Odendahl, Teresa, 28–29
Of a Fire on the Moon (Mailer), 54
Office of Technology Assessment, 49
Olympic: Games, 174, 191, 193–95, 199, 205, 207–9, 211 n.8; ideal, 194; movement, 193
Oral culture, 112–13
Organization culture, 13, 20, 106, 122

Morris, William, 219–20, 223
Motels, motel industry, 182–83
Motor touring, motor tourism, 181–83
Muckraking journalism, 77
Mulkay, M. J., 107
Multimedia deals, 123
Multinationals, 19, 114, 230
Multiple Personality and the Disintegration of Literary Character (Hawthorn), 5
Murdoch, Rupert, 121
Muscular Christianity, 192, 194, 201
Museums, museum shops, 186, 225–28, 231 n.5

Organizational: power, 107; structure, 108; systems, 122; utopia, 218; values, 108
Orwell, George, 213, 216
'Out-of-Fashion Trauma Syndrome,' 163
Owen, Robert, 27, 218
Owners, business ownership, 124, 126, 130, 132, 197, 202, 214

Pac Man, 70
Pacific cricket, 17
Pacey, Arnold, 51–53
Packer, Kerry, 17–19
Paige, Satchel, 20
Paris Exhibition, 1855, 154, 227
Parry, Jonathan, 33, 231 n.3
Participatory market economy, 231 n.3
Pastoral society, 219
Patent medicines, patent medicine industry, 74–78
Patent medicine advertisements, 75, 77
Paternalism, 27
Patriarchy, 90
Patton, Phil, 182–83
Peacock, Thomas Love, 48
Pears Soap, 69–70
Pecuniary truth, 77–80, 115
Permissible lie, 77–80
Personal privacy, 224
Personalized trading, 29
Personality as commodity, 35, 164

Personality of machines, 58
Personality market, 38, 164–65
Pharmaceutical industry, 78
Philanthropic trusts, 28
Philanthropy, 28–29, 39
Play, 187, 198, 200, 218, 226; in
    human culture, 198
Plays, 164
"Plays" in American football, 193, 202
Pluralism, 50, 224
Poison of the gift, 33
Political: action, 214–17, 223;
    advertising, marketing, 115, 224;
    dresses, 155; freedom, 35
Politicians as commodities, 115
Politics, morality of, 197
Popular culture, 60, 70, 226
Ports of trade, 33, 229
Post-industrial society, 11, 61
Postmodern, postmodernism, 186, 223–
    28, 230 n.1, 231 n.6
Potlatch competition, 24, 26
Power, 10–11, 19–20, 28, 30, 39, 131,
    141, 165–66, 202, 214; dressing, 165;
    elite, 29; games, 105
Press barons, 119
Printing technology, 112
"Private Vices," 36, 39
Production: ethic, 187; for exchange,
    33; for use, 33; psychology of, 187
Professions, professionalism,
    professional sport, 4, 12, 195, 200–
    207, 214
Profit: -making, -seeking, 31–34, 38–39,
    42; maximization, 221, 229; motive,
    31
Protestant Ethic, 28, 63, 80, 146, 187,
    220
Pseudo-events, 184
Psychobabble, 65
Psychology: of consumption, 67, 187–
    88; of humor, 100; of machines, 57;
    of production, 187; of the team, 197;
    of tourism and travel, 4, 183–88
"Publick Benefits," public good, 36, 39,
    224
Public relations, 56, 208
Public space, 227–28

Publishing: profession, 119; traditions,
    122
Publishers, publishing industry, 3, 73,
    78, 88–89, 117–24, 214
Puff, puffery, puffing, Mr. Puff, 72, 79
Puritanism, 141, 175

Quant, Mary, 137, 150, 168

Radcliffe-Brown, A. R., 102
Rae, Fraser, 175, 179
Railway: journeys, 179–80; time, 62
Railways, railway development, 27, 46–
    47, 60–63, 152, 154, 176–82, 188
    n.3, 201
Rational dress, 147
Rationality, rational science, 64
Ready-to-wear, ready-made clothing, 3,
    157–62, 167–68
'Real' holidays, 'real' travel, 184–85
Redfield, James, 24
"Revolution in rising expectations," 187
"Revolution in rising frustrations," 187
Reynolds, Mack, 218
Riess, Steven, 196–97
The Right Stuff (Wolfe), 54–55
Robber barons, 27–28, 77, 128, 130
Robinson, Dwight E., 137
Robotics, 61
Rodgers, William, 145
Role socialization, 128
Romantic ethic, 187
Romantic movement, romanticism, 55–
    56, 58, 60, 64, 188
Rosen, R. D., 65
Rosenwald, Julius, 158
Ross, Harold, 101
Rugby football, 201–3

Saenger, G., 90
"Sage-fool," 102–3
Saint-Simon, Henri, 216–19
Salesmanship, principles of, 81
Schivelbusch, Wolfgang, 61, 63
Schuller, Robert, 83
Schumacher, E. F., 47
Schwarzenegger, Arnold, 193
Science, 1–2, 45–46, 49–50, 55–57, 60,

65, 95, 112, 215–23; genderization of, 60
Science fiction, 49, 59, 223
Scientific: knowledge, rationality, thought, 46, 57, 61, 84, 217–18, 223–24; man, 55; revolution, 199
Sears Roebuck, 158–59
Self: -advertisement, 163; -help books, manuals, 36, 80, 165; -made men, 126–29; -regulation, 78
Semiological analysis, 68–71
Semiology, semiotics, 67–71
Sex roles, sex stereotyping in dress, 146–49, 151
Sexual competition, 148
Shakespeare, William, 85, 103
Shakespeare's plays as business case studies, 85–86
Shamateurism, 195
Shareholders, stockholders, 98–99
Shawn, William, 125
Shelley, Mary, 49
Shepard, Leslie, 117
Sheridan, Richard Brinsley, 72
Shopping centers, shopping malls, 226–28
Shops, shopping, 187, 225–28
Silicon Valley, 45, 58
Skinner, B. F., 221–23
Slop clothes, slop shops, 157–58
Small business enterprise, 221
Smith, Adam, 36, 175
Smith, Henry Nash, 128
Smither, Robert, 37
Snooker, 206, 211 n.7
Snow, C. P., 1–2
Snowmobile, 51–52
Soap, soap advertisements, 69–70
Soccer, 199–203
Social: change, 9–12, 46, 50, 63, 170, 215–16; control, 3, 10–12, 19, 21, 24, 29, 34, 139–43, 222; structure, 3, 10–12, 19, 21, 24, 29–33, 100, 103, 108, 140, 195, 214, 224; values, 20, 88, 140, 143, 151, 172, 224
Social Darwinism, 194
Social value theory of business, 231 n.2
Socialism, 217, 220

Socialist market economy, 231 n.3
Socialization, 10, 12, 20, 97, 128, 132, 195–96
Society, social system, 10, 33, 39, 50, 216, 229; definition of, 9; key elements, 10–11
Sociocultural time, 63
Sociology of business, 19–20
The Soul of a New Machine (Kidder), 58
Space, space age, 11, 45, 55, 59; program, 2, 52, 58, 65; technology, 52–57
Sponsorship, 225–26, 228, 231 n.5. See also Sport, sponsorship and
Sport(s), 1, 4, 21, 51, 191–211; administration, 18, 209; aphorisms, 199–200; as big business, 197–98; and Christianity, 15, 192; commentary, 206; commercialism in, commercialization of, 200, 202, 209; as culture, 191–95; and education, 192, 195, 199; as entertainment, 203–7, 210; entrepreneurs, 197; ideology and values of, 195–200, 210; industry, 196; languages of, 206, 210; and managers, management, 209–10; marketing, 206, 208; metaphors, 193, 210; and moral behavior, moral codes, 192, 194, 197, 199, 201; and the market, 200–203; and the media, 196, 203–11; professionalism in, 17, 195, 197, 200–204, 226; promotion, 204, 208; reporting, 203, 206; sponsorship and, 4, 17, 195, 207–10; and television, 17, 204–11, 227; and war, 193
Spot advertisements, 115
Staged authenticity, 184
Status, 3, 10, 19, 20–35, 95, 98, 103–4, 108, 112–13, 141–43, 162, 166, 199; competition, 23–26, 105, 141, 148, 151, 166, 199; symbol, 52, 69, 95, 97; symbol-out-of-control, 95
Statutes (Definition of Time) Act, 62
Stein, Ben, 130–31
Stephan, John, 150
Stewardship of wealth, 28, 38–39, 80

Steig, William, 104
Street: fashion, 161; literature, 3, 116–
    19
Sterne, Laurence, 175
Strauss, Levi, 157, 209
Streicher, Lawrence H., 100–101
Subjective computer, the, 64
Sumo wrestling, 205
Sumptuary laws, 140–41
Super Bowl, 176, 199
Symbolic value, 166
Symbolism: of blood, 40–41; of
    computer names, 58; of cricket, 16;
    of denim jeans, 161–62; of dress,
    163–64; of executive desks, 94–95; of
    gift giving, 19; of human control, 55;
    of the martini, 13; of money, 34;
    sexual, 51, 148
Symbolling, as key element of culture,
    13–15
Symbols, 2, 30, 33, 134, 187–88;
    advertising, 3, 51; baseball, 196;
    business, 20–21, 67–86, 111, 213,
    225, 227, 229; commercially
    produced, 114; of motor tourism,
    182–83; of religious belief, 13; status,
    52, 69, 95, 97

Talmudic tradition, 32
Tanii, Akio, 122
Taylorism, 197
Team: business organization as, 210;
    games, sports, 192, 198, 201, 210;
    player, 197, 210; psychology of the,
    197; spirit, 210
Technocratic: literature, 217; society,
    system, 61, 217–19; utopia, 216–19,
    223
Technological: accidents, 179; change,
    development, evolution, innovation,
    11, 46–50, 111, 138, 156–57, 167,
    178, 187, 216–17, 223, 231 n.3;
    culture, 60; culture, language of, 56;
    determinism, 50–51; systems, 52–55,
    60, 213, 218, 223
Technology, 1–2, 20, 70, 134, 230;
    assessment, 49; and business, 11; and
    consciousness, 60–65; of cricket, 16;

and culture, 21, 46–51, 214–17, 219,
    223–26; and fashion change, 167,
    170; genderization of, 60; humanizing
    of, 55, 58, 65; newspaper, 117;
    practice, 2, 51–54; printing, 112;
    railway, 179–80; social construction
    of, 50; television, 204; theories of,
    50; and tourism, 186–87; transport,
    183
Telecommunications, 46, 61
Telegraph system, 62
Televangelism, 6, 21, 83
Televised reality, 133
Television, 1, 4, 12, 113–15, 123, 126,
    130–35, 168, 172, 219;
    advertisements, commercials, 115,
    123, 132–33, 226; business of, 132;
    and consciousness, 132–33; and
    construction of social reality, 132;
    and cultural imperialism, 133–34;
    and culture, cultural values, 132;
    industry, 132, 134; news, 116, 131,
    133; ownership and control, 119,
    123; power of, 132–33; as socio-
    cultural agency, 130–35; and sport,
    17–19, 204–11, 227; rights payments,
    204–9, 211 n.8
Temperance movement, 147, 176–77
Tennis, 18, 199–200, 205
Thackeray, William Makepeace, 194
Thoreau, Henry David, 63
Thumb, Tom, 75, 188 n.2
Thurber, James, 92
Titmuss, Richard, 42
Time and space: concepts of, 3, 63;
    consciousness of, 61; industrialization
    of, 61, 63; mastery of, 47; psychology
    of, 61
Time as money, 63
Time zones, 62
Tobacco companies, tobacco industry,
    79, 207
Totalitarianism, 217, 222
Tourism, 4, 52, 173–89, 227; cultures
    of, 179–83; industry, 4, 227;
    promotion of, 184; psychology of,
    183–88; sociology of, 183–88. See
    also Travel

Tourist attractions, 4, 173, 227
Tourists, 178–79, 183, 185
Trade unions, 12
Traders, 30, 33
Trading relationships, 12, 46
Train travel, 179–80; structures of, 180;
  technology of, 180
Transactional orders, 39, 231 n.3
Transport technology, 3, 46, 60–63,
  176, 183
Travel, 1, 176, 178, 186–87; cultures
  of, 179–83; industry, 184; promotion
  of, 184; psychology of, 183–88. See
  also Tourism
Travellers, 185
Trobriand cricket, 15–17, 19, 23, 51
Trobriand Islands, Islanders, 15–17, 19,
  23–24, 191
Trollope, Mrs., 126
Trudeau, Garry, 88
Truffles, 65 n.3, 70
Tunstall, Jeremy, 134
Turkle, Sherry, 63–65
Twain, Mark, 80–81, 102, 185
"The Two Cultures," 1–2
Typographic culture, 112–13

Ueberroth, Peter, 208
Ungentlemanly conduct, 15, 92
Unitary management ideology, 210
United Nations Universal Declaration
  of Human Rights, 37
Urry, John, 184, 225
Use value, 37, 164, 166
User-friendly, 59
Usury, 31–32, 38
Utopia, utopian literature, 45, 215–24
Utopian Socialists, 216, 218–19

Van Nostrand, Albert, 124–25
Vanderbilt, Cornelius, 27

Victoria, Queen of England, 139
Veblen, Thorsten, 142
Veblen effect, the, 142, 170
Virtual reality machines, 187
Voigt, David, 199
Vreeland, Diana, 150

Wall Street (Stone), 38
Walvin, James, 201
Warburg, Fredric, 119–21
Wardrobe engineering, 165
WASP culture, 197
Wasserman, Lew, 122
Water travel, 180
Watts, Emily, 129
Weber, Max, 146, 187
Wells, H. G., 76, 119
Welsford, Enid, 103
Whannel, Garry, 202
Whiteside, Thomas, 122
Willeford, William, 102
Williams, Raymond, 12
Winick, C., 104
Winner, Langdon, 49
Winning images, 165
Wolfe, Tom, 2, 54–55, 83, 142
Work, work ethic, 187, 214–16, 218–
  20, 222. See also Protestant Ethic
World Series Cricket, 18
Worth, Charles Frederick, 142, 150,
  153–56, 167, 178, 227
Wuthnow, Robert, 36

Yankee peddler, 75
Yates, Norris W., 103
Yeager, Chuck, 54
Yinger, Milton, 214–15
Youthcult fiction, 226
Yuppie, 38, 185

Zeitgeist, the, 149
Zilch, Elmer, 73

About the Author

JOHN DEEKS is Associate Professor in the Department of Management Studies and Labour Relations in the Faculty of Commerce and Economics at the University of Auckland in New Zealand. He is a graduate of Cambridge University and the London School of Economics and Political Science and has been employed in management and research posts in business and the public sector. His previous books include *The Small-Firm Owner-Manager: Entrepreneurial Behavior and Management Practice* (Praeger, 1976) and, jointly edited with Nick Perry, *Controlling Interests: Business, the State and Society in New Zealand* (1992).